The *NapaLife* Insider's Guide to Napa Valley

A Travel Guide for the Connected Age

Paul Franson

*To Ken
Paul Franson*

The *NapaLife* Insider's Guide to Napa Valley:
A Travel Guide for the Connected Age

Paul Franson

ISBN-13: 978-1479258444

ISBN-10: 147925844X

The cover photograph is by Mars Lasar www.picfrommars.com

Foreword

I moved to Napa Valley in 1996, first to St. Helena, and then to the small city of Napa. Since then, I've made my living writing mostly about wine and Napa Valley.

That includes writing a weekly column on life in Napa Valley for the *Napa Valley Register* for 11 years, publishing the weekly insider newsletter *NapaLife* for eight years (and a free version before that), plus features for the *Register, Napa Valley Life, Inside Napa Valley, Napa Sonoma, Wine Country Living, Food & Wine, Senior Connection, Decanter*, the *Wine Enthusiast, San Francisco Chronicle* and many more publications.

I've also hosted radio programs about wine and wine country on two local radio stations.

In the first years in St. Helena, and more recently in Napa, I've seen a huge change in the Valley. Thankfully, little has changed in its rural vineyards and undeveloped land, but there have been many changes in its cities and towns. Most significantly, the city of Napa has grown from a bypassed turnoff on the divided highway to the major destination of the valley.

Now, many visitors don't see much reason to go all the way upvalley 27 miles to Calistoga, which means they're missing a treasure, but there are so many attractions in Napa that they could spend whole vacations there.

When I first visited Napa Valley in 1968, and on many trips as well as when I first moved here, wine was *the* attraction. As wine lovers and home winemakers, my former (and now sadly, late) wife and I spent many weekends here in the '70s visiting friends, making wine and enjoying cookouts and dinners at their home on Niebaum Lane in Rutherford. In those days, there weren't many more appealing places to eat or stay.

How things have changed. We've seen food become so much an almost-equal partner with wine in attracting visitors that Napa Valley with its population of only 135,000 demanding people has become an unquestioned gourmet center for America.

More recently, arts and entertainment have become big draws, both with ongoing attractions and important festivals. Now, many visitors are recognizing that it also holds many opportunities for outdoor and wellness activities, too.

In the process, Napa Valley's imagined lifestyle has become the aspiration for many Americans, and some have even moved here to enjoy that lifestyle.

Much of the emergence of Napa itself has been due to restaurants and other attractions that were created largely as the result of a massive project to control a periodic flooding of the small city that previously discouraged investment downtown.

With that change, new projects and developments have transformed the once-sleepy city without destroying its inherent historic charm – and even enhancing it.

Fortunately, you need drive only a few miles from Napa to be in vineyards or truly wild space, or in quaint towns that remind you of America's past, too.

After writing so much about the valley and the changes that have come to it, I decided to collect my observations and opinions and share them with others.

This isn't your usual travel guide, for it is written from a local insider's viewpoint, not a writer who parachutes in for a few days. It's light on information about lodgings, for I don't stay at them, but heavy on the real local experiences.

And it is opinionated. I make no claim to be objective. I don't depend on advertising or free trips, lodging or meals to write about Napa Valley, so I can say what I want.

This book is also prepared with a nod to today's technologies and tastes. It doesn't include detailed listings of restaurants, lodgings and wineries and their contact information, for almost everyone turns to the Web for that these days.

You'll also find inconsistencies in style and depth, as part of this material was written for different uses over a few years. The good news is that you may find undiscovered gems lurking in its pages.

Some of the material in the book has appeared in other forms in the *Napa Valley Register, Napa Valley Life, Senior Connection, Wines & Vines, Food & Wine* and the NapaStyle web site. The section on the agricultural preserve was written for Napa Valley Vintners. I especially want to think Sasha Paulsen and Kari Ruel.

I thank all for letting me write for them and using the edited material. Much was written specifically for the *NapaLife Insider's Guide to Napa Valley*, however, and ironically, almost none came from *NapaLife*, the timely weekly insider's guide to Napa Valley.

I hope you find *The NapaLife Insider's Guide to Napa Valley* interesting and useful. I invite you to share your opinions with me, as well as the inevitable errors and omissions. And if you want an on-going record of life in Napa Valley, consider subscribing to *NapaLife*. Get details at www.napalife.com.

Paul Franson
Napa Valley 2012

Primary web sites for information about Napa Valley

This book is intended to be used with a smart phone, computer or tablet to get details like opening times, costs and other information, which changes rapidly. Here are the best sources to consult:

- Visit Napa Valley (Official visitors organization) www.visitnapavalley.com

- Napa Valley Vintners (exhaustive listing of wineries and their offerings) www.napavintners.com

- Napa Valley Arts Council (Full listing of everything happening) www.nvarts.org

- Napa Valley Register (The local daily paper) www.napanews.com

- NapaValley.com (Best private listing service). www.napavalley.com

- NapaStyle (Napa to You section) www.napastyle.com

Map of Napa Valley

Calistoga ⓘ

• Angwin

St. Helena ⓘ

Lake Berryessa •

Rutherford •

Oakville •

Yountville ⓘ

ⓘ Guest Services

Napa ⓘ Napa Valley
        Welcome Center

American
Canyon ⓘ

Map courtesy Visit Napa Valley

The *NapaLife* Insider's Guide to Napa Valley

Food and Restaurants 164

Where to stay in Napa Valley....................................276

The Lay of the Valley

A Quick Tour of Napa Valley

If your image of Napa Valley is America's wine and food playground, the destination vacation of sophisticated travelers, you're only partly right.

Yes, it's all those things, but fundamentally, the rural valley an hour from San Francisco is full of farms and farmers; we call them vineyards and grape growers, but the beautiful valley has more in common with life in Iowa than with Las Vegas or Miami. It's just that the scenery is better and the end products of the farmers' efforts is more appealing than pig food or fuel.

Napa Valley is a narrow valley – two to five miles wide –30 miles long. It's defined by steep mountain ranges on each side capped at the north by 4,344-ft. Mount St. Helena.

That's fitting, for Napa Valley's geology, geography and climate are a direct result of its open exposure to San Francisco Bay and its northern lobe, San Pablo Bay.

At the south, Napa Valley opens into a broad plain and the rolling hills of Carneros, then into marshes and San Pablo Bay. It barely touches the bay, but its influence is great.

The river runs through it

Where the valley opens and the mountain ridges end at the south is the small but attractive city of Napa. Napa sits where it is because of the Napa River, a rare navigable river in California. The town was built as far as bay-going ships could venture upstream to pick up the flour, fruit and meat raised in the Valley. A large mural at First and Main Streets in downtown Napa depicts these early days.

Though the Napa River was once the lifeblood of the valley and town, it was long neglected and cursed for its frequent floods. Now that it has been largely tamed, it has become one of Napa's top attractions. A pathway, parks, shops and cafés are blossoming along the river – though it's a work in progress that won't be completed for years.

Napa was long bypassed by tourists heading for the more picturesque towns up valley, but that has changed. With the river no longer a threat, chic lodgings, fine restaurants and other attractions have made Napa a major destination.

Napa also offers many wine-tasting venues for wineries that can't host visitors, and a special treasure, The Oxbow Public Market. The market and the area it occupies are named after a horseshoe bend in the Napa River. The market is filled with eateries, shops, markets and wine-tasting opportunities and is a must stop for locals and visitors alike.

Next to the market is a large white elephant. Copia, the ambitious American Center for Wine, Food and the Arts, sits closed while the mortgage company that now owns it ponders it future. Fortunately, it's one of few dark spots in an otherwise-bright picture and recent activity suggests it may soon open with a new purpose.

Likewise, the Napa Mill and adjacent Riverfront complex at the south end of Main Street are also filled with similar delights including the upscale Napa River Inn.

Napa's West End at First and Franklin is also booming with shops, wine tasting restaurants and the boutique Andaz hotel.

Heading upvalley

North of Napa, the valley becomes rural and county ordinances prohibit new buildings except wineries and homes, and both those are highly restricted. Locals call everything north of Napa "upvalley".

Because of the influence of the bay, the valley is cooler than upvalley, notably south of Yountville where the valley's narrow waist and hills constrict the cold air from venturing north.

The first town north of Napa is tiny Yountville, which makes a claim to be the nation's per-capita food capital. The star is the French Laundry, which some consider the best restaurant in the world, but Bottega, Bouchon, Bistro Jeanty, Bardessono's Lucy, Redd, Ad Hoc, étoile at Domaine Chandon and other restaurants are superb, too.

The freeway ends at Yountville, and that's where the wine country seems to begin for many people who don't realize that excellent wine comes from southern Napa Valley.

Next are two hamlets whose names shine far larger on the wine scene than their size: Oakville and Rutherford. Once, each had stores, taverns, hotels and other businesses. Now most of those are long gone. Some of America's most revered wines come from these areas, however.

The heart of the valley

Widely considered the heart of America's wine business is 8,000-resident St. Helena, a picturesque town becoming a playground of rich residents, second-home owners and well-heeled tourists. It boasts fine restaurants and chi-chi shops. Any visitor will find its two-block downtown and Victorian neighborhoods appealing.

At the northern end of the valley is Calistoga, which started out as a center of hot springs and mud baths, and grafted on a wild-west look. Many tourists don't make it this far north, but they're missing one of the valley's most pleasant towns. Not yet the haunt of the rich and famous, it has plenty of affordable attractions for visitors.

Of course, "Napa Valley" means wine to most people, specifically its rich Cabernet Sauvignons. Almost as famed are its buttery, oak-tinged Chardonnays, and many locals claim its Sauvignon Blancs are the best in the world. A number of producers make excellent sparkling wines from cooler-region grapes, too, and the Pinot Noirs from Carneros deserve attention, too.

If you are making your first visit to Napa Valley, you should certainly hit the classic wine attractions, notably the Robert Mondavi Winery in Oakville, Beaulieu Vineyards in Rutherford, Beringer Vineyards and Louis Martini Winery in St. Helena and Sterling Vineyards atop a knoll south of Calistoga and looking like a Greek Monastery. You ascend to the winery via a gondola from the base of the knoll.

You should surely visit the amazing Castello di Amorosa winery near Calistoga. The authentic-looking $35-million vision of a 13th-century castle took eight years to build as homage to vintner Dario Sattui's Italian heritage. The winery has impressive vineyards and makes excellent wine, too, including some sweet wines appreciated by the estimated 30 percent of Americans who don't like the excellent but tannic Cabernets Napa Valley is famous for. The Castello makes those, too, however.

Combining fine wine and amazing art is the Hess Collection in the mountains west of Napa and Clos Pegase near Sterling.

Three temples to Napa wine are worth visiting, too. Wines from Chateau Montelena Winery north of Calistoga, and Stag's Leap Wine Cellars on the Silverado Trail in Napa won the famed Paris tasting of 1976, beating the best of France. The Montelena Chardonnay that won was made by Miljenko "Mike" Grgich, who has his own Grgich-Hills Estate Cellars in Rutherford.

Off the main roads in the mountains are two of Napa's most-amazing and rarely visited wineries, Kuleto Estates and Long Meadow Ranch. Both are veritable self-contained estates that raise olives, vegetables, fruit and livestock as well as wine grapes – and boast interesting architecture as well.

Long Meadow has the largest rammed-earth building in America. It's both a winery and frantoio (olive press). Long Meadow's owners, Ted and Laddie Hall, also own Farmstead Restaurant in St. Helena, where they offer food largely sourced from their farm.

Kuleto is worth a visit, but like Long Meadow Ranch and all newer wineries, requires appointments.

Though best known for wine, Napans take their food seriously, as demonstrated by the many fine (and expensive) restaurants, the gourmet shops, farmers markets and even the offerings in local supermarkets.

Two special gourmet attractions are the Oxbow Public Market in Napa and the Culinary Institute of America campus in the old Christian Brothers Greystone Cellars in St. Helena.

The range of food is amazing. Gott's Roadside Gourmet in St. Helena (formerly Taylor's) and at Napa's Oxbow Market sells cult wines along with gourmet burgers, for example, but the tacos at modest La Luna market in Rutherford are as appreciated locally.

At the other end of the spectrum in dining is the French Laundry, which requires jockeying for reservations exactly two months ahead. Other luxury competitors include the Restaurant at Meadowood, which like The French Laundry boasts three Michelin stars, Auberge du Soleil, étoile at Domaine Chandon and La Toque in Napa, and many other restaurants offer exquisite gourmet meals.

Napa isn't only wine and food, however. Art fills the valley from the huge and eclectic di Rosa Preserve in Carneros to many wineries and galleries.

The valley is also home to more and more arts and entertainment. Napa Valley is still best known for its wine with food close behind, but the valley is also becoming a destination for entertainment and the arts.

The valley has a whole new schedule of exciting wine, food and art events, too, including the Napa Valley Film Festival and Flavor! Napa Valley, the valley's first big food and wine festival, both held in a normally slack time, November.

During "Cabernet season" in the quiet months of January through April, the valley hosts Napa Valley Restaurant Month and the Napa Valley Truffle Festival in January, Arts in April with the Arts Council and Napa Valley wineries. Festival del Sole in July is one of the music celebrations; the valley hosts two chamber music series, in fact.

After all the wine and food, you might enjoy more active pursuits. You can canoe or kayak on the river, hike in the hills and mountains, bicycle along the river, play golf or tennis or even work out at many gyms.

You might also enjoy an early-morning balloon ride over the vineyards, attend concerts at the Napa Valley Opera House or Uptown Theatre in Napa, learn more about the valley and its history at a number of museums, or enjoy cooking demonstrations and more at the CIA.

Whatever your interest, Napa Valley holds many attractions. It's a great place to visit for a day, preferably for far longer.

Napa Valley: Glitz Grafted on Deep Roots

Though you wouldn't know it from most of the articles you read, Napa Valley isn't really the glitzy scene you see for a few days each year during Auction Napa Valley, the world-famous charity wine auction.

It's a farming community, not a retirement community or a destination resort. There's a very strong sentiment among local residents to keep the Valley as it is, and people in the valley zealously protect the farm land and fight incursions. There's as much distain among residents toward those who want to make Napa Valley a trendy playground for the wealthy as there is for those who want to fill it with housing developments, strip malls and tourist attractions.

A wealthy newcomer who spurns environmental laws is a pariah among most of the valley community – including other wealthy newcomers – for arrogantly flaunting environmental and other county regulations as well as their success: A local grower who legally but unnecessarily killed bears and vintners who polluted creeks were heavily pressured by their peer community; the bear-killer sold his vineyard and left town. Michael Mondavi bought the vineyard and calls it Oso, bear, in tribute.

The county has fined wineries up to $500,000 for environmental offenses, and a judge reportedly promised jail to one vintner if she repeated her offenses.

By contrast, the way to gain acceptance and respect in the valley is to protect the environment or help the needy. The local heroes are people like Joseph Phelps, who donated valuable land for farmworker housing, and the late Robert Mondavi, who's given so much to education and the arts.

Many growers and vintners (the local name for the owner of a winery, not the customary usage of a wine merchant) have donated their valuable land to the local Land Trust or placed it in permanent agricultural or natural preserves. Local landowners pride themselves on restoring the rivers and creeks, and they value the wildlife.

Everyone is close to the soil and even the rich act and dress more like farmers than sophisticated city dwellers.

 The agricultural roots of Napa Valley are never far away, from dinner parties that start at 6 p.m. and are over by 10, to the jeans and boots and pick-up trucks favored by residents and the roar of wind machines protecting the grapes on chilly spring mornings.

Most vineyards in Napa Valley, moreover, are being farmed the "old" way, with few or no chemical pesticides, herbicides and fertilizers, even without irrigation. Many are organic or reflect the truly retro Biodynamic path of planting and harvesting by the phases of the moon and using archaic homeopathic potions.

It's often difficult to tell the wealthy vintners - owners of wineries – from the hired winemakers who make their wine, and in fact, in some cases they are the same people. There's no hierarchical society like that found in most cities; the life of the valley is wine, and if you're involved in the wine business, you belong. The former schoolteacher bootstrapping a winery or the Mexican-born vineyard manager is as welcomed as the rich developer, though naturally people tend to develop friends with similar interests and assets.

The "aristocracy" is the old-time families who've owned property for decades – even generations – but they're not that exclusive and seem to welcome others if they play by the rules: Respect the environment, don't flaunt your wealth and do good things for the valley and its people.

The way for newcomers to get accepted is to participate in charitable and wine organizations. Giving lots of money to good causes (including big purchases at the wine auction) helps, of course: Wealthy people here spend a lot of time and money supporting each others' favorite causes.

During the summer, the elite we read about in the San Francisco society columns like to party in Napa Valley, with former San Francisco mayor and now Lieutenant Governor Gavin Newsome, a part owner of PlumpJack Winery in Oakville, Cade in Angwin and Odette in Stags Leap, joining the Gettys and Trainas at the home John Traina once shared with ex-wife and novelist Danielle Steele.

Some locals like the Swansons of frozen dinner and winery fame are members of that informal club. City swells do invite locals to their parties, but Napans don't take that too seriously.

A price to belong

Land in Napa Valley is expensive. It typically costs $150,000 to $3 million an acre, depending on its potential for a grand estate, though you can find property in outlying areas for $50,000 to $75,000.

There's always property for sale in Napa Valley, and current listings range up to $35 million for star quarterback Joe Montana's home near Calistoga and the same for Carl Doumani's Quixote Winery and modest but elegant home.

The price is dependent on the amount of land involved, whether it contains or can support a vineyard and whether it includes or is

18

suitable for an estate. A modest one-bedroom cottage with a small yard can cost $200,000, and the most interesting houses start at around $1 million. It takes 10 acres to get a permit for a physical winery, so that's a magic number for many people and the price jumps dramatically there.

New parcels on the valley floor have to be 40 acres; in the hills and mountains, 160 acres, daunting figures – on purpose.

The most prestigious area is around St. Helena, but mountaintop property is naturally desirable, and there's another whole unincorporated community around Silverado Resort just northeast of city of Napa that could never be developed today.

Napa itself is becoming the cultural and entertainment center of the valley, and it attracts many newcomers with its Victorian homes at more moderate prices.

Everyone agrees that the best properties never hit the public market. They're scooped up by insiders who've developed relationships with realtors like Barry Berkowitz of St. Helena Real Estate, who knows what's going to become available almost before the sellers do.

Other top brokers include Chuck Sawday at Pacific Union in Yountville, Cindi Gates and Steve Gregory in Napa.

Some people buy temporary homes while they're looking, staying on weekends or even moving permanently while they look for the right place. Many pay cash to ensure success.

Most people look for an existing house, and a sizeable number undertake significant remodeling, often obliterating any sign of the original. Others must build their own.

For building or remodeling, you need an architect, and Howard Backen of Backen & Gillan of St. Helena rules. His list of homes, wineries and restaurants seems endless, most relatively simple contemporary designs attuned to their settings and often the valley's heritage. Also popular is Jon Lail, but many other architects also work in the valley.

People seeking typical Napa Valley homes look for a huge great room with a large fireplace at one end and an open showplace kitchen designed by a top local chef at the other. They like professional or home-style professional appliances and favor the rustic look of wood more than stainless steel.

A large island that can also seat people, a built-in espresso machine, one or two wineglass washers and a wine cave carved into a hillside are very desirable.

Of course, the climate in Napa Valley draws people outside, and many estates have bocce courts, pools and cabanas. Everyone has elaborate outside cooking grills, and a wood-burning pizza oven is the ultimate for entertaining. It does get cool in the evenings, even in the middle of the summer when daytime temperatures lap at 100 degrees, so outdoor fireplaces and heaters are almost a necessity.

Many families belong to the Meadowood Country Club and enjoy the fellowship with vintners as well as the pool, tennis, golf and even croquet – as well as the resort's two restaurants.

Napa Valley favors reverse snobbery, and showing off is considered in bad taste. In general, even regulars don't have "reserved tables," though smart maitre d's know locals and treat them well.

You need to make reservations if you want to eat at busy times in popular places, though some vintners have invested in restaurants, which helps ensure attention and access.

For daily eating, vintners and winemakers go to Cook, Market and Cindy's Backstreet Kitchen in St. Helena, Rutherford Grill, Hurley's in Yountville and Fumé Bistro in Napa.

Everyone loves Bistro Don Giovanni and Angèle in Napa, while Bottega and Redd in Yountville, and Press in St. Helena are also local favorites.

People often go to places where they aren't charged corkage, like Rutherford Grill or Hurley's, particularly for their own wines. Many restaurants let vintners to bring their own wine for free, and some restaurants don't charge anyone corkage.

Most restaurants forgive one corkage for every bottle bought, so many parties order a white or sparkler, which needs to be chilled anyway, and bring in a big Napa red. Corkage ranges from trivial to $75 at the French Laundry. You hardly need to take a bottle there, however, as they have 10,000 selections. If you care about money, you wouldn't be eating there anyway.

It should be noted that other than vintners entertaining, many locals rarely buy or drink Napa wines, which they consider expensive. Particularly if they're in the wine business, they're also curious to try other regions' wines. Wine shops sell expensive Napa Cabernets to visitors and modest Rhônes and other imports to locals.

People tend to entertain at home, particularly on weekends when the tourists are around. Though many people can cook well, the status caterer is the chef from a good restaurant or a winery. If you're a good customer and the event is right (and you pay enough), you can attract almost anyone from Thomas Keller down. Other than that, one of the top caterers for private dinners is the Invisible Chef, Michelle Cheatham. The charge for private chefs is typically $150 to $250 per head, often with a minimum of a few thousand dollars.

Everyone in who can shops at Sunshine Market in St. Helena, though they may buy cat food and paper towels at the Safeway.

Most people support local businesses as much as they can, a challenge as an increasing number of businesses in St. Helena court the tourist trade. Everyone shops at Steve's classic ACE hardware store and its adjacent kitchenware shop.

Furniture Erin Martin, a top local interior designer, has a store and showroom in St. Helena.

In Napa, Trader Joe's attracts everyone, and the nearby Whole Foods Market provides upscale groceries. Many residents frequent locally owned Vallerga's and Brown's Valley Markets, which offer more personal service and superb butchers, cheese, produce and delis. During the summer, everyone visits the Farmers Markets in each town, which are as much about socializing as shopping.

Yes, it's the good life.

How the Ag Preserve Saved Napa Valley

If Prohibition was society's worst social experiment, Napa Valley's Agricultural Preserve is one of its best.

For more than a century, our country had set aside land for national parks, scenic byways, historic sites, cultural attractions and recreation areas, but never for agriculture. That changed in 1968 with the establishment of the Napa Valley Agricultural Preserve.

2008 marks the 40th anniversary of the act that protected much of Napa Valley for agriculture. You only need to look around the valley to recognize its success: the valley is lush with grapevines, not tract housing and shopping malls. It has maintained a rural character long lost by adjoining counties around San Francisco Bay.

If the act hadn't succeeded, there's little doubt that Napa Valley would have gone the way of Santa Clara Valley, which was called the Valley of Heart's Delight for its orchards and vines long before it became a symbol for technology and urban development.

If Napa Valley hadn't been saved, a major divided highway would run through what are now some of the world's finest vineyards, and Yountville, St Helena and Calistoga would be a sea of housing development and their quaint downtowns would be bypassed and largely unused.

Instead, Napa Valley is America's premier wine destination, and its communities offer the lifestyle that both residents and visitors value so highly.

The fact that Napa Valley wasn't lost is primarily due to the vision of the vintners and growers of Napa Valley's wine community. That vision has led to great success, and the world-wide acclaim for Napa wines has helped support ever-heightened protection and leadership.

Napa's unique environment

To understand why Napa Valley has maintained its unique character while much of coastal California has been overtaken by development, you have to start with its environment. Part of the answer is in Napa Valley's unique suitability for growing premium wine grapes.

It boasts an incomparable combination of climate, geography and geology ideal for producing some of the world's best wines. And the valley's natural beauty has captivated visitors to return time and again.

Though they live in one of the nine counties that front the San Francisco Bay, Napa County residents don't often consider themselves part of the Bay Area. Residents feel on the fringe, but distance from the hub would not have kept the valley safe from development, as neighboring counties attest.

As the Bay Area prospered in the years after World War II, progress inevitably spread. Though Prohibition had ended in 1933, there were only about 25 wineries in Napa Valley in the mid-1960s, and Napa County's landowners and farmers could see development creeping toward them.

The state of California talked of building a major highway through the valley while regional planners had considered placing the Bay Area's fourth major airport in the marshes south of Carneros, and the Army Corps of Engineers suggested turning the Napa River into a concrete channel like the once-flowing Los Angeles River.

Projections envisioned 200,000 people in the city of Napa by 2000, half a million by 2020. Most people here think it's fine with today's 85,000.

Locals saw that rising land values would soon mean that property would be worth far more for development than for the nuts, fruit, dairy and cattle, grapes and other agricultural products then grown in the county.

Grape growers were getting only $300 a ton for Cabernet Sauvignon but the most widely planted grapes were Napa Gamay, Petite Sirah and other varieties that sold for even less.

In 1968, the county had less than 12,000 acres planted to grapevines compared to about 45,000 acres planted today. The average price per ton for Cabernet Sauvignon has risen to more than $4,000 and the value of the grape crop from $6 million to nearly half a billion dollars.

From 25 or so wineries in 1968, today there are more than 400 producing wineries, and more than 1,000 brands.

L. Pierce Carson came to the valley as a cub reporter only a month or so before the original proposal for the Ag Preserve was formulated, and he wrote the article about it when it was passed in April of 1968. "It sounded reasonable to me," he says. "I couldn't understand why some people were so adamantly against it." He says that emotions ran high, and as written in the local headlines, long-time friendships dissolved.

> "Dirt Farmers Rebel Against Ag. Pres."
>
> *St. Helena Star*, Feb. 25, 1968
>
> "Landowners Launch Heavy Attack On Ag. Preserves"
>
> *St. Helena Star*, Feb. 22, 1968

"Agricultural Preserves: Why They Are Needed"
St. Helena Star, Jan. 11, 1968
"Agricultural Preserves Under Heavy Fire Here"
St. Helena Star, Jan. 4, 1968

Back in the '60s, many landowners felt that their only attractive economic course was to sell their land to developers, or develop it themselves, as had already occurred on prime farm land from San Diego to Redding. Others wanted to maintain the special environment that is Napa Valley — beautiful views slow pace and enchanted lifestyle. They recognized that Napa Valley had unique properties for growing fine wine grapes: people could live most anywhere, but rare few places allowed noble grapevines to flourish.

Conservationists felt that the highest and best use of the fertile valley and foothills of the county was in growing grapes — not in homes and development. They also knew that it would take a strong legal change to preserve that environment.

Basing their argument on the Williamson Act that allowed lower valuation, and hence lower taxes on land kept in agriculture, they mounted a campaign to create an agricultural preserve. Opponents charged that the measure would destroy the value of their land, restricting it to the low $2,000 to $4,000 per acre of farmland, not the far higher amount that would be paid by developers. Carson notes that the county assessor, George Abate, kept telling people that land would be worth more in agriculture than in subdivisions, but many didn't believe him. Ironically, later as the county's viable vineyard property approached its limit, land value skyrocketed.

Scarcity combined with the mounting reputation of Napa's wines, and its attractive lifestyle, had created land prices 100 times what they were. It's unlikely that even the original supporters of the preserve could have anticipated such a benefit. "A lot of people believed that Napa Valley was a good spot for agriculture, but I don't think anyone expected the rise we've seen," says Carson.

Thus in 1968, encouraged by a small group of vintners and growers, Napa enacted tough-won, forward-thinking changes in its county code that implemented an agricultural preserve. The best-known part is called the Napa Valley Agricultural Preserve (zoning AP). It lies primarily between Napa and Calistoga. It originally protected 26,000 acres of the valley floor and foothills and has since grown to more than 38,000 acres. No land has ever been taken out of the preserve.

Beyond the protection of the valley floor, the county also designated a huge area as Agriculture, Watershed and Open Space (AW zoning), which is also protected, and in some ways, even more so. Together, the two total 482,000 acres and represent 91 percent of the county's 505,859 acres.

According to the county general plan, the "...Agricultural Preserve classification is intended to be applied in the fertile valley and foothill areas of Napa County in which agriculture is and should continue to be the predominant land use... the Agricultural Watershed classification is intended for areas of the county where the predominant use is agriculturally oriented, where watershed areas, reservoirs and floodplain tributaries are located..."

This latter designation covers most of the mountainous areas as well as developed and undeveloped farm and range land, forests and some very remote areas indeed. Only most visitors see a fraction of Napa County. More than half of the county lies over the mountains of the Vaca range to the east and another large portion is contained in the Mayacamas range to the west.

In these areas, the minimum new lot size is 160 acres, but that's only the start of the obstacles to building the allowed single-family home or winery, since intense environmental review must be passed to build or even plant vineyards in most cases.

Agriculture rules

Beyond county regulations, Napa landowners, many of whom are vintners and growers, formed the Land Trust of Napa County in 1976. They have placed their property in trust, some of which could have been used for vineyards, forever saving it from development. Now more than 50,000 acres of the county are in the Land Trust and will forever remain in agriculture or open space.

The success of establishing regulations to preserve Napa County for agriculture in 1968 led to further protection. In 1980, county voters adopted Measure A, which restricted growth in the unincorporated areas of the county via building permit limits to 1 percent per year.

Again restating their approval of agricultural preservation, in 1990 voters approved Measure J, which requires a two-thirds vote of the county's citizens to rezone any Ag land. Only a handful of these rezoning attempts have passed, and all were very specific, such as allowing the sale of pumpkins and produce in a rural site and allowing Bistro Don Giovanni to serve meals on its existing patio.

The resistance to rezoning attempts clearly reflected the residents' desire to maintain the integrity of the Ag Preserve. No one wants to let that camel's nose in the tent, fearing that its body would soon follow.

Though seemingly innocuous, the challenges to the measures have historically been condemned as the first steps to weakening the protection and have been soundly defeated.

25

Another contentious point was defining what is a "winery." In other regions, wineries are sometimes considered to be in the entertainment and hospitality businesses as much as winemaking. Some offer extensive gift shops, restaurants, inns and wedding chapels, and derive much of their revenue from parties, wedding receptions, corporate dinners and non-wine retails sales.

In Napa County, this issue was resolved with a hard-fought battle that ended in 1990 with the Winery Definition Ordinance that prohibited new wineries from engaging in ancillary activities like weddings, restaurants, inns and gift shops, and required all visitors to make appointments.

Many wineries have severe restrictions on the number of visitors allowed, some not even allowing the public to visit at all.

As a result of the establishment of the Ag Preserve, agriculture remains the leading source of revenue in Napa County, unlike other Bay Area counties where farmland has largely been displaced by development.

In an analysis of agricultural resources, approximately 45,000 acres, or about 9 percent of the county is planted to vineyards, with very limited opportunity for expansion.

It seems as though 1990 was a watershed year for Napa County, for that year, the county adopted a hillside erosion control ordinance, too. Also adopted were rules regarding setbacks from streams designed to protect the waters and wildlife. The wine community largely supported the stream setbacks even though the rules reduced plantable acreage in many vineyards.

Again in 1998, Napa County voters followed the wine community's lead and endorsed the common good by approving another measure, a project to control the periodic flooding of the Napa River in a forward-thinking plan that chose natural controls such as wide floodplains and acceptance of occasional flooding of certain areas instead of the all-or-nothing approach of fighting nature that has historically been favored by the Army Corps of Engineers.

In this effort as in the others noted, vintners and growers were strong supporters even though any of these measures could potentially affect their individual property rights.

The Ag Preserve inspires leadership

Protecting the land is just one part of protecting Napa Valley. The success Napa has enjoyed by protecting its agricultural heritage, restricting development and focusing on its wines has encouraged Napa Valley Vintners to persist in their quest — and provided them with the resources to continue. The Napa Valley was the first recognized American Viticultural Area or appellation in California, and it remains by far the best known here and abroad.

"Napa" means quality, so much so that consumers understand the value and rely on the reputation for quality when a label reads "Napa," and outsiders have repeatedly tried to hijack the name.

In 2000, a state law prohibited the selling of wines labeled "Napa" or its geographic subdivisions unless the wine contained at least 75 percent Napa grapes. This was contested by Bronco Wine Company, which had bought the Napa Ridge and other Napa place name brands and produced and marketed wines made from grapes from outside Napa, leading consumers to believe the products to be from the Napa Valley Appellation.

The Napa Valley Vintners fought this practice all the way to the US Supreme Court and after a six-year court battle, Bronco lost.

California state law SB25241 is now fully enacted requiring brands with a Napa place name on the label to contain at least 75 percent fruit from Napa County. Following Napa's lead, last year, Sonoma County requested and received similar legislation from the state.

Even the European Union has recognized Napa's renowned role, and granted Napa Valley status as a Geographic Indication in 2007.

It was the first wine region outside a member state of the EU to receive this designation. Indeed, it's the first American product of any kind recognized with this status in Europe, and hence guaranteed protection from counterfeiting.

In the same way, Napa has also been a leader in protecting all wine appellations. It was a founding member in the Joint Declaration to Protect Wine Place and Origin signed by leading European and New World wine regions.

The quality of the wine, and the leadership of Napa's vintners, led them to create the first consumer charity wine auction in the United States in 1981. Auction Napa Valley has given more than $100 million to local healthcare and youth services, and it's also been the inspiration for every other charity wine auction in the U.S. Napa Valley vintners have also donated wines and experiences that have helped make these other charities successful.

Napa Valley Vintners has also been at the forefront of wine education, including programs to teach consumers, educators, the media and the trade about the region's wine through programs like Master Napa Valley for advanced level MS and MW candidates, Napa Valley Wine Educators Academy for professional educators, Napa Valley Rocks for on- and off-premise trade and the Symposium for Professional Wine Writers for journalists. The Vintners also supports the Rudd Center for Professional Wine Studies at the Culinary Institute of America in Napa Valley through part of the proceeds from Premiere Napa Valley, a trade auction.

Sustainable agriculture applies to a sustainable work force as well, and Napa County vintners and growers have been leaders in working conditions, pay, housing and opportunities for their workers.

About 6,000 farm workers and 7,000 winery workers are employed by Napa's wine industry. Wages are higher than average in the Napa Valley, but housing costs are also higher, and Napa's leaders initiated a local, self-assessed tax whereby vineyard owners tax themselves nearly $10 an acre to subsidize the valley's three farm worker housing centers for seasonal workers. This tax along with a very affordable daily rate for residents provides the funding for this work force's housing.

The NVV is also setting the standard with green programs such as Napa Green Certified Land. This program, begun in 2003, looks at all aspects of a grower's property from vineyards to roads, buildings and non-farmed land to curtail erosion, reduce or eliminate pesticide use and adopt practices that will ultimately enhance the Napa River watershed and preserve or restore wildlife habitat through sustainable agriculture practices.

Currently, 22,000 acres are enrolled in the program. Nearly 90 percent of the Napa River watershed is in private ownership and this public/private partnership is vital to the long term viability of the Napa Valley winegrowing community.

As a complement to Napa Green Certified Land, the Napa Valley Vintners developed a companion program for winery production facilities. Napa Green Certified Winery extends Napa Green through the winemaking process into the winery. The program covers such issues as water and materials recycling and energy conservation to reduce the carbon footprint of wine production facilities.

One example is the many Napa Valley wineries powered by the sun. A winery's solar power system can generate as much power as that used by 20 to 30 homes, and will keep more than 7 million pounds of greenhouse gasses out of the atmosphere.

Napa Green Certified Land and Winery go beyond compliance, meeting or exceeding environmental regulations to help the businesses become more sustainable through economically viable, environmentally sensitive and socially equitable practices.

As Napa looks ahead, one major concern is potential changes in climate that could affect grape growing. Some climate models suggest Napa Valley might be heavily affected as global temperatures rise, therefore, the Vintners created a Climate Study Task Force and hired two of the state's leading climate researchers from Scripps Institute and Stanford University to investigate the situation, project climate models specific to Napa Valley and help prepare tools for the future.

What the future holds

Napa Valley continues to maintain its commitment to agriculture with leadership from the NVV. The county sets a very high priority on maintaining the agricultural preserve and its recent draft of a new general plan states clearly: "Napa County in 2030 will remain a world-famous grape growing and winemaking region, with a viable and sustainable agricultural industry. Under this General Plan, the amount of land designated for agriculture will increase, assuming no further annexations of county land by incorporated cities and towns. New non-agricultural development will continue to be focused in the incorporated cities and already developed areas." The report continues, "Policies supporting agriculture include the long-standing 'right to farm' that ensures that new residents and new users of land understand they inhabit an agricultural area where the viability of agriculture comes first. These policies also define all the components of agriculture encompassed by the right to farm, and perpetuate the county's longstanding commitment to protections for agricultural land."

The plan also establishes agriculture and rural residences as the principal users of ground water aquifers and calls for data collection and long-term monitoring to ensure adequate supplies remain in the future and states that vineyard development is expected to continue, and will become increasingly environmentally sensitive as business practices and conservation priorities converge. The Napa River will increasingly run clean and healthy, supporting native fish, plants, and animals and serving as an important part of the life of the county's people. The plan emphasizes, "Napa County in 2030 will retain its rural character and outstanding quality of life."

The Napa Valley Agricultural Preserve, established 40 years, ago did more than protect the land and make Napa Valley a desirable place to live and grow grapes. Long-time observer Carson believes the preserve has played a key role in helping create Napa's reputation as the top spot in the United States to make wine. "After it passed, growers could concentrate on what they do best, growing grapes, not fending off the tax collector or worrying whether their neighbors were going to sell out or develop their land."

The experiment was a complete success. Carson concludes, "It was the foundation for great winemaking in Napa Valley," and the foundation for other leadership efforts that followed.

The Couple Who Created Napa Valley

Many people have worked to make the Napa Valley of today: early pioneers like George Yount and John Patchett, who planted the first grapes, and Charles Krug and Patchett who created the first commercial wineries; the Beringer brothers, Jacob Schram and Gustave Niebaum in the 19th century, then John Daniel, Georges de Latour, Louis Martini, and Andre Tchelistcheff who sought to restore Napa Valley's wine culture and industry after Prohibition. Mike Grgich, Jim Barrett and Warren Winiarski showed the world that Napa wines could match and beat the best from France.

But it was Robert and Margrit Mondavi who created the Napa Valley we see today.

Bob, as everyone called him, was a visionary who started his own winery in 1966 at the age of 54 after being ejected from the family winery, Charles Krug, after long disagreements with his family.

Bob adopted modern winemaking techniques to make superior wines, but he was also a tireless and selfless promoter: He first promoted wine as part of a healthy lifestyle, then California wine, then Napa Valley wine. Only then did he promote his own products.

Partnering with people as diverse as Baron Philippe de Rothschild and Julia Child, he sung the praises of wine and the good life. His iconic winery – patterned after missions that never existed in Napa Valley – became the symbol for Napa, even California wine. He promoted wine tasting as a way to snag customers, and created a wine world that has permeated American culture today.

Partnering with Bob to create today's Napa Valley was his second wife, Margrit, who taught him – and he was a quick and avid student – to tie wine to food, art and culture. Together, they started the Napa Valley Wine Auction, today's Auction Napa Valley, which has raised more than $100 million for local charities.

She initiated concerts at the winery, including the long-running summer music festival that has supported local music, installed sculpture and exhibited art that introduced the valley to an appreciation for arts the Tuscans developed centuries ago.

Perhaps most important, Margrit persuaded Bob to found the great chef's series, in which the best chefs of America traveled to Napa Valley to Napa Valley to teach classes, but really to be indoctrinated into the culture and wine of Napa Valley – and Robert Mondavi Vineyards. Jack and Dolores Cakebread expanded that mission with their American Harvest Workshop, as did many others like

Donald Hess and Jan Shrem who picked up the cultural heritage Margrit espoused, cleverly getting Bob to turn her vision into his.

Bob and Margrit contributed so much: The restoration of the Napa Valley Opera House, the Mondavi Center for the Arts at UC Davis, the Robert Mondavi Institute for Wine and Food Science at UC Davis, the Oxbow School, Lincoln Theater, even Copia, a grand vision poorly executed.

Even today, every visitor to Napa Valley who tastes fine wine, enjoys a concert or art show, and especially those who enjoy a fine meal, owe a heartfelt thanks to Bob and Margrit Mondavi.

Getting Around

Though you can get to Napa Valley by public transit, it's inconvenient. A car or a driver is almost a must.

Evans Transport runs regular buses from the San Francisco and Oakland Airports to Napa. Oakland is a bit more convenient and often cheaper. If you're adventuresome, you can take a ferry or BART from San Francisco and parts of the Bay Area, then an express bus to Napa and beyond up to Calistoga. The ferry is a very pleasant trip, by the way.

Amtrak also runs buses from its Martinez station to the Napa Valley Wine Station Depot and downtown Napa, and the Wine Train offers packages that include pickup at the Vallejo Ferry Terminal.

Once you get to Napa, a car or driver is almost vital if you want to see much of Napa Valley outside of town. Most attractions and all the towns are along highway 29, and a convenient public bus line runs up highway 29 to Calistoga, and stops close to most attractions, but buses are infrequent so check the schedule.

Tours and limousines

One way to avoid driving is to book a limousine or van to take you around, or arrange for a knowledgeable guide to design a tour. The valley has a wide variety of these transportation companies that do everything from driving you around in your own or rental car, like Designated Driver, which I've had good experience with (www.designateddrivernapa.com (707) 483-0123), to big buses that take crowds around. My Napa Valley Driver does the same.

Other companies customize a tour. One example is Verve Napa Valley designs personalized itineraries curated to your interests and passions. Its guides will share their insider access to exceptional boutique wineries, private art collections, secret gardens, special venues, events and more. (707) 287-2777

Don't drink and drive

One warning to take seriously is "Don't drink and drive." The wonderful wines invite overindulgence even though all wineries offer buckets to taste and spit and their staffs are trained to ferret out those who shouldn't drink more.

A designated driver is ideal. You can also hire drivers or cars for about $50 per hour, though limos full of drunken bachelorettes and buses aren't generally welcome at wineries.

It's unfortunate that there's not more convenient public transit in Napa Valley. You can actually reach all wineries along Highway 29

– most of those of major interest to tourists – via the public Vine bus, but the schedules are inconvenient and few tourists want to stand along the road waiting for a bus.

Ironically, the founder of the Napa Valley Wine Train, Vince DiDomenico, wanted to run a train that would let tourists visit wineries, but the county nixed that: They said it would attract equally undesirable commuters and tourists... The Train does have some excursions to wineries, however.

One alternative is to taste at tasting rooms in Napa, Yountville, St. Helena and Calistoga, where you can hit many wineries on foot.

One attraction of the city of Napa is that you can walk to so many places, and taxis are becoming quite available, but a trip up valley can be expensive in a cab. And though it's hard to accept, even a $100 taxi ride from Calistoga to Napa is a lot better than an arrest for drunk driving, which may involve a night in jail, fines and insurance costs of $12,000 and maybe a weekend in county jail.

The local papers publish the name of people arrested for driving while intoxicated and it costs plenty and probably jail time, though it can often be reduced to a charge called "wet reckless," which is as expensive or more so compared to a DUI charge, but with fewer repercussions.

Some visitors think local law enforcement agencies give tourists slack, but don't believe it. Drunk driving causes many accidents and takes many lives here, though probably no more than elsewhere, and the police, sheriff's deputies and highway patrol want to reduce those accidents and injuries.

It's especially important to be careful in St. Helena, which has a reputation for aggressive action.

Tours and Transportation Suppliers

Car Rental
- Budget. (800) 527-7000. Napa
- Enterprise. (707) 253-8000. Napa
- Enterprise Rent-A-Car St. Helena. (707) 968-0816.
- Hertz. (707) 265-7575. Napa

Helicopter Tours
Wine Country Helicopters. (707) 226-8470. Napa

Pedicabs
NV Hoppers. (707) 224-4677. Napa (pedicabs)

Taxicabs
- Black Tie Taxi. (707) 259-1000. www.blacktietaxi.com. Napa
- Napa Valley Cab. (707) 257-6444. Napa
- Northbay Taxi. 707-259-1000.
- Valley Valet. www.valley-valet.com. (707) 942-9009.
- Upper Valley Wine Valley Taxi. (707) 251-9463. Napa
- Yellow Cab Napa Valley. (707) 226-3731. www.yellowcabnapa.com. Napa

Winery Tours
- A Limo Excursion & Wine Tours. (707) 655-6053. www.alimoexcursionwinetours.com. Rutherford
- Alegro Private Tours. (415) 668-1864. Napa
- Alliance Wine Country Tours, Meetings & Events. (707) 333-8340. St. Helena
- Backroads. (510)-527-1555. Napa
- Beau Wine Tours and Limousine Service. (707) 257-0887. www.beauwinetours.com. Napa
- Bordeaux Limousine. (707) 257-4501. Napa
- Butler Limousine. (925) 682-5466. Napa
- California Wine Tours. (707) 253-1300. www.californiawinetours.com. Napa
- Celebrity Limousine. (707) 552-7752. Napa
- Classic Convertible Wine Tours. (707) 226-9227. www.ccwinetours.com. Napa

- Classic Limousine. (707) 253-0999. www.classiclimousine.50megs.com. Napa
- Consort Wine Tours. (707) 631–6775. www.consortwinetours.com. Yountville
- Cristal Blue Carriage. (707) 927-3141. Napa
- Designated Driver Napa (707) 483-0123. www.designateddrivernapa.com (Can drive your car)
- Designated Driver Napa Wine Tours. (415) 251-4183. www.designateddriversnapa.com.
- Destination: Napa Valley Tours. (707) 256-3307. www.tournapavalley.com. Napa
- Esperya: The Wine Country Experience. (707) 253-1797. www.winecountryesperya.com. Napa
- Elegant Tours. (707) 312-1352. www.elegantwinetours.com. Calistoga
- Elite Limousine Service. (925) 825-1800. www.elitelimonapa.com. Napa
- First Classic Limousine. (707) 320-0008. Napa
- Group Outings. www.groupoutings.com. Napa
- Knight Wine Tours & Travel. (707) 738-4500. Napa
- Limos of Napa. (707) 334-0411. www.limosofnapa.com
- Luxury Tours. (707) 254-7467. www.luxurytours.info. Napa
- Magnum Tours. (707) 753-0088. St. Helena
- My City Tours. (415) 531-8724. 991 St. Helena Highway, Rutherford
- My Napa Valley Driver (707) 254-5115. www.mynapavalleydriver.com(Drives your car)
- NLS Limousine & Sedan Services. (650) 364-0118. Napa
- Napa Insiders. (707) 254-1814. Napa
- Napa Limousine. (707) 637-4399. www.napalimousine.com
- Napa Valley Chauffeurs. (707) 253-2029. Napa
- Napa Valley Crown Limousines. (707) 226-9500. www.napalimo.com
- Napa Valley Off-Road Tours. (707) 257-6680. Napa
- Napa Valley Tours & Transportation. (707) 251-9463. Napa
- Napa Valley Tour Company. (707) 224-4949. www.napavalleytourcompany.com

- Napa Valley Wine Country Tours. (707) 226-3333. Napa
- Napa Valley Wine Tours. (707) 265-8204. Napa
- Napa Winery Shuttle. (707) 257-1950. www.wineshuttle.com. Napa
- Perata Luxury Tours. (707) 227-8271. www.perataluxurytours.com . Napa
- Platypus Tours Limited. (707) 253-2723. www.platypustours.com . Napa
- Prestige Limousine. (925) 691-7000. Napa
- Pure Luxury Wine Tours. (707) 253-0296. www.pureluxury.com.
- Royal Coach Limousine Service (800) 995-7692. www.royalcoachlimousine.com. Napa
- St. Helena Wine Tours. (707) 963-9644. St. Helena
- Swirl And Sip Wine Tours. (707) 363-7717.
- Tours D'Elegance. (707) 252-6568. Napa
- Verve Napa Valley (707) 287-2777 www.vervenapavalley.com. Napa Can arrange art tours.
- VLS Tours. (707) 929-3555. www.vlstours.com Napa.
- Wine & Dine Tours. (707) 963-8930. www.wineanddinetour.com. St. Helena
- Wine & Vine Ways. (707) 254-9982. Napa
- Wine Country Jeep Tours. (800) 539-5337. Napa
- Wine Country Safari. (707) 265-7683. Napa
- Wine Country Tour Shuttle. (415) 513-5400. Napa
- Wine Country Tours. (707) 322-3733. Napa

The Napa Valley Wine Train

You'll notice the train tracks along the Highway 29 as you drive up valley. They now end north of St. Helena at Deer Park Road (in the Charles Krug Winery property).

Napa Valley used to have two train systems, a steam train and an electric train, both going all the way to Calistoga (you can see the tracks for the electric in the road at the main intersection by Brannan's Restaurant and the steam depot a block away.)

Both systems gave up passenger service long ago, and unfortunately, the tracks were removed north of St. Helena and the rights of way abandoned.

Though much of the old route is now in vineyard roads, at least one building is in the way, a warehouse at Sterling, and most owners would probably be opposed to having trains restored through their property. It's a shame, for Calistoga would dearly love to have a train ending in its suffering downtown.

The former owner of the Wine Train originally wanted to run service from the Vallejo Ferry Terminal and drop people off at wineries, but most wineries and many others in the valley fought him; the wineries like people to arrive with cars with big trunks for cases of wine! They also were assessed for restoring tracks they had often paved over.

St. Helena even prohibited visitors from getting off the train to shop or eat, though its opposition has softened slightly and it now lets some passengers debark on street parties on Friday nights during the summer.

The owner of the train also offered to run passenger service using self-propelled cars, but the county turned it down, saying it would encourage tourists and commuters, which it considered undesirable.

Now, some local entrepreneurs are trying to figure out how to finance passenger service, though it seems a long shot.

Though it doesn't offer true passenger service (except for trips to St. Helena's Cheers street festival on Fridays once a month during the summer), the Napa Valley Wine Train is still a delightful if expensive way to enjoy the valley.

The trains consists of beautifully restored antique cars, though at least one engine is converted to run on clean natural gas. Half the passengers typically taste wine on the 1½-hour trip up valley, then eat on the way back (or vice versa).

The food is excellent, and is prepared onboard in the kitchen car by chef Kelly Macdonald. The wines are primarily from Napa Valley, and the train has a selection of seating options and many special programs for holidays and different interests like Murder Mystery Theater, winemaker dinners and appellation meals.

The views out the train are delightful (once you leave Napa!). In the summer, dinner trips are great ways to get a lay of the land, but the trip is largely in the dark during the winter (when the schedule is restricted) and lunch is probably a better option then.

The train does have programs with some wineries that allow passengers to get off and visit the wineries including Grgich-Hills, a short walk, and Domain Chandon, a short bus ride.

The Vine Trail

One alternative to driving or the bus is bicycling. Plans are in place for a bike train from Vallejo to Calistoga (about 50 miles), and some pieces are in place.

Originally planned to follow the Napa River, that's proven too complicated and now the best bet is a path along the railroad tracks but separated by a fence for safety.

For now, it's easy to get from Napa to north of Yountville on bike trails or little-used roads. From there north to a mile south of Calistoga – about 20 miles – you're on narrow and busy Highway 29, which doesn't have bike lanes in many places but does have a lot of distracted drivers.

Silverado Trail is striped for bikes, but traffic moves fast and it's not very comfortable for most bicyclists.

The Cities and Towns of Napa Valley

American Canyon – Gateway to Napa Valley

Almost anyone driving to Napa over the Carquinez Strait Bridge passes through the small city of American Canyon and may not even realize that it's part of Napa County. It is, but has more in common with usual subdivision and strip-mall cities than Napa Valley, and in fact, isn't actually in geographic Napa Valley.

That doesn't keep the operators of the pleasant but modest hotels in American Canyon from suggesting they are in the "gateway to Napa Valley."

Unless you happen to be staying in one of those hotels, there isn't much of interest to visitors. It's mostly subdivisions and a few shopping centers with a Wal-Mart and various fast food restaurants and chain merchants.

If you look carefully to the east, however, you might see the ruins of an old basalt plant with its intriguing giant, cone-topped kiln. Developers have proposed a town center in those interesting ruins including a theater in the kiln, but nothing has come of that so far.

Vineyards start just north of the city of 25,000, good vineyards of grapes that like the area's relatively cool climate.

Napa – No Longer a Cinderella

What a difference a few years makes! Napa used to be a place visitors drove through on the way upvalley, but now it's a must-visit destination.

The change is due largely to an election by voters more than a decade ago to fix the city's frequent flooding.

Napa regularly flooded because of its largely overlooked treasure, the Napa River. That river is one of the few navigable rivers in California; ships once came to Napa to load the grain and other crops grown in the valley before it became famous for wine, and Napa was about as far up the river as they could go before it turned into a creek.

Unfortunately, nature's way of keeping the valley fertile was to flood regularly, and that was very inconvenient. No one would invest downtown near the river when they knew they property would soon flood.

The vote to fund a massive flood-control project changed everything. Or we should say, is changing everything. It's mostly completed, but funding slowdowns have taken their toll and more work lies ahead.

The project was a unique one for the Army Corps of Engineers, too. Instead of trying to confine the river to concrete channels and levees, it created flood plains and bypasses that would let the river spread – not to populated areas, but part-time parks.

With the river being tamed, investors started spending money downtown. Margrit Mondavi dreamed of a Napa festival to match Salzburg or Spoleto, which has come in Festival del Sole, but it's mostly held upvalley. Her late husband Robert mostly anticipated a better way of life for Napa's residents.

Most notably, however, the Mondavis put up a large gift to fund the now sadly closed Copia: The American Center for Wine, Food and the Arts, a large interactive museum and learning center in the river's oxbow bend.

Development followed the progress of the flood control project. The popular Oxbow Public Market, a small version of San Francisco's popular San Francisco Ferry Building food and shopping center, lies next door and The River Terrace Inn and Westin Verasa were built nearby. The Mondavis also funded the innovative Oxbow School for the arts across the river.

The best way to see Napa is to just head downtown. The Visitor Center in the Riverfront development is a great place to start, and has a large raised-relief map of the valley as well as interactive and human help. It also offers advice to visitors, books rooms for procrastinators and sells some Napa-oriented books and merchandise.

The Visitor Center is only blocks from most of the other attractions as well. The new Napa, if filled with delights, is compact enough for walking, measuring about half a mile in each direction. The must-see district stretches along the river roughly from the restored Napa Mill in the south to the Jarvis Conservatory, from the Oxbow Public Market at the eastern end of the Oxbow to the booming "West End" near Franklin Street downtown.

Downtown Napa is schizophrenic, with lovely old buildings — and a few clever new ones — mixed with ordinary or forbidding government buildings. Fortunately, much old remains, and the town is slowly reclaiming its heritage. The Napa Downtown Association publishes an excellent map and booklet listing walking tours.

Among the gems are the Hatt Building or Napa Mill, an old grain mill on the river reborn as a small version of San Francisco's Ghirardelli Square. Its heart is the boutique Napa River Inn, an elegant hotel with 65 rooms in the old mill building as well as two modern structures so well integrated they look as if they've been there for a century. Silos for grain rise above the complex and lend their name to intimate Silo's Jazz Club.

The Mill contains an outside concert area by Silos's Jazz Club on the river and inviting patios where you can enjoy a meal alongside the river in elegant Angèle French restaurant and bar or casual Napa General Store, in Celadon with its fusion comfort food, Sweetie Pies bakery and Vintage Sweet Shoppe. The Napa General Store is a shop off the hotel lobby sell gifts, too. The owner has proposed expanding the hotel and adding a spa.

Most recently, the multi-use Riverfront complex has risen next to the Napa Mill. It contains restaurants, the Napa Valley Visitor Center and many shops on the ground floor, with offices and condominium homes on the upper floors.

The Riverfront development hosts the first western location for Iron Chef Masuharu Morimoto, and the trendy big-city décor and innovative food is drawing scores of elegantly dressed young diners from San Francisco and beyond but it's also a favorite of locals and caters to them with special deals during the week.

The hopping bar area has comfortable lounges for sipping and meeting. The main room is lively if loud, while a side space is quieter and the tables outside along the river are perfect for couples.

The food is a combination of traditional Japanese and the chef's famed innovations, and all are good.

By itself, Morimoto raised the hipness level of Napa, and it's always busy – and open late.

Also in the Riverfront complex is Fish Story, an outpost of Lark Restaurant Group. Both restaurants have outside seating along the river. TV chef Tyler Florence opened a restaurant, but it didn't take off and closed after failing a health inspection, though it fixed that problem. It's a great location, if a bit small for a restaurant. It would be a great bar – or combined with the closed Tyler Florence kitchenware shop as a restaurant.

A new gelato and coffee shop has also opened on the river patio, and a number of upscale clothing stores and other shops are open, too.

A short pedestrian path lines the river and will be extended. The east bank contains sloped parks that allow the river to rise gently when it feels rambunctious rather than flood downtown.

A dry channel across the river's oxbow bend will provide parks and sports space, allowing river overflow if needed. Longer, higher new bridges also give the river room to romp while providing greater access to the boats that will arrive when construction is complete.

Some of the most interesting developments in Napa not surprisingly lie along Main Street, but only a few years ago Main St. was anything but main. Numerous restaurants line now Main, with others on the way.

The real jewel of Napa is the Napa Valley Opera House just off First Street and Main, the corner immortalized in the musical *The Most Happy Fella* where the boys stood on the corner and watched the girls go by.

Bob and Margrit Mondavi helped pay to restore the Napa Valley Opera House, a gem built in 1879 but abandoned for almost 70 years following World War II.

Now lovingly restored, the 550-seat theater features frequent eclectic performances from folk music to musicals to lectures and even cabaret and vaudeville acts. It even hosts an occasional small opera production, something that never happened in its early days as a vaudeville theater.

All seats in the upstairs auditorium lie 22 rows or less from the stage, so all performances are intimate. Downstairs is the Café Theater used for small performances and offering refreshments before performances and during intermissions.

Further up Main lies one of the best cookware stores anywhere (Shackford's), and the Jarvis Conservatory, an old winery used for performances and art films, as well as a number of popular eateries and tasting bars.

New Cielito Lindo restaurant offers authentic Mexican cocina and local favorite Azzurro Pizzeria and Enoteca are on Main Street, with Bui Bistro offering Vietnamese cuisine and Uva Trattoria with Italian-American food and jazz nearby.

The old Goodman Library on First Street is a historical museum now. A gem nearby is venerable Uptown Theater, which developer George Altamura has turned into a top venue for live music.

Napa has also become a prime destination for wine tasting, with many tasting rooms, wine bars and retail shops offering tastes as well as glasses and bottles. Many of these venues offer wines from wineries that can't or don't have their own tasting rooms at wineries. Some are from "virtual wineries" that make their wines at other wineries, while others can't get permits for tasting rooms due to the fact that their locations are too remote.

Downtown Napa also boasts many other fine restaurants, most of them new, and some shops and galleries with a big effort by a new owner to attract new retailers to the shopping mall, " The Shops at Town Center."

Just south of downtown, stretching back from the river, lies Napa Abajo Historic District, filled with lovingly restored Victorian homes from just after the big earthquake of 1906 as well as houses from later times. It is home to numerous beautiful bed and breakfast inns.

Napa's West End

Not far away in Napa's hot "West End" at First and Franklin around the Avia hotel, which was bought by Hyatt and will become part of its Andaz boutique brand.

The West End's restaurants include comfy Norman Rose Pub and Grace's Table serving global comfort food, and Eiko's Japanese sushi bar with a dark lounge that's a magnet for younger patrons.

Tarla Mediterranean Grill serves food with a Turkish-Greek tilt and Oenotri southern Italian food and wine that has garnered raves from both food critics and locals. Its outside seating in the plaza is like being in Palermo, if a less worn.

The area also includes art galleries, the tasteful West End Napa gift and lifestyle store, and the John Anthony tasting salon, more an elegant wine bar than the usual tasting room.

The new Napa Tourism Information Center is a private operation that does offer advice, but also a reasonable wine bar, a branch of venerable Napa Valley Olive Oil Co. and a gift store.

About 20 winery tasting rooms and wine bars dot downtown Napa, too. My favorites are Carpe Diem on Second Street and ZuZu tapas bar. New 1313 Main attracts locals, too.

Back Room Wines has popular themed tastings on Thursday and Friday, and they're always filled with locals.

It's not downtown, but on highway 29 just north of Napa, but Bistro Don Giovanni is a favorite restaurant of almost everyone in Napa Valley, including me.

Today, Napa remains a work in progress. It features old and new attractions for the tourist and resident alike, yet there's promise of far more to come. Napa is already a vital destination for visitors, but it will become even more so.

Outside downtown Napa, Silverado Resort's new owners are upgrading the rooms and facilities, including the two golf courses and tennis program.

The Oxbow Public Market

The Oxbow Public Market is one of the treasures of Napa Valley. After a slow start due to 9/11, Copia's closing and a troubled economy, it is now very successful and is now filled most of the time with happy eaters, drinkers, shoppers and gawkers.

A smaller version of San Francisco's Ferry Building Market, Faneuil Hall in Boston or Pike's Market in Seattle, it's an amazing collection of restaurants and shops.

Most are in the main hall, though the Model Bakery, Fatted Calf, Gott's Refresher and Poor House furnishings are across a small parking lot and face McKinstry Street.

The Market isn't a food court, and Ca' Momi, C Casa, Hog Island and Kitchen Door don't allow you to bring food into their space, though part of the river deck is open to anyone – but they have to buy wine from Hog Island, Wine Merchant or Kitchen Door due to the business' licenses.

Otherwise, you're welcome to take your food (and beverages) to the tables in the middle of the market and front deck (but not wine or beer there...)

Tuesday is lively Locals Night with lots of specials and big crowds of happy people, and music resounds some nights and weekends.

During the summer, Farmers' Markets are held on Tuesday and Saturday mornings next to Oxbow Public Market.

Anette's Chocolates

Anette's is a retail outlet for Anette's Chocolate factory only a few blocks away on First Street. It sells exquisite morsels of chocolate and a few other sweets. 1321 First St., Napa. (707) 252-4228. www.anettes.com

C Casa Taqueria

C Casa is a taqueria that combines tradition authentic soft tacos from southern Mexico with innovative touches, all made with fresh, natural ingredients. It sells salads, side dishes, roasted rotisserie chickens and sometimes ducks. On Sundays during the summer, you can enjoy music and specials on the deck. 610 First St., Napa. (707) 226-7700. www.myccasa.com

Ca' Momi Winery & Enoteca

Ca' Momi is an Italian restaurant focusing on authentic Neapolitan and other pizzas as well as other Italian food including appetizers and pastries. It's also a retail outlet and tasting location for Ca' Momi's many affordable wines, many from Napa Valley, which are sold at retail prices with meals.

It also sells imported Italian ingredients for cooking at home. 610 First St., Napa. (707) 257-4992. www.camomienoteca.com

Five Dot Ranch

Five Dot Ranch specializes in free-range natural beef as well as specialty cuts and some beef charcuterie. It only sells beef; paradoxically, the Fatter Calf at the Market doesn't sell beef (including veal) but pork, lamb and poultry.

Five Dot Ranch also sells a limited selection of excellent sandwiches to eat at the market. 610 First St. # 2, Napa. (707) 224-5550. www.fivedotranch.com

Gott's Roadside

Gott's Roadside, a sister to the popular eatery in St. Helena, is a unique, high-end drive in without the cars. In addition to offering upscale drive-in food and healthy California alternatives like fish tacos, it sells artisanal wine and beer including some from the Gotts who own the small chain. 644 First St., Napa. (707) 224-6900. gottsroadside.com

Heritage Culinary Artifacts

Heritage Culinary Artifacts sells premium culinary antiques that are both aesthetically pleasing and functional. The emphasis is on American work, but not to the exclusion of European pieces, with all relating to food, wine and cooking. 610 First St. # 14, Napa. (707) 224-2101. www.heritageartifacts.com

Hog Island Oyster Company

Hog Island Oyster Company is a small restaurant that serves oysters on the half shell and cooked, as well as other shellfish and fish, much from its oyster beds in Tomales Bay. Hog Island also sells the live shellfish.

Call ahead for more than small quantities of shellfish. 610 First St., Napa. (707) 251-8113. www.hogislandoysters.com

Kanaloa Seafood

Kanaloa sells only sustainably caught or raised seafood. It offers many varieties you won't find many places as well as live crabs and lobsters.

It also prepares sushi to eat at the Market and a number of ready to eat items to talk home. 610 First St .# 3, Napa. (707) 224-3474. www.kanaloaseafood.com

Kara's Cupcakes

The craze for expensive, elegantly decorated cupcakes shows no sign of subsiding. Kara certainly makes her share, many looks more like works of art than something you'd eat. 610 First St., Napa. (707) 258-2253. www.karascupcakes.com

Kitchen Door

The Kitchen Door is a casual restaurant that serves upscale food in simpler presentations – and cost. Chef Todd Humphries has long experience including at the former Martini House in St. Helena. He's especially known for his treatments of fungi. The deck is a great place to sit in the usual good weather. 610 First St., Napa. (707) 226-1560. www.kitchendoornapa.com

La Crepe!

La Crepe is owned by a Frenchman with great experience at restaurants and his wife. They prepare authentic sweet and savory crepes and fill them with traditional and California ingredients. 610 First St., Napa. (707) 925-5410. www.lacrepenapa.com

Olive Press

The Olive Press is a retail arm of The Olive Press, which is at the Jacuzzi Winery in Sonoma's Carneros region. It sells a variety of olive oils, olives, vinegars, accessories and other items. You can also taste the oils and buy by the ounce even in your own container. 610 First St., Napa. (707) 226-2579. www.theolivepress.com

Oxbow Cheese Merchant

Oxbow Cheese Merchant shares space with Oxbow Wine Merchant. It probably has the largest selection of cheese in Napa Valley and knowledgeable experts to help you decide what to buy. They're happy to cut samples and pieces, including for a picnic or snack with wine there. 610 First St., Napa. (707) 257-5200. fpwm.com

Oxbow Produce and Grocery

When there's no Farmers Market in the parking lot (they're on Tuesday and Saturday mornings during the summer), you can shop the virtual farmers market at Oxbow Produce and Grocery. It includes locally sourced produce as well as gourmet items form elsewhere. 610 First St. # 20, Napa. (707) 257-6828. www.oxbowpublicmarket.com

Oxbow Wine Merchant & Wine Bar

Oxbow Wine Merchant & Wine Bar has a good selection of wines including both local wines and imports, but as big a draw is the popular wine bar. The bar offers tastes, flights, glasses and more.

It shares space with the Cheese Merchant, and they'll happily provide cheese to pair with your wine. 610 First St., Napa. (707) 257-5200.www.fpwm.com

Pica Pica Maize Kitchen and Pica Pica Bar

Pica Pica Maize Kitchen sells arepas and other food from Venezuela. The arepas look like English muffins, but are made with corn (maize), as are their breads, so they're gluten free.

Pica Pica Bar serves interesting tropical drinks as well as wine and beer. It has many special nights when it highlights various wines or beer and also sometimes hosts Latin musicians. 610 First St. # 5, Napa. (707) 251-3757. www.picapicakitchen.com

Poor House

Poor House sells distinctive furniture and house furnishing, some designed by the owners. It's in a metal building on McKinstry with a separate entrance. 1046 McKinstry St., Napa. (707) 294-2066. info@poorhousenapa.com

Ritual Coffee Roasters

Ritual Coffee Roasters is the anti-Starbucks, with distinctive, strong coffee much appreciated by connoisseurs. It also makes various coffee beverages and has a few pastries and cookies on hand, though there are many other options in the Market. 610 First St., Ste. 12, Napa. (707) 253-1190. www.ritualroasters.com

The Fatted Calf

The Fatted Calf doesn't sell fatted calf (veal) or other beef products in the Oxbow Public Market, but it does carry and make a wide variety of pork products as well as lamb and some other proteins. It also sells a few other gourmet items like Rancho Gordo beans. The charcuterie also sells excellent sandwiches to eat at the Market or take away for a picnic. 644 First St. # C, Napa. (707) 256-3684. www.fattedcalf.com

The Model Bakery

The Model Bakery is one of Napa Valley's two superb artisanal bakeries (The other being Bouchon Bakery). It make a wide variety of breads and some pastries. It also makes sandwiches for lunch and sells slices of thick-crust pizza. It bakes bread in the afternoon so it's fresh for dinner, and has specials at the end of the day, too. 644 First St. # B, Napa. (707) 259-1128. www.themodelbakery.com

Three Twins Ice Cream

Ignore the silly name. Three Twins Ice Cream makes incredible ice cream. It even makes fresh waffle cones for pure decadence. Note that the kiddie cones are enough for many people... 610 First St. # 1, Napa. (707) 257-8946. www.threetwinsicecream.com

Tillerman Tea

Tillerman Tea offers a wide selection of over 60 loose-leafed teas in addition to a special "house flight" of five teas: green, oolong, black, jasmine and puerh. All Tillerman teas are from small growers and producers and represent the very best in quality and in value. It holds free monthly introductory classes and, by reservation, customers can book a private tea tasting and education program complete with ceremonial and cultural elements. They also have a selection of teapots, cups, infusers and tea-making paraphernalia. 610 First St. # 8, Napa. (707) 265-0200. www.tillermantea.com

Whole Spice Company

Whole Spice Company finds the best spices from around the world, import fresh products and custom grind them and creates custom blends of spices. Nearly 30% of their spices are certified organic. From the usual to the exotic, allspice to vanilla and ajowan to zhug, Whole Spice also offers a broad scope of salts and mushroom powders. It offers 300 different spices and 50 to 60 blends, both bulk and pre-packaged, and all in small quantities to ensure freshness. 644 First St. #D, Napa. (707) 226-6529. www.wholespice.com

The Market is at the corner of First Street and McKinstry, backing up to the Napa River and close to the Napa Valley Wine Train Depot and the Westin Verasa hotel.

Across the street from the Oxbow Public Market is Filippi's Italian-American Restaurant, and there are five wine-tasting rooms within a quarter block.

Next to it is closed Copia, which we hope will rise like a phoenix in the near future.

The Historic Napa Mill

In addition to the Oxbow Public Market, Napa's has another special destination for visitors, the Historic Napa Mill, often called the Hatt Building locally. It's only a few blocks walk away and also on the Napa River.

It was indeed a mill. In the 19th century, Napa County produced far more grain than grapes. The Bale Mill north of St. Helena is an impressive reminder of that, and still grinds corn and wheat on weekends with water power.

The Napa Mill was build by Captain Albert Hatt in 1884. It's the last vestiges of the large industrial and commercial center in the area in the late 1800's and early 1900's, including two large wineries.

Developer Harry Price has the vision to repurpose the old buildings, which had laid unused for decades and even slated for demolition.

He lovingly restored the existing Hatt Building, adding two new buildings along the river that complement the old structure and appear to have been originals.

These new buildings include rooms for the Napa River Inn, which has its lobby, meeting room and some suites in the old building.

Also in the complex are a riverfront plaza popular for events and a cantilevered river walking trail.

Fittingly, the historic silo still tops the building, serving a reminder of Napa's grittier past.

The Hatt Building contains two excellent restaurants, Angèle and Celadon; the informal Napa General Store with gift items, a wine-tasting bar and café with inside and outside seating; Sweetie Pies Bakery and Café; Vintage Sweet Shop, which also offers wine and chocolate tastings; La Pelle Skin Spa and Boutique, and Amelia's Gifts.

A special favorite is Silo's Club, which features jazz and eclectic performances.

Owner Price has approval to replace the small spa with a larger building and add a third floor to the Embarcadero building with its guest rooms.

The Riverfront

Next to the Historic Napa Mill is a new complex designed to look old. That illusion is fleeting, but it's a worthwhile addition to the city with many attractions to visitors and locals alike.

It consists on two buildings interconnected with a bridge above an opening in the middle. The upper floors are offices and condominiums. Downstairs are shops and restaurants. The eateries along the river offer desirable outdoor seating in the shade during the warm summer and generally have heaters for cool evenings.

Unfortunately, the city dock is temporarily missing; when it returns, this will be a prime destination for boating enthusiasts from around San Francisco Bay.

A prime destination for visitors along Main Street is the Visitor Center, which includes a large raised-relief (3-D) map of Napa Valley, plus computerized guides, helpful volunteers, a concierge and even a gift shop with items relevant to Napa Valley.

Next to it is the exceptionally popular Morimoto Restaurant, which is always busy – and for good reason. Also along this stretch is Michael Holmes' Ivy Twig & Twine home and garden accessory shop.

Scott Lyall's men's shop, and his mother Helen Lyall's women's shop and B. Real Women's Apparel have brought chic clothing to downtown Napa.

Also along Main Street is Fish Story restaurant, part of the Lark Creek Group chain.

Continuing along the Napa River frontage is the patio of Fish Story, the Pearl Southern Bistro, Frati Gelato with panini and coffee as well as iced treats, Napa River Velo; Michael Holmes' Gallery, Liken; and Morimotos' outside seating.

Yountville – America's Tiny Gourmet Capital

Now dubbed, "America's per-capita gourmet capital" because of its many fine restaurants, Yountville once boasted California's *lowest* per-capita income because of its California Veteran's Home, a residence for retired and infirm veterans.

The Veteran's Home is still in Yountville, but the small town – one of few official "towns" in California – is now full of well-off retirees who only fought business wars, upscale inns and shops – and all those great restaurants.

Yet it wouldn't be a stretch to call Yountville a one-street town. There are homes on other streets, but virtually all the businesses and attractions lie along Washington Street, once the route of the railroad running up Napa Valley.

Yountville is so close to the relatively large city of Napa that it doesn't have much in the way of local businesses, though its Ranch Market Too sells grocery and produce and a good deli is grafted on. What it does have is the aforementioned restaurants, starting at the top with the French Laundry, often called the best restaurant in America.

Also at the top tier is étoile Restaurant at sparkling wine producer Domaine Chandon, and the town boasts two authentic French bistros, urban Bouchon and country Bistro Jeanty.

Michael Chiarello's Bottega is one of my favorite restaurants anywhere with its upscale casual southern Italian-based food. His NapaStyle store across the plaza also serves deli food and wine.

Redd is owned by chef Richard Reddington, the acclaimed chef from Auberge du Soleil, and he recently opened Redd Wood pizzeria in the North Block Hotel.

Then there's Hurley's comfortable Italo-French-California restaurant. Bouchon Bakery, Pacific Blues Café, new (soon to open) Ciccio and the grill at the golf course complete the more informal eateries, while Napa Valley classics Brix and Mustards lie just north of town.

Yountville contains some of Napa Valley's most popular inns, including Tuscan-inspired Villagio and French-styled Vintage Inn, plus newly expanded and upgraded Hotel Yountville, luxury environmentally sensitive Bardessono, boutique North Branch Hotel, Napa Valley Lodge and a host of smaller B&B's in and just outside of town. Luxury Poetry Inn affiliated with Cliff Lede Winery has only three suites on a hillside overlooking Napa Valley.

The town also contains interesting shops, many in V Marketplace, an 1870-era former winery turned into a shopping center with gift shops, a chocolate maker, art galleries and clothing stores as well as Bottega and Chiarello's NapaStyle lifestyle store. Other galleries, antique stores and other shops line Washington Street.

The Napa Valley Museum is on the attractive grounds of the Veteran's Home. The Museum is worth a visit to learn more about winemaking and Napa Valley. Nearby Lincoln Theater is a state-of-the-art performance center that unfortunately is closed at present.

Being in Napa Valley, Yountville naturally contains a number of wineries. The most notable is Domaine Chandon with interesting tours that explain how sparkling wine is made – and offers tastes in an elegant salon or on its patio. Because it's connected with a restaurant, the salon stays open far later than most Napa Valley wineries, which typically close between 4 and 6 p.m.

About a dozen wineries have tasting rooms in Yountville, while other wineries lie nearby.

Yountville also has some nice parks where you can enjoy a picnic, and the historic Pioneer Cemetery where town-founder George Yount lies buried.

Yountville is the home to a number of balloon companies; a leisurely trip aloft in a balloon may be one of Napa Valley's best indulgences, perhaps followed only by a massage.

The Shops at V Marketplace

V Marketplace is a unique shopping center. It's built in and around the 1870 Groezinger Wine Cellars at 6525 Washington St. in Yountville.

A little history of Groezinger Wine Cellars

On June 23, 1870, German-born vintner, Gottlieb Groezinger, acquired 370 acres in Yountville from Henry C. Boggs and began construction of what would become one of the largest operating wineries in California.

The buildings that you see were part of the elaborate Groezinger Winery complex, which included a large brick wine cellar and detached distillery, brick livery stables and barns, a creamery, a steam power plant and the three-story, brick Groezinger mansion to the north of the property.

Unfortunately, Groezinger's great enterprise was due for a setback. On the night of Sept. 20, 1876, a mysterious explosion and a fire in the distillery destroyed all that would burn in the building. Groezinger carried no insurance. In spite of the disastrous loss of his distillery, Groezinger successfully continued his winemaking operation until 1889, when he ultimately sold the property.

Under successive ownership, the winery remained in operation until 1955. The Groezinger Winery, known today as V Marketplace, is listed in the National Register of Historic Places with the U.S. Department of the Interior. The buildings have had little alteration and most of the original ones stand here on the 20-acre site.

Now, the main building and surrounding ones are filled with shops and other businesses of interest to visitors. It features unique businesses, and most of the shops are owned by local people, living and making their living here in the Valley. One gallery is owned by a San Francisco firm. Many people would be surprised at the longevity of our shops. The children's shop, for instance has only had two owners in its 42-year history. Most shops have been there more than 10 years, many 15 and some over 30.

It's worth visiting the shops and eating at one of its restaurants.

Shops

- A Little Romance; gifts and rare finds of comfort. (707) 944-1350
- California & Vine; where whimsy meets the vineyard. (707) 945-0344
- Ielle; contemporary women's clothing and accessories. (707) 944-2282

- Kāne; resort wear and accessories for men. (707) 945-5263
- Kollar Chocolates; taste something new. chocolate, gelato, espresso. (707) 738-6750
- Lemondrops; children's boutique and toys. (707) 947-7057
- Montecristi, A Legend: a lifestyle - hats and accessories made in Ecuador. (707) 944-2870
- Napastyle; lifestyle retail, café, wine tasting. (707) 945-1229
- Sisters; fashion apparel for women & men, unique jewelry and gifts. (707) 944-8400
- Soluna Boutique Salon; hair, make-up, lash extensions and esthetic services. (707) 944-8589
- Tay & Grace; fabulous collection of women's novelty clothing. (707) 944-8307
- Vianett; Bridal • couture• evening. (707) 944-1505

Galleries

- Blue Heron; wine country art by wine country artists. (707) 944-2044
- Dennis Rae Gallery; discover the secret art of Dr. Seuss. (707) 944-2523
- Gallery 1870; fine art from the heart of Napa Valley. (707) 944-9670
- North Bay Gallery; art glass, bronzes, wall art and jewelry. (707) 945-0145

Wine Tasting

- NapaStyle; Chiarello Family Vineyards and many others. (707) 945-1229
- V Wine Cellar; historic boutique wine shop and tasting bar. (707) 531-7053

Restaurants

- Bottega; Michael Chiarello's rustic farm-to-table Italian cuisine. (707) 945-1050
- NapaStyle Paninoteca & Wine Bar; panini, salads, salumi e formaggio. (707) 945-1229
- Pacific Blues Cafe; "Maverick American" cuisine. (707) 944-4455

Ballooning

Napa Valley Aloft; Hot air balloon rides. (707) 944-4408

Oakville & Rutherford – Big Names, Tiny Towns

Oakville and Rutherford were once real towns, with stores and hotels as well as train stations, but now both are tiny hamlets. They both still have post offices, but that may not last as the Postal Service contracts.

Oakville and Rutherford are best known for their wineries, which will be covered in a later section.

The Oakville Grocery is about all else is of interest in Oakville other than wineries. It, however, is a gourmet destination that's recently been extensively renovated. Owned by Leslie Rudd, who also owns Dean & DeLuca in St. Helena, it sells gourmet food and wines and also makes sandwiches and offers other picnic items as well as coffee and pastries. It even has tables and chairs to enjoy your purchases.

Rutherford has a little more: Rutherford Grill, Italian Alex restaurant in the Rancho Caymus Inn, and locally popular La Luna Market, which also makes tasty tacos. Large Beaulieu Vineyards (called BV locally) dominates the town, while Francis Ford Coppola has reclaimed the name Inglenook Vineyards for his historic estate across the road. Tony Auberge du Soleil resort in the eastern hills has a Rutherford address.

St. Helena – the Heart of Napa Valley

Most people think of St. Helena (never *Saint*) as the heart of California's Wine Country and it sure looks the part.

If the cars in the compact downtown were replaced with horses and buggies, it would look as if nothing had changed in a century, with beautifully restored historic buildings still bearing the signs of Elks, a sidewalk honor to the Grand Army of the Republic and a park where bands still play from the ornate bandstand during the summer.

Wander off the main street and you'll encounter beautifully restored Victorians but if you look a bit more closely downtown, you'll note fancy shops aimed at visitors among the auto parts, the drugstore and the podiatrist that serve locals. Steve's Hardware cleverly mixes the shovels and pest traps of country life with fancy kitchenware and gifts.

The small town is definitely Napa Valley's center for upscale shopping, with most of its stores featuring understated country chic. This includes numerous antique stores, art galleries and casual clothing and shoes. Even if you don't buy, there's plenty to look at.

Some of California's favorite wine destinations are in St. Helena, and no visitor should miss the historic Culinary Institute of America at Greystone Cellars, with cooking demonstrations, a store full of kitchen toys, a café-bakery and a fine restaurant.

Naturally, visitors to St. Helena love to eat and drink. Though small, it has a varied collection of excellent restaurants. They're almost all within a few blocks of each other, encouraging a virtual progressive dinner, with cocktails at one place, appetizers at another, and after-dinner drinks still elsewhere. Just make sure you have reservations, or you may find yourself waiting in line for a burger at retro Gott's Roadside Gourmet drive in.

Among the restaurants is Farmstead, which serves meals incorporating produce and meat from nearby Long Meadow Ranch, Tra Vigne, an elegant Italian restaurant with a lovely patio, Cindy Pawlcyn's Wood Grill and Wine Bar and Cindy's Backstreet Kitchen from Cindy Pawlcyn and Terra and Bar Terra, two of Napa Valley's best and most innovative eateries.

Also popular are Cook and Vercelli serving mostly Liguria-American favorites, Market, Ana's Cantina, Armadillo with gringo Mexican food, Villa Corona, Gillwood's for breakfast and lunch and Model Bakery.

French Blue opened recently and it's already a local favorite, serving breakfast, lunch and dinner in a casual and inviting atmosphere.

Fancy Meadowood Resort and its Grill and three-star Restaurant lie to St. Helena's east.

St. Helena has a beautifully restored old-time movie theater, the Cameo Cinema, that shows both currently popular and foreign, art and classic films nightly.

Calistoga – the Wild West in Napa Valley

Calistoga is no one's vision of a "Wine County" town; it looks like the Old West with its one-street downtown, covered sidewalks and definitely informal ways.

The tiny city – it has a population of only 6,000 – lies at the far north of Napa Valley, just below towering Mount St. Helena and about 30 miles from the Valley's mouth at Napa.

Though ringed by vineyards and wineries, many in the steep hills that surround it on three sides, Calistoga is best known for what lies underground – hot water. The town has been a center for hot springs, mud baths and even a geyser since the 19th century, and it first developed as place to go to take the baths.

The pioneering promoter of Calistoga, Mormon Sam Brannan, reportedly gave it that name when he twisted "the Saratoga of California" after enjoying a bit too much local wine at a dedication of his spa.

The mud baths and spas are still prominent, though most of the old-time resorts are long gone. The last reminder, Indian Springs, is remarkably similar to the places visitors once frequented, and most of the spas are basic and functional rather than opulent like the spas in other Napa Valley resorts.

Aside from massages and mud baths, people visit Calistoga to shop in quaint stores, taste wine and relax. The town has a number of good restaurants, too, including Brannan's named after the aforementioned pioneer, All Seasons and Solbar at Solage, plus casual restaurants offering many choices.

The Calistoga Inn serves meals inside and along the Napa River – here a creek – during good weather, and its lively microbrewery and bar host music on weekends. The Hydro Bar is the other local hangout.

The small local museum contains interesting dioramas showing the old Calistoga and even boasts the last surviving unmodified guest cottage of the type Robert Louis Stevenson once occupied.

Auberge's uber-chic Calistoga Ranch resort lies just outside of town, and it's become one of the valley's top hideaways for celebrities and the rich. Auberge Resorts also built more casual – but hardly downscale – Solage resort, and two other fancy resorts are proposed in town.

To Calistoga's west is famed Diamond Mountain, home of many renowned wineries. South of town, Clos Pegase with its temple of art and Sterling on a knoll looking like a Greek monastery are some of the biggest wine destinations in Napa Valley as is Chateau Montelena north of town. And Castello di Amorosa is a must visit.

Also in the area is Schramsberg Winery, one of America's top sparkling wine producers, where you can tour the old caves hand-dug by Chinese laborers and taste a variety of wines by appointment.

One of the few regularly erupting geysers in North America lies just north of Calistoga. You can pay to get up close, though it's also visible from outside if you're lucky.

Angwin – Teetotaler's Haven in Wine Country

Only the need to be consistent requires a page on Angwin, but the unincorporated town on flat-topped Howell Mountain is interesting.

Angwin grew up around a Seventh-Day Adventist community that now includes the only four-year college in Napa County, Pacific Union College, and nearby St. Helena Hospital.

If it seems ironic to have a teetotalers' community on the edge of the most famous wine region in America, the relationship is now peaceful. The college leases land used for vineyards while the hospital receives considerable funding from the Napa Valley Vintners' Auction Napa Valley. Fittingly, the hospital has a respected center for alcohol and drug addiction.

Angwin has a small shopping center worth a visit; it's vegetarian (other than pet food) and until recently, didn't sell any products containing caffeine. It still doesn't carry wine, of course. However, don't visit on Saturday; that's when it and all the other local businesses – even the post office – are closed.

Continue east from Angwin and you end up in Pope Valley, "East of Eden."

The Land East of Eden

The Napa Valley says that Napa Valley is an Eden for grapes, and they're probably right. But what lies east of Eden? A large underdeveloped paradise in its own right, though there are unfortunately a few snakes to deal with.

Cross the Vaca Range east of Napa Valley proper, and you descent into one of a number of other valleys, though all were included in the Napa Valley AVA by someone who obviously wasn't a geographer.

The southernmost valleys, which you can reach over Monticello Road from Napa, includes Wooden and Green Valleys. Only part of the latter is in Napa County. Both have climates similar to Napa Valley even though they're clearly distinct. A few vineyards and wineries dot the area, which produces fine grapes and wine. North of there is Capell Valley.

If you travel east on Highway 128 from Rutherford, you skirt Lake Hennessey, Napa's reservoir, and the roads leading up to famed Pritchard Hill, then ascend steep Sage Canyon, passing the entrance to Kuleto Winery and Nichelini Winery, both worth a stop.

At the top of the canyon, turn left into small Chiles Valley, higher in altitude than Napa Valley itself but a fine place to grow grapes. RustRidge, Green & Red and Eisele are here. You can even stay overnight at RustRidge; it has a small B&B.

Go straight at the intersection, and you enter Soda Valley – not to be confused with Soda Canyon – that contains Somerston and Brown Estate Vineyards, also both worth visiting. Continue on and you get to Lake Berryessa, of which there is more later.

If you continue north through bucolic Chiles Valley, which once had four one-home schools, and you climb a ridge and drop into Pope Valley.

You can also get to Pope Valley by driving east from St. Helena on Deer Park Road, passing through Angwin and descending into Pope Valley itself.

A large fertile valley, Pope Valley has many vineyards supplying grapes to Napa Valley wineries across the mountains but only a few wineries open to the public.

Pope Valley is home of Lido's Hubcap Ranch, a landmark boasting thousands of hubcaps nailed to fence posts.

The valley also contains the almost-abandoned Aetna Springs resort perpetually about to be restored. The resort consists of a few large buildings that might have been designed by famed architect Bernard Maybeck or his pupils, and a number of cottages and other buildings in states from beyond repair to sound.

You can see its remains from dead-end Aetna Springs Road. The nine-hole golf course there was reportedly the first in California. It's been restored and a clubhouse built. It's open but seems in limbo awaiting future events at adjacent Aetna Springs and nearby.

The hearty can hike over Oak Hill Mine Trail to Calistoga, and ponder that this rough trail was once traversed by stagecoaches taking guests to Aetna Springs. It was once so prominent that Ronald Reagan announced his run for governor there.

If you continue north from Aetna Springs on Butts Canyon Road, you pass Snell Valley Road, the turnoff to the isolated but well-kept subdivision of Berryessa Estates, one of the least expensive places to live in Napa County. No one has flowers or garden plants here; deer lounge in front yards and eat anything that dares to pop out of the ground. A small store sells basic supplies.

Pope Valley is the gateway to Lake Berryessa, a large man-made lake. The large lake began to fill in 1957, drowning what everyone agrees was one of the most fertile agricultural communities in California, Monticello. The town was razed, trees cut down and even the bodies in the cemetery were moved to create the lake that damned Putah Creek to collect water for Solano County agriculture. Yes, Napa County gets none of the water; all it gets are the police, fire and other problems around the lake.

Lake Berryessa was once rimmed with funky "resorts" (really trailer parks) that have been cleared to create facilities for overnight visitors.

The plans are ambitious but a long way from realization, and at present, there are few facilities for visitors in the areas – notably no gas.

There are some shops and restaurants around Berryessa, even an Italian restaurant run by a chef from Parma at Spanish Flat, plus boat launching ramps, hiking trails and picnic and camp grounds with portable toilets and no water. You can only drive up the west and south sides of the lake. The east is privately owned.

The plans for the lake include luxury resorts as well as modest cottages, and gourmet restaurants as well as casual eateries.

For now, here are the businesses that are open:

- Cucina Italiana 4310 Knoxville Rd. (707) 966-2433www.lakeberryessanews.com
- Hand-Made Store & More, 4300 Berryessa Knoxville Rd.

- Lake Berryessa Boat and Jet Ski Rental, 7521 State Highway 128, (707) 966-4204
- Monticello Valley History Exhibit, 4300 Berryessa Knoxville Rd.
- Spanish Flat Country Store & Deli, 4310 Berryessa Knoxville Rd. (707) 966-1600
- Turtle Rock Bar & Restaurant at intersection of Hwy 128 and Knoxville Road.

Only time will tell if any of the great plans come to pass. The next edition of this book might even have a section on the Lake.

Wine in Napa Valley

Grapes and Wine in Napa Valley

Napa Valley is clearly the best-known wine region in the Americas, and one of the best-known in the world. It's that way because of a number of fortuitous circumstances:

- The valley has the ideal weather for growing fine wine grapes, a Mediterranean climate with a long growing season enjoyed by only 2 percent of the world's surface.
- It's compact and beautiful.
- It's close to a major urban center and tourist destination, San Francisco.
- Its grape growers and winery owners (called vintners locally) and winemakers work together for the common good in a way unknown elsewhere.
- Its growers and wineries work constantly to improve their knowledge and sophistication.
- Its growers and wineries intentionally farm for low, hopefully optimum, yields that averages 3.5 tons per acre. Some growers in the Central Valley harvest more than 20 tons per acre, albeit of mediocre grapes.
- The Napa Valley Vintners is an exceptionally able organization at promoting and protecting its wines.
- Robert Mondavi. The late winemaker was a tireless advocate of wine and Napa Valley first and his own winery second.
- Auction Napa Valley (formerly the Napa Valley Wine Auction), one of the world's leading charity wine auctions, which has raised the visibility and perceived value of Napa Valley wines for more than 30 years.

This small valley produces only 4 percent of the wine made in California from less than 10 percent of the vineyards in California, about 45,000 acres, yet represents an incredible 34 percent of the economic impact of wine in the state.

Only about 10 percent of the county is actually planted in vineyards, and strong restrictions make it unlikely that that amount will grow significantly as much of Napa County is mountainous and basically off limits to new vineyards.

Other parts are public land, in conservation easements to keep it undeveloped, under water (Lake Berryessa), or lacking water, or have soil unsuitable for vines.

Napa Valley boasted about 12,000 acres of vines in 1888 when the vine louse Phylloxera arrived. By 1900, only 2,000 acres remained.

Then came the San Francisco earthquake and fire of 1907, World War II and Prohibition. Most wineries went out of business. A few made legal sacramental and "medicinal" wines. Growers switched to tough-skinned grapes that they could ship safely back east; it was legal for families to make wine for their own use.

A few wineries were founded after Prohibition ended, but it was much later before many stared up. One was Stony Hill in the '40s. It became the first cult winemaker.

The big boom started with Robert Mondavi's founding of his winery in 1966.

This chapter will look at the grapes used to make wine, the distinctive wine regions of the Valley, the best wineries to visit and even a bit on growing your own grapes and making wines.

One important note: The Napa Valley American Viticultural Area or AVA, the federally recognized definition of the region, includes the mountains on either side of the valley proper as well as large tracts (Pope Valley and Chiles Valley) that are geographically not really in the valley surrounding the Napa River. That benefits owners of vineyards in Pope and Chiles Valley, who can label their grapes and wines with the valuable Napa Valley designation, and benefits wineries in Napa Valley itself since the grapes from these outlying areas are cheaper but still count as Napa Valley grapes.

A few areas of Napa County that aren't in the actual Napa Valley AVA grow grapes, which are labeled "Napa County."

Ironically, the best grapes grow in the mountains and benchlands or piedmont, not in the valley floor itself.

Wine Varieties

There are thousands of wine grapes in the world, but only a few dominate Napa Valley.

Napa Valley was once planted mostly to hearty reds like Petite Sirah ("Pets"), Carignan and Zinfandel that augmented vapid Central Valley wines for Gallo, but now the Valley is best known for its intense Cabernet Sauvignons, the "king of wines." Few of the old vines survive though they make superb and much-appreciated wine.

Cabernet Sauvignon is the most widely planted and valuable grape grown in Napa Valley. Cabernet's "cousins" Merlot, Cabernet France, Petite Verdot and Malbec are also popular.

White Sauvignon Blanc excels here, too, while Chardonnay, the queen of wines, and Pinot Noir are planted in cooler areas like Carneros.

The following sections discuss the most popular wines and other wines and varieties ("varietal" is an adjective, by the way, though widely misused in the industry as a noun.)

Sauvignon Blanc – Napa's Best White

If it weren't for Cabernet Sauvignon, Napa Valley would probably be famous for its Sauvignon Blanc. Though the grape plays second fiddle to Chardonnay in the marketplace – and of late, even Pinot Grigio and Moscato – Sauvignon Blanc is the preferred white wine to pair with food among many wine experts and lovers.

It's made in many styles, from the herbaceous New Zealand style of late fashion to oaky, overripe wanna-be Chardonnays.

Many Napa Valley producers make Sauvignon Blanc, but many try to figure out how to make a bigger wine that justifies a higher price – and growing the grape instead of replacing it with more lucrative Cabernet.

As a result, the "regular" (i.e., cheaper) Sauvignon Blancs of many wineries in Napa Valley better exhibit its strengths than their reserve (i.e., more expensive) bottlings. To justify higher prices, the producers tend to pick the grapes later, resulting in higher alcohol and less acid, as well as overripe flavors more suited for dessert wines than to match with food.

Ferment in barrels, stir the lees and put the wine through malolactic fermentation and you end up with a second-rate Chardonnay; worse, on its own Sauvignon Blanc has more assertive flavors than neutral Chardonnay, and these flavors seem to conflict with all the manipulation.

Fortunately, plenty of Napa Valley wineries make crisp, clean Sauvignon without mucking it up with excessive ripeness and alcohol, oak, yeastiness and malolactic mellowing. You can usually identify them by their price – under $20. Frog's Leap, Honig and Napa Wine Company in Oakville make two excellent examples.

Chardonnay – America's Favorite Wine

To many people, the epitome of Napa Valley Chardonnays are rich, buttery wines made with new oak barrels, extended contact with yeast and malolactic fermentation to mellow the acids while contributing buttery flavors. Ironically, Chardonnay is a relatively bland grape and contributes relatively little flavor to this mix; most of the character is created by winemaker manipulation.

The most "typical" Napa Valley Chardonnay is Rombauer, which shouts that big style.

Many wineries in the Valley, however, make another more traditional Burgundian style that's crisp, leaner and better with most food. These wines are made with few or no new oak barrels used in fermentation or aging, so they don't exhibit the rich vanilla and caramel flavors introduced by the toasted oak. They also undergo little or no malolactic fermentation.

Among the producers of these leaner wines are Stony Hill, Grgich-Hills and Chateau Montelena. Interestingly, Mike Grgich made the Chateau Montelena that bested the best of Burgundy in the famous tasting of 1976, and he clearly hasn't lost his touch. Likewise, old-timer Stony Hill illustrates that fashions may change, but good wine remains.

Most Napa producers emulate the rich style, but many are starting to reduce their oak and malolactic manipulation as some consumers tire of such wines. Unfortunately, there's no simple way to tell from the label without trying the wine or seeking advice. No matter which you prefer, however, Napa Valley's more than 400 wine producers make a wide variety of wines, and some are sure to please your palate.

Pinot Noir – the Choice of Kings

Napa Valley is most famous for its intense Cabernet Sauvignons, but it also produces other excellent red wines. Notable among these is Burgundy's famed Pinot Noir, a finicky grape that excels in cooler climates than robust Cabernet and its Bordeaux cousins.

As any wine lover knows, Pinot Noir received a heady boost from the cult movie *Sideways*, which celebrated Pinot, particularly that from the cooler parts of Santa Barbara County. Other fine Pinots come from the cool Santa Lucia Highlands of Monterey County, the cool Russian River Valley of Sonoma, cool Anderson Valley of Mendocino County and equally chilly Oregon.

Anyone who has been in St. Helena or Calistoga during the summer knows that Napa Valley isn't cool, and that part of the Valley isn't suitable for growing good Pinot, which developed in the temperate climate of Burgundy in France.

However, parts of Napa County are cool; even the hot parts are too cool in the evenings to enjoy dining outside, in fact.

Most notably, southern Napa County lies close to San Pablo Bay, the northern reach of chilly San Francisco Bay, and it has an overwhelming impact on the climate of the area. It notably cools Los Carneros, the grape-growing appellation that stretches across southern Napa (and Sonoma) County.

Carneros is home to most of Napa's Pinots, and many of them match the best of other famed areas. Much of the land was first planted by the makers of sparkling wines such as Domaine Chandon, Mumm and Domaine Carneros. They use their Pinots for those wines, and picked riper, for excellent still wines as well.

The cool air affects all of southern Napa Valley; the areas south of the Yountville Hills and Stags Leap outcroppings are considerably cooler than those north, so grapes grown in Oak Knoll (like Trefethen), Napa, American Canyon, Jameson Canyon and the areas east of Napa in Coombsville also share this cool weather, though not as intensely.

A few mountainous areas also produce good Pinot, including Kuleto Estate east of Rutherford.

Merlot – Unappreciated Stepsister

Merlot has took a hit of late, notably in the movie *Sideways*, but it remains one of America's top wine varieties.

That's not surprising since Merlot has many of the luscious characteristics of Cabernet Sauvignon, but is typically a little less tannic and a bit more luscious.

In truth, most wine lovers associate Cabernet with the top wines of Bordeaux, but many of the most famous Bordeaux contain more Merlot than Cabernet, and the most famous and expensive of all the Bordeaux is Pétrus, mostly Merlot.

By contrast, the Merlots that critics scorn are overripe, are *too* lush and flabby without inadequate tannic backbone. Merlot is sensitive to weather, and doesn't excel in an excessively hot location where many Merlots are planted in California's Central Valley (and Chile and Australia, for that matter.) In warmer years, the best Merlots can come from cooler areas, and in Napa Valley, that includes Stags Leap, Carneros, Oak Knoll and east Napa's Coombsville AVA.

In any year, the mountaintops and hillsides produce superb wine, so look for vineyards from Mount Veeder, Atlas Peak, Howell Mountain, Spring Mountain and Diamond Mountain first – though because of difficult growing conditions, these wines tend to be more expensive.

Even in weaker years, some producers make excellent wines by managing their vines. Many top wineries drop extra clusters of grapes to allow those remaining to ripen fully and not exhibit the "green" flavors rejected by those who like riper wines.

The first Merlots labeled as such came from Louis Martini and Sterling, and while Martini is now focusing more on Cabernet, Sterling remains an excellent Merlot producer. If any one winery created the demand for fine Merlot, however, it was Duckhorn Vineyards. Its Merlots are still among the best.

Other excellent producers include Chimney Rock with its mostly Merlot blend Elevage, Hartwell, Lewis, Pahlmeyer, Paloma, Pride Mountain, Provenance, Shafer, Swanson and Switchback Ridge. Most are less expensive than Cabernets.

Cabernet Sauvignon – the King of Wines

Cabernet Sauvignon, one of the major grape varieties used in Bordeaux, has become the grape of choice in Napa Valley. There are a number of reasons it has become preeminent, unlike in Bordeaux, where many wines have little if any Cabernet Sauvignon in them but are blends of related varieties.

Historically, Cabernet Sauvignon didn't ripen fully in cool years in Bordeaux and other varieties did, and they were used to create a balanced wine. It almost always ripens fully here, however, creating a good wine on its own. In addition, it can produce a lush, intense wine, and that style is preferred by many critics and consumers.

In the right location, which includes much of Napa County, a Cabernet Sauvignon that's picked ripe can be an impressive wine, and that style has become the epitome of California wines.

These highly extracted, dense wines tend to be high in alcohol, however. A few decades ago, the standard wine – including Cabernet – had an alcohol level of 12.5 percent. The fashion now is to let the grapes get riper to obtain more intense fruit and avoid any trace of vegetal, "green" flavors that were once characteristic of most Cabernets. Many growers also starve the vines for water, which concentrates flavors and sugar. The standard is now about 14.5 percent, and many wines are even higher.

Many people find these wines taste hot and unbalanced, so some producers use artificial means of removing alcohol or even dilute the grape juice or must with water during fermentation to compensate for the dehydration.

These riper wines also have more subdued tannins, the bitter flavors that once were softened by long aging. Winemakers have learned other techniques to reduce harsh tannins, and most Cabernets today can be drunk and enjoyed soon after release.

Many also add other varieties to obtain desired flavors. Petite Verdot, for example, not only provides intense purple color but violet aromas, while Merlot is softer and Cabernet Franc ripens at a cooler temperature and Malbec can take even more heat.

The Cabernets of Napa Valley come in many styles, from lean, traditional "European" styles mostly from older winemakers to easy-to-drink-young styles to massive cult favorites that are better in tastings than with dinner for they overwhelm most food.

The leaner wines tend come from cooler regions like southern Napa and mountainous areas. There are more than 400 wineries (and far more labels) in Napa Valley, and almost anyone can find a style they like.

Zinfandel – America's Own (Croatian) Grape

Though Zinfandel was once one of Napa Valley's most widely grown grapes, today Cabernet is king. Few growers plant Zinfandel when they can get twice the return for Cabernet, but many pockets of old Zin still dot the valley. They make remarkable wine.

Because of their rarity, however, top Zins tend to be pricier than many wine drinkers expect from the rustic grape. Many Zins from Napa Valley producers come from other areas, notably Lodi, itself famed for its Zinfandels.

Zinfandel is a versatile grape, however. It's used to make everything from "white" (often pink) sweet Zin to light table wines, inky high-octane monsters and even port-like wines with high alcohol and residual sugar.

Today's red Zinfandels, like today's other wines, tend to be alcoholic. Many are over 15 percent alcohol, some 16, beyond the level for table wines suitable for pairing with most food. They're at their best as what the Italians of Puglia, who make wine from an identical grape called Primitivo, call "meditation" or social wines, perfect for after-dinner discussions with friends.

At any rate, the best Zins exhibit brambly raspberry and blackberry character when young, but it tends to fade quickly, leaving a Claret-like wine in the best cases. Most Zins are best consumed fairly young, at 2 to 5 years, and few seem to improve with age.

Many of the big producers offer Zin, but it's often from other regions where the economics make more sense – and the wine is also very good, such as Dry Creek Valley, Lodi and the Sierra Foothills. And some of the best wines come from the outskirts of Napa Valley, such as Chiles Valley, home of excellent Green & Red, D Cubed and Brown Family.

In Napa itself, some of the most impressive Zinfandels come from Turley Wine Cellars, a company owned by the physician brother of famed winemaker Helen Turley. Other top wines include Biale, Buehler, Elyse, Storybook and Grgich-Hills Cellars; winemaker Mike Grgich comes from Croatia, the ancestral home of Zinfandel where it's the obscure grape called Crljenak Kastelanski.

It's ironic – and no coincidence, really, that Napa Valley is also the home of white Zinfandel, which was first produced almost by mistake by Sutter Home's Bob Trinchero. It and Beringer Vineyards, also based in St. Helena, together dominate the market for the sweet pinkish wine that remains a popular if not critical favorite, but both wineries also produce serious red Zinfandel as well. Zin grapes for red wines have recently passed those used for white Zin due to the increased popularity of red blends based on Zinfandel, growing demand for Moscato among drinkers who once favored white Zin, and growing appreciation for the real stuff.

Blends and Meritage Wines

The reputation of Cabernet Sauvignon as the King of Wine has led many wine lovers to believe that the greatest wines in the world are made from that grape.

And some are – mostly. In Bordeaux, home of the world's most famous wines, many wineries do use Cabernet Sauvignon to make wines – but most add other grapes to the blend. Some famed wines like Pétrus are primarily made from other grapes, in this case, much- maligned Merlot.

In reality, many of the best wines made are blends. In Bordeaux, for example, five grapes are widely grown, though Merlot and Cabernet are most prominent.

The same is true in many other wine regions. In Chianti, the wines are primarily made from Sangiovese, but generally include other grapes. They even traditionally included white grapes that were discovered long-ago to have the paradoxical property of intensifying and stabilizing color in the blends with the cultivars of Sangiovese then popular. Today's versions of Sangiovese stand alone better.

In the Rhône region, Syrah is the most famous grape, but many wines such as Châteauneuf du Pape are blends of up to 13 different grapes, again often including white Viognier, which can set red pigments, and Grenache and Carignan. These two are often considered inferior here, though Grenache is regaining its reputation as vast fields of high-yielding vines are pulled out and the remaining vines are managed better.

Sometimes a wine of one grape can excel in the perfect vineyard, but often other grapes can overcome deficiencies in flavors. In the United States, however, we've chosen to lionize pure varieties in spite of facts, and a "Cabernet Sauvignon" wine from an appellation such as Napa Valley, for example, must contain 85 percent of that grape. But what if that wine is better with 20 percent Cabernet Franc added? Then it can't be called Cabernet Sauvignon, but only Red Table Wine, the same as Carlo Rossi Paisano in 4-liter jugs.

To address this situation, many top producers give such wines proprietary labels, and others have adopted the Meritage name.

Meritage, which rhymes with heritage, describes blends of the eight accepted Bordeaux varieties (Cabernet Sauvignon, Merlot, Cabernet Franc, Malbec, Petite Verdot, Gros Verdot, Carmenere and St. Macaire, the latter three almost unknown).

You have to belong to the Meritage Association and pay a nominal fee to call your wines Meritage, and not all producers of such blends bother.

Whether labeled "Meritage," a proprietary name or called a "Bordeaux blend," however, most such wines are excellent. They typically show more depth and complexity than wines labeled with varietal names (most of which incorporate a little of their cousin grapes anyway).

The granddaddy of such wines was Joseph Phelps' Insignia, still a standout. Other outstanding Bordeaux blends from Napa Valley include Dominus, Opus One, Robert Craig Affinity, Merryvale Vineyards Profile, Dalla Valle Maya, Flora Springs Trilogy, Franciscan Magnificat, Quintessa, Inglenook (Niebaum-Coppola) Rubicon, St. Supéry Élu, Beaulieu Tapestry and Viader.

All are expensive – but exceptional. They represent some of the best wines made in Napa Valley – and that's saying something.

Other Varieties in Napa Valley

In Napa Valley, where Cabernet is king and Chardonnay queen, why would you grow other grape varietals and make them into wine?

Yet growers here raise grapes from Albariño to Zinfandel including popular grapes like Pinot Grigio and Pinot Noir as well as grapes as obscure as Nero d'Avola, Grignolino, Vermentino and Montepulciano.

Growers grow these grapes, and wineries sell these wines, for a lot of reasons.

In some cases, they're from old vines and represent varieties once popular in Napa Valley. At one time, Zinfandel, Chenin Blanc, French Colombard, Charbono, Mondeuse, Carignane and Petite Sirah were widely planted here, in some cases mixed together for crushing and fermentation in a field blend as was a common practice.

No one sold varietal wine; they generally made blends, and often, the flavors of the grapes complemented each other. Casa Nuestra still sells a wine made from a field blend of such grapes and Stags Leap Winery's Petite Sirah is such a blend if mostly "Pets."

Nichelini, which has been in the same family's hands longer than any other winery in Napa County (and perhaps California), still grows Sauvignon Vert, which the government makes them call Muscadelle, the third white grape of Bordeaux after Sauvignon Blanc and Semillon. Chimney Rock uses it in its white Meritage.

Other growers maintain the old vines for nostalgia, or like people restore and drive old cars, and lavish money on old houses.

In some cases, wineries choose varieties to reflect their passion, such as the Italian grapes favored by some growers of Italian background or Italophiles.

Gianni Paoletti grows the Sicilian grape Nero d'Avola, for example.

Dario Sattui honors his Italian heritage at his Castello di Amorosa winery with Sangiovese, Pinot Grigio and Muscat di Canelli. Bennessere features Italian varieties, including Sangiovese, Aglianico, Muscat di Canelli, and Sagrantino

These wineries also sell other wines, of course – this is Napa Valley – but will point out that Merlot and Pinot Bianco (Pinot Blanc) are traditional varieties in Northeast Italy, too.

Other growers are looking for grapes that might excel in our environment. The climate in most of California including Napa Valley is far more like that of most of Italy, Spain and

Mediterranean France than of Burgundy or even Bordeaux, so it seems that grapes from those countries should excel here.

Traditionally, Mediterranean varieties such as Grenache, Carignan, Mataro (Monestrell or Mourvedre) and even Syrah and its cousin Durif (Petit Sirah) were popular, not to forget Zinfandel.

There are original zinfandel vines planted in the 1870's by the Slovenian Ogulin family still grow in Lake County, as well as Syrah vines from the same period on vast Langtry Estate there.

Many of these grapes are still popular in the Central Valley, where they are irrigated and produce prodigious amounts of overripe grapes that go into jugs and boxes, but anyone who's tasted the intense Garnachas and Cariñenas of Prioat and some other areas of Spain, or the same grapes from the Rhône, know that they can produce remarkable wines.

A number of wineries and growers are experimenting with Tempranillo, the top Spanish red grape, and a number of producers have planted traditional Portuguese Port varieties in attempts to make wines more similar to those wines; here, wineries traditionally used what they had, for "port," often dark grapes like Petite Sirah.

The Spanish white variety Albariño, called Alvarinho by the Portuguese, has become extremely popular and is in short supply even in Spain. It has been planted here.

Italian Pinot Grigio has become the second most popular white wine in America, too, with an explosion of local grapes joining the imports.

Italian red varieties have fared more poorly in general, however. A huge wave of planting Sangiovese subsided when even the Antinori family, which makes some of the best Sangiovese wines in the world in Tuscany, gave up to focus on Cabernet at its vast Antica estate in the Atlas Peak appellation here. That might partly be due to the cultivars planted; even the Tuscans have replanted their vineyards to better clones.

Nebbiolo is used for Barolo and Barbaresco, again some of the best wine in the world, yet here, it's been used for a rosé by a frustrated winemaker who claimed it just wouldn't ripen.

Another rare variety is Grignolino. In a homage to history, Heitz Vineyards makes a Grignolino, Grignolino rosé and a Grignolino "port."

But that brings up a good reason for offering odd varieties. Wineries often make small quantities as an exclusive inducement to club members and winery visitors, and they often charge more for these wines than for arguably better Cabs and Chards. Some people get bored with Cabernet and Chardonnay.

Another reason for the continuing popularity of these grapes is that winemakers and growers get bored, too. Famously experimental, both like to try new things.

If the wineries make enough to distribute the wines, the unusual wines can be fun to restaurant and bar patrons, too.

In some cases, unusual varieties bring in more money to growers than popular varieties. Rarity and its value as an intense flavoring component makes Petit Verdot the highest-priced red grape grown in Napa Valley. Rarity and demand made the tiny amount of Roussanne and Marsanne more valuable per ton than Chardonnay.

Francis Mahoney, who performed much of the original research to determine which Pinot Noirs grow best in Carneros and California, grows Vermentino, a white variety from western Italy (Liguria, Tuscany and Sardinia), as well as Albariño, Sangiovese, Montepulciano (a type of Sangiovese), as well as Tempranillo and Nebbiolo. Winemaker and manager Ken Foster admits that part of the reason Mahoney Vineyards grows these varieties is curiosity.

Heidi Peterson Barrett, who makes some of the most famous and pricey Cabernets in the business, also makes a small amount of a delicious dry white Muscat called Moscato Azul. "I couldn't see much sense in introducing another Chardonnay," she once said.

Sparkling Wine from Napa Valley

Though I love almost all wines, I must admit that sparkling wine is my personal favorite. In America, sparkling wine is served mostly on special occasions, but Tuesday is special enough for me.

I can happily drink it with brunch, talking with friends on a warm afternoon, as an aperitif, with many meals, and after dinner, even watching a Bruce Willis movie eating popcorn.

Visit my house, and that's likely what you'll be offered to drink, just as in the most civilized parts of Europe.

I almost never drink an alcoholic beverage before noon (other than tasting) unless it's a good sparkling wine, either.

Of course, the standard for sparkling wine is Champagne, but having a long-developed California palate, I generally prefer the best California sparklers to those from France.

Some of the fine Champagnes are wonderful experiences, but the fresh lively flavors from the New World seem to go better with most experiences other than those focusing on appreciating the wines themselves.

There are many producers of quality sparkling wines in California, including the biggest, Korbel, which cranks out vast amounts of okay stuff and some very good wines. There are also a number of good producers in Sonoma County and Anderson Valley in Mendocino County.

But Napa is ironically California's center for sparklers. I say ironically because Napa's climate isn't ideal for the delicate grapes used to make fine sparkling wines. Fortunately, southern Napa, including the Carneros region, is quite cool due to its location by San Pablo Bay, the northern lobe of San Francisco Bay.

San Francisco Bay is infamously cold, of course. All the jokes about San Francisco being cold in the summer aren't jokes. Visitors soon learn that shorts and t-shirts aren't appropriate there — and Carneros is almost as cool. It also endures chilling strong winds, again cooling the grapes so they maintain good acidity and ripen slowly, with flavors developing faster than sugar content, ideal for sparkling wines.

That said, Napa sparkling wine producers like Schramsberg also buy grapes from cooler Sonoma, Mendocino and even Marin Counties.

Grapes for sparkling wine in Champagne are picked at as little as 14 or 15 percent sugar, but in California, where the intense sunlight develops sugars faster, it's usual to pick at 18 to 20 percent, less than grapes for still wines picked at 22 degrees (percent) or above.

The traditional grapes for Champagne are Pinot Meunier, Pinot Noir and Chardonnay. The Pinots are red- or black-skinned varieties, the latter called white, though it's really green. All have clear juice — we call it white — and if the red grapes are pressed quickly, none or little of the grape color pigment ends up in the juice, so the wine is very light in color.

Pinot Meunier is popular in Champagne, where it's surprisingly the most widely planted grape because it ripens early. That's not necessarily an advantage in California, and most sparklers are made primarily with Pinot Noir and Chardonnay. At least one producer, Mumm, throws in a little of the Pinots' pale cousin, Pinot Gris.

Many companies in America make sparkling wines, and quite a few make excellent products. One company, however, stands out: Schramsberg Vineyards.

The winery virtually created the market for top-of-the-line sparkers in America, and it has continued to evolve, always a step ahead of the market in producing premier sparkling wines. Some match the best from Champagne.

Napa is also home to three European-owned sparkling wine producers. Domaine Chandon, which is owned by LVMH (Louis Vuitton Moët Hennessey), is the second largest American producer of wines made by the traditional secondary fermentation in the one bottle.

Mumm Napa Valley, which has had a number of owners, is now reunited with its French sister as part of Pernod Ricard. It also makes excellent wines.

Smaller Domaine Carneros is owned by Taittinger and focuses on high-end wines. Its La Rêve is among the world's best sparkling wines.

Most of the producers of sparklers are also increasing production of still wines, recognizing that Americans drink sparklers for special occasions and the market is limited.

It costs more to make sparklers, especially financing inventory for years, yet many consumers won't pay as much as they will for Chardonnays and Pinot Noirs made with the same grapes.

Other Napa producers also make small amounts of sparkling wine including Frank Family Vineyards, Bell Cellars, Artesa and V. Sattui.

Growing Grapes in Napa Valley

Napa Valley contains about 45,000 acres of vineyards, 10 percent of the county's area. Not much more property can be planted to vineyards because of limitations on planting on slopes in the mostly hilly county as well as unfavorable soils and water issues.

Though the valley has a few large owners of vineyards, most of the actual vineyards are relatively small and heavily divided into different grape varieties and farmed with different growing practices.

Unlike in many parts of the world, wineries only own about half the vineyard acreage. They buy, or "source," grapes from independent growers, some of whom also make wine themselves.

Napa Valley has almost ideal climate for growing grapes. It's sunny most of the year and warm to hot during the summer with a large diurnal swing so that temperature drops 30 to 40 degrees at night. Even on a 90-degree day, it's chilly at night. Grapes like that. The sun and heat ripen the grapes and the cool helps maintain acidity necessary for good wines.

Early morning fog also keeps the grapes cool except at higher elevations above the fog line.

Actual temperatures vary significantly over the valley, however. It's coolest in the south next to San Pablo Bay, but the cool air is partly trapped by the Yountville Hills and it's warmer in the northern valley, though a little Pacific air sneaks through the Chalk Hill gap into Calistoga to the far north. There's easily a 10- to 15-degree difference between Napa and St. Helena on hot days.

The mountains are cooler, too, of course. Though Mount St. Helena reaches over 4,300 ft., no one grows grapes there. The others are more typically 2,000 to 3,000 feet high and quite a few vineyards are planted above 2,000 ft.

Napa County gets about 30 inches a year on average, just enough for healthy vines. However, it receives almost all its rain during the winter when vines are dormant. This has a number of benefits for growing grapes: It reduces the likelihood that rain could damage young buds, lessens moisture that can encourage fungus and rot, and allows growers to give vines just the amount of water they need, forcing them to put their energy into producing grapes rather than sporting lush vegetation.

However, this lack of rain during the summer makes it difficult to farm grapevines without irrigation except in some parts of the county. The Napa Valley floor, for example, has a deep water table close to the surface, and vines can exploit it. If they're not irrigated, they tend to dig deep, perhaps 15 to 20 ft., and can sustain themselves without irrigation during the summer.

A few hearty souls like Frog's Leap don't irrigate except to establish vines (in their case with buckets!), and most vineyards have irrigation systems but use them sparingly. Fortunately, grapevines don't require much water compared to other crops – or grass or trees – but water is a big issue for growers now and will become more so in the future.

Fundamentally, Napa Valley is an arid region. Some older vineyards have rights to use water from the Napa River and its tributaries, but more and more restrictions are keeping growers from drilling wells or collecting water that would run into the river system. Many build ponds – but it's expensive, hard to get permits – and takes valuable land out of production.

In general, the valley floor has plenty of water, but outlying areas like Carneros and Coombsville don't. Both areas are looking into using recycled water and a pipeline is heading east from Napa's water treatment plant for that purpose.

Soil is also important to vines. They tend to like lean, not rich, soil, with decent water-holding capacity but not too much. Napa Valley allegedly has more distinct soil types than any other comparable region in the world, 33 types, half the world's soil varieties and some are better than others for growing fine wine grapes.

In general, the benchlands and hills surrounding the valley floor, and the mountains, produce the highest-quality grapes, but growers are resourceful. They've learned to grow fine grapes even in rich bottomland that would be better suited for annual row crops – Napa was once filled with fields of wheat (Think of the Napa Mill and Bale Mill) – and vegetables.

The rich valley floor does produce the fruity, rich Cabernets and Merlots that many people love, while the wines from the mountains and benches are leaner, elegant and more complex.

Napa grape growers are exceptionally sophisticated and use a lot of advanced technology in their efforts, but still depend primarily on hand labor for pruning vines and harvesting grapes as well as other vineyard operations mechanized in many places. There are a number of reasons for this.

One is tradition. Another is the historical access to a large force of inexpensive Mexican immigrant labor.

In the past, moreover, mechanical harvesters, for example, were pretty crude and damaged grapes and tossed too much "MOG" (Material Other than Grapes) into bins, but today's equipment is very gentle and can deliver perfect destemmed berries to the wineries.

Economic forces and restrictions on immigration will likely force greater acceptance of mechanical harvesting, but growers and wineries aren't likely to trumpet it as they like to talk about their hand-crafted products.

It should be noted that many of those workers are not only citizens, but well-paid full-time employees. Supplemental workers are brought in for harvest and other labor-intensive tasks, but many return to the same vineyard each year. The vineyards of Napa Valley are considered prime employers to most workers. A number of housing sites supported by the industry offer low-cost housing and food, too. The industry assesses itself to pay for them.

You'll note a huge variety of schemes for managing vines and different orientations to the sun in Napa Valley. Old vines grow like bushes in the "California sprawl," while newer vineyards are trained in neat rows with wires used to hold their canes up like bandits with their arms in the air.

A recent craze is for tiny, Bonsai-like vines planted very close together, and while that's attractive, it's tough on the workers, requires a lot of "hedging," and is probably not really suited for most of our soils. Long cordons (branches) with lots of grape clusters are probably better in the richest soils, for example, but they aren't considered chic and modern and they don't look as neat.

In any case, growers will tell you that their method is best, but even researchers don't really agree. The truth of the matter is that all can – and do – produce fine wine.

Stealth Organic Growers

Many grape growers in Napa Valley farm their crops organically, but you wouldn't know it by reading wine labels.

Organic growing uses no synthetic chemicals, whether fertilizers of improving vigor, pesticides for killing harmful insects, fungi and diseases, or herbicides for eliminating weeds. They depend on natural organic (which means of living origin) products for these purposes or better, seek to avoid them by the way they manage their crops.

Most encourage beneficial insects and even hawks, owls and bluebirds to counter pests, and plant complementary plants that attract these allies.

Yet while many people are willing to pay more for organic food as they believe it's healthier or better in taste, the same isn't true of wine.

Most food producers that farm organically herald the fact and charge more for their products, but many wineries hesitate to say much about the subject. Most grape growers can't get paid better for organic grapes, in fact.

Most growers in Napa Valley use very few chemicals anyway, but many of those dedicated to growing strictly organically keep a low profile.

Among the wineries growing all their grapes organically are Frog's Leap, Long Meadow Ranch, Grgich-Hills, Staglin Family and Robert Sinskey, while the 600 acres of vineyards owned by the Pelissa family is all organic. Its grapes go into many wines, including its own Napa Wine Company. The Novak family lives among their vineyards at Spottswoode, too, and they don't want to be subjected to chemicals.

Nevertheless, the wineries don't claim the organic farming. There are reasons for the silence even though all are devoted environmentalists who believe growing organically is the right thing to do.

But requirements for labels for organic claims on wine have been confusing. Until recent changes were announced, wines could claim to be made with organically grown fruit, and they could be labeled organic only if no sulfur was added during winemaking (and the natural level was very low).

Nevertheless, many producers aren't sure they want to use the label "organic." Though organic foods are considered superior by most people, in the past, "organic wines" got a bad reputation. It's difficult to make a stable, long-lasting wine without adding a tiny amount of sulfur dioxide, which acts as a preservative. Frankly, many organic wines were disappointing.

Improved filtering technologies has reduced that problem, but the stigma remains. Even natural food stores often downplay organic wines.

Growers and wine makers may also not want to go to the bother and cost of certifying their vineyards, which takes three years after the end of chemical use, and frankly, many want to keep their options open. They may be committed to natural farming, but aren't prepared to lose their whole crop if some new insect or disease pops up to threaten them, as seems to happen almost every month.

When you come right down to it, however, most growers farm organically simply because they believe it's the way to grow the best grapes. They grow the way our ancestors did using cover crops and composting but with improved viticultural practices. They skip the pesticides, herbicides and inorganic fertilizers once so popular.

Fortunately, grapevines are tough, perennial crops, and it's easier to grow grapes organically than most other food crops. It's also easier to grow organically in our dry climate than in many winegrowing regions. Organic growers believe that they'll have healthier vines that produce better grapes over time, and reap the environment and psychic benefits, too.

Biodynamic and "Natural" wines?

Biodynamic and "natural" wines are getting a lot of attention in the wine press, but many people don't understand what they are and what their benefits are, if any.

Let's take them separately, though they're related.

Biodynamic wines are produced from grapes farmed with exotic practices recommended by an Austrian "philosopher" named Rudolf Steiner. He proclaimed that crops should be raised in a natural balance with nature, and that meant planting, pruning and harvesting by the phases of the moon, using animals in the vineyard for fertilizer, avoiding synthetic chemicals, and treating the vines with various homeopathic "preparations" or potions. These portions include teas made from decomposed cow manure buried and aged in a cow horn, and dug up, at certain phases of the Moon.

Some of these practices strike scientifically trained viticulturists as superstition, even "voodoo."

Few if any scientific trials have attempted to determine whether these practices make a difference, but many top winemakers have adopted the protocol. As some say, "It can't hurt..."

One thing is clear: Most Biodynamic growers devote great care and attention to their vines. That alone could create some differences.

"Natural" winemaking could be considered the winemaking version of Biodynamics. The winemakers try to affect the wines as little as possible, crushing the grapes for red wines and then hoping natural yeasts convert the sugar in the grapes into wine before harmful yeasts and bacteria ruin it (Most winemakers kill wild bacteria and yeasts with sulfur dioxide and inoculate their musts with cultured yeasts.)

In truth, wild yeasts can ferment sugars, but none will produce stable wines by fermenting to an alcohol level of 12 percent or more, so even if wild yeasts start the fermentation, it's likely finished by "feral" yeasts that inhabit old wineries and even wine regions.

The wild yeasts can create some distinctive flavor and aroma compounds, but not all are desirable.

The "natural" winemaker also doesn't filter or fine the wine, and doesn't add sulfur dioxide to stabilize it. Needless to say, many "natural" wines I've tasted have been distasteful, though some have been excellent if not better than wines made in a safer way.

After all, wine is food, and we all take steps to protect and preserve our food; alcohol and acidity in wine certainly help preserve it, but some bacteria can thrive even in that hostile environment.

One possible solution would be to treat wine like dairy products and keep it cold, but that would be very expensive and cause a huge change in distribution and sales of wine.

By contrast, use of small amounts of sulfur dioxide has served the job well for millennia, and in spite of some people's belief, very few people are allergic to it. In fact, many other foods like dried fruit contain much higher levels of this chemical that's common in nature and benign in the tiny doses used.

Many Napa growers farm Biodynamically. Few winemakers, however, attempt rigorously "natural" wines.

The Gentleman Grower from Virginia

Many people who learn about Napa Valley are surprised to find that about half the grapes used by the average winery are bought from others including independent growers. But there's a definite trend for those growers to make wine, too.

Presently, the majority of Napa County's vineyard acreage is owned by companies that make wine, more than half by large international and non-local wine companies.

Standing out among the minority are the vineyards owned by Andy Beckstoffer, a native of Virginia who has taken another strategy. Promoting the quality of his vineyards, he's persuaded many of the Valley's best-known wineries to highlight the use of his fruit, in effect creating a strong brand that says high quality as much as does the name of the winery itself.

Beckstoffer now owns more than 1,000 acres of vineyard land in Napa County, including some of the Valley's most respected historic vineyards like the former Beaulieu Vineyard Georges III vineyard in Rutherford, the former Charles Krug Cabral Ranch and Louis Martini Vineyards in Carneros, part of the historic To Kalon Ranch and Missouri Hopper Vineyard in Oakville, and Dr. George Crane's original vineyard in St. Helena.

He also owns about 1,300 acres in adjoining Lake County and 1,000 acres in Mendocino County.

At a time when huge wineries make so many wines and own so much diverse property that the 'estate' designation that indicates that they own the land and make the wine has lost much of its exclusivity, Beckstoffer regards the designation of a specific vineyard as the new indication of pedigree. He sells wine to about 50 wineries, and 20 designate Beckstoffer Vineyards on the label.

These include Acacia, Atalon, Clos du Val, Merryvale, Provenance, Chalone's new Napa brand, and Stag's Leap Wine Cellars

Beckstoffer has been active in Napa Valley for more than 30 years. First joining liquor giant Heublein in 1966 after graduation from Dartmouth with an MBA, he soon recommended the company enter the super-premium wine segment of the California wine business.

Under his direction, in 1968 Heublein bought United Vintners, owners of once-famed Inglenook and Italian Swiss Colony wines, then acquired venerable Beaulieu in 1969. Beckstoffer moved to Napa Valley that year and soon created a subsidiary, Vinifera Development Corporation, to supply grapes to Beaulieu and Inglenook.

In what was clearly not a great business decision, Heublein decided to exit the grape-growing business, and Beckstoffer was able to execute a leveraged buy of 75 perfect of the grape-growing business in 1973, partly financed by Heublein. Beckstoffer put up only $7,500 in cash – all he had.

He then acquired additional land, and as business improved, sold some land to reduce debt, and ended up with full ownership of the company.

He's been busy buying vineyard land ever since.

All has not been buying, however. Beckstoffer sought advice from some of California's most talented experts, including legendary winemaker André Tchelistcheff, viticulturist Bob Steinhauer, later head of vineyards for Beringer, Steve Yates, Kendall-Jackson's head of vineyards, and others.

He was the first to install drip irrigation in Napa Valley, and the first to replant heavily to Cabernet Sauvignon, anticipating replacing the 'generic' grapes that had filled the Valley at the time.

Active in local and state farming politics, he also pioneered tying the cost of grapes to the price of a bottle of wine, preaching that grapes should sell for 100 times the retail price per ton, i.e., $8,000 per ton for an $80 bottle.

He helped establish the law that now requires that new wineries in the Napa Valley Agricultural Preserve (most of Napa County) must include 75 percent of Valley fruit.

More recently, he donated an easement on some of his land to the Napa Land Trust, ensuring it will never be developed.

He's been an advocate for identifying and recognizing historic vineyards, many of which he owns, of course.

Though many locally remember his role in the loss of local ownership of Inglenook and Beaulieu to Heublein, and the subsequent debasement of those famed names (since gratefully restored under Diageo at Beaulieu, and now Inglenook by Francis Ford Coppola), Beckstoffer was acting in his employer's interest.

And as for the sharp deal he cut to acquire the vineyard land — don't we all wish we were so fortunate. Stupidity among corporate executives is nothing new, as we can read in the paper every day.

One thing is clear: Andy Beckstoffer has made a huge contribution to making Napa Valley wine what it is and equally in boosting its reputation as well as its own, a strategy well practiced by none other than Robert Mondavi.

He offers incentives for the wine companies to mention the name, but in the long run, it's likely to become a big advantage to him. His dream is that people will see 'Beckstoffer Vineyards' on a bottle of wine and know it's excellent, no matter the company that produces the wine. And that means he can get more from his grapes. It's a sound strategy, and one that seems to be working.

You can learn more about Beckstoffer at www.beckstoffervineyards.com.

And Beckstoffer isn't even the largest independent vineyard owner in Napa Valley. The Laird family owns about 2,000 acres, but they keep a very low profile.

Plant Your Own Little Bit of Wine Country

You don't have to be rich or famous to own a little piece of wine country. Increasingly, home owners from San Diego to Seattle are turning their yards into miniature vineyards where they can watch the fascinating yearly cycle of grape growing — and enjoy their own wine as a bonus.

Some home grape growers even go commercial. They sell their grapes to a winery for cash or a share of wine — or create their own label. Some of America's most famous wineries started with a few vines in the yard; Grace Family Vineyards began when the family planted an acre in its front yard in St. Helena and today its wines sells for hundreds of dollars per bottle.

A vineyard is the ultimate in rural chic; the yards of wealthy entrepreneurs and executives sport Chardonnay vines instead of lush lawns or tennis courts.

Even a smaller space can produce a worthwhile amount of wine. Mature premium grape vines typically produce about a gallon of wine per vine, so even 60 vines are enough for a barrel or wine — more than 20 cases.

Few homeowners actually expect to make money on grapes — it takes at least three acres to do so — but they may still find the economics attractive even though most hire experts to establish vineyards, which typically costs about $30,000 per acre.

Specialists generally maintain the vines, perhaps charging $5,000 per acre per year to fertilize, control weeds, remove excessive leaf cover and grape clusters, harvest, maintain irrigation systems and trellises and prune.

That may cost less than conventional landscaping and gardeners and there is a return: Prime Cabernet grapes sell for $4,000 to $10,000 per ton and an acre typically produces three to five tons of premium grapes when mature.

Some homeowners plant and tend their own vines, but may need help testing and preparing soils plus selecting varieties. Fortunately, grape vines are relatively easy to grow and the best quality fruit typically comes from poor soil, not rich loam. It's vital to get advice on the best varieties to plant for your climate and site, however.

Here are some suggestions from experts about small vineyards:

- Don't plant a variety just because you like the wine. You may have the wrong location.
- Don't overplant; 65 or 70 vines is enough for most home users.

- Try to keep 6 feet between vines to discourage rot and fungus.
- Use modern trellis systems if possible.
- Vines don't use much water, perhaps 4 to 6 gallons per vine per week.
- Organic grape growing is difficult and expensive. You need to use sulfur to avoid fungus, but insects aren't usually a big problem.
- Birds love ripe grapes and you may have to net the vines. Deer love vines, often requiring tall fences.
- Take a course at UC Davis or Napa Valley College to learn how to tend vines.
- Get the whole family to participate; it enhances the whole experience.
- Be patient. The vines don't produce right away and there's nothing you can do to speed them up.

Making Your Own Wine

You don't have to live in Napa to print your name on a label and plaster it onto some generic bottle. But those who move to Napa often plant a vineyard and then start to make their own wine. Here are various ways to go about it:

If you don't have a vineyard yet, you'll have to buy grapes. You'll need about half a ton for a barrel of wine, so it'll cost you about $2,000 worth of grapes for a barrel of typical Napa Valley Cabernet.

You can hire a winemaker to make your wine at a custom-crush facility.

Judd's Hill Winery services smaller producers in its "micro-crush" facility. Some other wineries also make wine for other wine companies or individuals. If you want to sell your wine, it can get complicated, for there are many local, state and Federal rules and agencies to deal with.

Judd's Hill will process as few as one or two barrels, which produces 24 to 48 cases of wine, charging $2,500 per barrel for the processing through bottling, but not for the barrels (up to $1,000 each), bottles or labels. That adds at least an additional $20 or so a bottle.

Labels can be expensive since the owner's ego is involved.

Those with greater ambitions might hire someone like Cary Gott, who founded Monteviña Winery at the age of 24, and served as head of winemaking at Sterling Vineyards before forming Vineyard and Winery Estates. He helps people get into the wine business. He assists with everything from locating land – which might also be used for an estate home – to dealing with government agencies and even hiring a winemaker. He often serves that function himself, at least initially.

A consulting winemaker costs from a few thousand to $10,000 per month, with the big names as much as $250,000 a year or requiring a share of sales.

Though having your own winery on your property (you need a minimum 10 acres to build a winery in Napa Valley) is obviously more prestigious than just making the wine elsewhere, physical wineries cost more than many expect. Cary Gott estimates it costs about $3 to $5 million, depending on the site, for a nice building that can handle 3,000 cases. A winery in a cave is a popular new option, hiding the workings for minimum environmental impact, which can help gain county approval if neighbors object to a winery building.

An alternative to setting up your own winemaking is to join Napa Valley Reserve, Bill Harlan's exclusive wine club just outside Meadowood Resort (1000 Silverado Trail, St. Helena; (707) 968-3140 or thenapavalleyreserve.com). It has a 50-acre vineyard.

It costs more than $150,000 to join and you sign up to make specific amounts of wine. You also instantly become a member of an inner circle with seminars, events and parties to match.

You can do as much or little of the work as you want, from picking grapes to doing barrel tastings, and noted winemaker Bob Levy, who also makes Harlan Estate and Bond, supervises the winemaking.

On a simpler level, Napa Valley abounds with home winemakers and winemaking clubs. It's not hard to find one and join the fun – but you can't sell the wine.

Wine Terms

Here are popular terms referring to wine that you may encounter in Napa Valley with am emphasis on local usage.

Acidity

One of the key measures of a grape is its acidity. Too little and the wine tastes bland and spoils easily. Too much and the wine tastes sharp. In general, grapes grown in warm climates are relatively low in acid. It is often augmented by winemakers for better balance. The typical level in a table wine is 0.6 to 0.7 percent (6 to 7 grams per liter).

Air lock

An air lock is a device that lets carbon dioxide produced during fermentation out of a closed tank but prevents air, which could oxidize wine, or undesired bacteria and yeasts from entering the tank. You can see locks bubbling on tanks and barrels early in the fermentation process.

Alcohol

Alcohol is a hydrocarbon containing carbon, hydrogen and oxygen atoms arranged in a certain pattern. The alcohol present in beverages is ethanol. Other alcohols like methanol (wood alcohol) and isopropyl are toxic.

American Viticultural Area

The American version of an appellation. It specifies a geographic area like Oakville but not grape varieties that can be grown or any production or quality standards as is common in Europe. The term suggests distinctive wine, but really is used primarily for marketing purposes.

Barrel

Most red wines here are aged in roughly 59-gallon oak barrels, and some white wines are fermented in as well as aged in them. The barrel, which is lightly toasted inside, imparts flavors of vanilla from the wood and caramel from the toasted sugars, and allows slow and desirable oxidation. Europeans call them barriques.

Barrel thief

A barrel thief is a long bent glass tube used to remove a small sample of wine from a barrel for tasting or testing.

Bin

Grapes are picked into bins. Small bins are more desirable since grapes at the bottom of big bins can be crushed prematurely and start fermenting or even spoil. Half-ton plastic bins are often used to ferment small lots of wine.

Biodynamic

Biodynamic farming was codified by the Austrian theosopher Rudolf Steiner. He combined traditional practices like use of compost, animal manure and planting and managing vines by phases of the moon with an array or teas and portions he called preparations that are applied homeopathically to plants. Some are very controversial, like cow manure buried in cow horns at certain phases and similarly dug up, then stirred in a specific matter to produce vertexes before sprinkling on plants.

Though having undergone almost no scientific testing, Biodynamic farming has been adopted by many growers and winemakers, some of whom produce superb wine.

Blend

Many of the world's most famous wines are blends of different grapes that complement each other. They are not necessarily inferior to wines made from single varieties of grapes.

Botrytis Cinerea or noble rot

Botrytis cinerea is a fungus that dehydrates and shrivels grapes leaving berries very high in concentrated sugar. They are used to make distinctive sweet dessert wines.

Brettanomyces

Brettanomyces (British fungus) is a strain of yeast that gives Heineken and some Belgian beers its distinctive character. It can contaminate wine with a barnyard smell, but some people think it provides desirable complexity in low concentrations.

Brix

Brix is the percentage of sugar in a liquid by weight. Grapes are picked for table wines at 22 to 26 Brix. A rough measure of the alcohol produced is 55 percent of that number.

Sparkling wines are picked at lower Brix levels when the grapes are more acid for flavor and because sugar is added to the wine during a second fermentation to create the bubbles.

Bung

A bung is a large stopper used to seal barrels.

California sprawl

A traditional form of growing grapes that lets the vine canes sprawl around the vine without training to supports.

Cane pruning

Cane pruning is cutting one or two canes from a vine's previous year's growth back to a few buds that will produce the next season's canes and grape bunches. Contrasts with cordon or California sprawl.

Carbon dioxide

Yeast breaks sugar in grape juice into alcohol and carbon dioxide. The latter is normally released into the air but some is retained for sparkling wines. Carbon dioxide emissions are culprits in pollution and global warming, but grapevines and other plants in vineyards absorb much of that carbon dioxide.

Cave

A wine cave is a tunnel dug to store wine, sometimes for production.

Chai

A chai is a barrel storage facility above ground.

Cordon training

Cordon trained vines have one or two woody arms extending from the top of the trunk. Short spurs extend from them, each with one or two buds that will form canes.

Cork

A cork is a traditional wine closure made from the bark of the cork oak tree. Most comes from Portugal and the Mediterranean. Corks allow subtle aging of wine, but can be contaminated with tricholoanisole (TCA) and its relatives, making the wine "corked."

Custom crush facility

A custom crush facility or custom winery produces wine for others. Many of Napa Valley's most noted small-volume wines are made in these shared facilities.

Crush

Crush means to break open the grapes to make them easy to ferment or press to extract juice. Many people confuse crushing and pressing; the famed statue at the bottom of Napa Valley shows a grape presser, not a crusher.

Many wineries actually only remove the stems from grapes using a destemmer, but most crushers can serve this function with adjustments.

Crush is also local slang for the harvest period when grapes are crushed.

Dry

"Dry" in wine terms means not sweet, though wines with 1/2 percent sugar can still be considered dry as they may not taste sweet to drinkers, particularly if the wine is acid.

Dry farmed

Grown without irrigation. Napa Valley gets enough water to grow grapes, but most falls as rain in the winter. Fortunately, the Napa

Valley floor covers an abundant aquifer, and vines can be trained to access it.

In other parts of the valley, irrigation is vital, but it can also be used to manage grape yield and properties.

Enologist

In local use, a person who works in a winery wine lab. Elsewhere, a winemaker.

Estate winery

A winery that produces grows grapes and produces its wine on its own property. Most wineries buy grapes from independent growers and other wineries.

Fermentation

Fermentation is the conversion of carbohydrates like sugars to alcohols and carbon dioxide or organic acids using yeasts or bacteria under anaerobic conditions (lack of oxygen).

It is one of the most important natural processes. It creates wine, beer, bread, cheese, yogurt, pickles, sauerkraut, soy sauce and many other important foods.

In wine, yeasts convert natural sugars to alcohol and carbon dioxide.

Grapes

Many varieties of grapes exist. Those used to make wine here and in most winegrowing regions are in the large vitis vinifera family.

They are green, pink or dark, generally called white or red. The color in most red grapes is only in the skin. The juice is clear and the pigment from the skin is extracted by soaking in alcohol, hence red wine is created by fermenting the crushed grapes with their skins.

For white wines, only the juice is fermented. For pink wines, the must is only kept in contact with the skins a short while.

Gravity feed

Many winemakers prefer to let grapes, crushed grapes and wine flow by gravity rather than pumping it, which can crush seeds and extract undesired tannins or heat the wine.

Harvest

Harvest is the process of collecting ripe crops.

Most grapes in Napa Valley are harvested by hand, but modern machines can perform the job efficiently and deliver almost perfect grape berries to the winery. It also allows harvesting at night, when the grapes are cool, which is desirable. This will become more widely used as labor shortages develop.

Late-harvest wine

Late-harvest wines are made from grapes that have been left on the vine longer than usual. They are usually sweet or dessert wines.

Lees

Lees are dead yeast dells and other wastes that settle to the bottom of barrels and tanks.) They can contribute "mouthfeel" (thickness) and desired flavors to the wine.

Malolactic fermentation

Malolactic fermentation (MLF) is a natural process that lowers acidity by converting malic acid to lactic acid and carbon dioxide. Many winemaker initiate MLF in white wines and almost all red wines undergo MLF by themselves.

In addition to reducing acidity (rarely needed in warm Napa Valley), MLF also introduces a "buttery" flavor, particularly noticeable in white wines like Chardonnay.

Meritage

Meritage are blended wines on the Bordeaux model. The term was developed for wines that don't contain at least 75 percent of one grape variety. The red blend is made from at least two of the eight Bordeaux grape varieties, while white Meritage is a blend at least two of Sauvignon Blanc, Sauvignon Vert and Semillon. The term is losing popularity to proprietary terms.

Microoxygenation

Very judicious application of oxygen can soften flavors and remove undesired substances in wine. Traditionally accomplished in barrels, it can be produced by bubbling a tank amount of air or oxygen through wine.

Must

Must is grape juice on the way to becoming wine.

Negotiant

A person or company that buys bulk or semi-finished wine, finishes and packages, then markets it.

Oak alternatives

Oak barrels are very expensive. The best from France cost more than $1,000 and can only be used a few times to extract flavors. Winemakers often mimic their flavors by inserting oak chips and sticks in used barrels or stainless steel tanks, particularly for moderately priced wines.

Off-dry

Off-dry refers to wines that are slightly sweet. Many popular American wines are off dry in truth though marketed as "dry."

Organic

In farming terms, organic refers to plants grown "naturally" using only derived from living sources (like compost) and naturally occurring minerals, not synthetic fertilizers, pesticides, herbicides and other chemical.

Oval

An oval is a large upright tank used for aging wines.

Oxidize

Oxygen can combine with other materials to oxidize them. Rust is an example. If wine is oxidized, it turns brown and becomes undesirable. Very subtle oxidization can eliminate undesired odors, however.

pH

pH is the measure of hydrogen atoms in a solution, a type of measure of acidity. Water is neutral at 7, and lower numbers indicate acid conditions, while higher are alkaline. It its pH is too high, wine is likely to spoil. A typical wine pH is 3 to 3.5.

Press

As a noun, it's the machine used to extract juice or wine from grapes with pressure. The venerable basket press is a good example, though most wineries use sophisticated presses in which a bladder filled with air squeezes the grapes against the walls of a cylinder.

As a verb, the act of pressing grapes. Also see crush.

Pump over

The cap of grapes that rises is a fermenting tank must be kept moist. One way it to pump wine from near the bottom of the tank over it.

Punch down

The cap of grapes that rises in fermenting red wine must be kept wet. One way is to punch it down in an open tank with a special tool.

Puncheon

A puncheon is a large wine barrel.

Racking

Racking wine is pumping or draining it off settled lees (dead yeast cells and other waste) and putting it in another or the same cleaned container.

Reductive or reduced wine

A stinky wine contaminated with sulfides. Can often be corrected with careful oxidation or even decanting.

Refractometer

A refractometer is an instrument for measuring the Brix (sugar content) or grape juice (must) using refracted light.

Reverse osmosis

Reverse osmosis systems are used to remove defects and excess alcohol from wines.

Sorting table

Many wineries now use a sorting table to remove defective grapes, stems (jacks) and material other than grapes (MOG) like leaves and lizards before fermenting grapes. The most modern are automated and operate automatically, but most use conveyor belts or shaker tables and patient humans to remove debris.

Spinning cone

A spinning cone is a low-pressure low-temperature still used to remove alcohol from wine, whether to make a wine without alcohol, or to reduce the alcohol level of wines.

Structured wine

Winemaker jargon for tannic wine, a term considered pejorative.

Sulfate

Copper sulfate can be added to wine to remove stinky sulfides.

Sulfide

Sulfides are nasty-smelling compounds that sometime form in wine. They include hydrogen sulfide, which suggests rotten eggs, and compounds like mercaptan, which smells like rotten cabbage.

Sulfite

Sulfites are used to protect wine, killing unwanted bacteria and yeasts. They can be introduced by burning elemental sulfur to create sulfur dioxide gas, introduced as a gas, or commonly, created by dissolving potassium bisulfite, potassium metabisulfite, sodium bisulfite, sodium metabisulfite or sodium sulfite in the wine.

Very small quantities of sulfites are used, and have been used for millennia. They are also used to preserve many other foods including dried fruit. Few people appear to be allergic to sulfites despite the required warning labels, and it's challenging to make a long-lasting wine without them.

Sulfur

Elemental sulfur dust is sprayed on vines to protect grapes from fungus and mildew.

If sulfur is burned, it gives off sulfur dioxide. Burning sulfur "candles" in barrels was once used to disinfect them.

Sulfur dioxide

See sulfite; a benign disinfectant for wine and food.

Tank

Tanks are large vessels, generally now made of stainless steel, used for fermenting, aging, blending and storing wine. Historically, wood and concrete tanks were used, and they are making a bit of a comeback for perceived advantages like temperature stability and induced convection currents, particularly in concrete "eggs." Another name for is a tank is vat.

Tannin

Tannins are bitter polyphenols found in grape skins, seeds, stems and some juice. They are also found in oak barrels. Tannins contribute age-worthy properties and complexity to wine, but many people find them very distasteful. They may also contribute healthful properties to wine.

Tricholorosanisole (TCA)

Tricholorosanisole is an earthy, wet-Airedale-smelling contaminant generally introduced from defective corks, hence such spoiled wines are called "corked." Wine drinkers vary dramatically in sensitivity to these smells.

Toast

Oak wine barrels are "toasted" like bread to a varying degree to mellow their tannins and provide desired flavors. This is less extreme than the charring of whiskey and rum barrels, which contributes color as well as caramel flavors to the spirits.

Topping off

Topping off is replacing the wine that inevitably evaporates or is absorbed in wooden wine barrels.

Varietal/variety

There are many varieties of grapes. Varietal is the adjectival form; it's correct to refer to a varietal wine produced mainly of one variety, but not to refer to grapes or vines as varietals.

Vineyard

A farm that grows grapes.

Vintner

In Napa Valley, the owner of a winery. Elsewhere, a wine merchant. In general, not the actual winemaker.

Virtual winery

A company that produces wine from bought grapes in a rented facility or has the wine produced for it. Legally, a wine retailer that can also distribute its wines.

Winemaker

The person who actually makes the wine; not usually the owner of the winery.

Winery

A company that produces wine or the building used to produce wine.

Yeast

Wine yeasts are tiny Saccharomyces cerevisiae fungi used to ferment wine (other strains used for beer or bread). Most winemakers inoculate their musts (grape juice) or crushed grapes with carefully incubated strains, but some depend on "feral" yeasts present everywhere in winemaking regions and wild yeasts on grape skins.

True wild yeasts may introduce off-odors and can't ferment all the sugar in a typical wine, but they can introduce complexity, though Saccharomyces cerevisiae is needed to complete the process and make a stable dry wine.

Wine smells and tastes

The *Wine Advocate* publishes a good glossary of terms primarily related to wine tastes and smells at www.erobertparker.com/info/glossary.asp.

The Wineries of Napa Valley

The Legacy of Napa Valley Wineries

Three-fourths of Napa Valley wineries make less than 10,000 cases per year. Fully 63 percent make less than 5,000 cases, a tiny amount in the wine business.

95 percent are family owned, though admittedly, far more of the wine is produced by larger companies, though some like Gallo, Trinchero (Sutter Home), Bronco and Jackson Family Farms are also family owned.

Many wineries in Napa Valley require reservations and appointments for visits, and most do for tours and special tastings like food pairings.

In many cases, these appointments are required by law, for Napa County ordinances prohibit public (open) tours and tastings for any wineries created after 1990. Many older wineries operate under grandfathered regulations, however.

In this day of cell phones, that's usually not a problem, but note that the phones may not work in remote, mountainous areas.

A Note on Visiting Wineries

This book isn't about wine, but about Napa Valley. You notice no gushing over wines or even much discussion of the winery's products unless they're different from the usual Napa lineup of (excellent) Cabernet, Chardonnay, Merlot and Sauvignon Blanc.

Virtually all wineries in Napa Valley make superb wines, and a misstep is so rare as to be remarkable. Tastes differ, however, and you might prefer some more than others. I've noted a few I particularly like but that doesn't mean that I don't also consider many others top wines.

For that reason, I've focused more on the experience than the wines. If you want to enjoy a particular style of wine, consult the *Wine Advocate* or *Wine Spectator*.

I can almost guarantee that my favorite wines won't be theirs.

Napa Valley's Major Appellations

Though excellent wines – some arguably the best in America – are made in less-known appellations, many in the mountains, the best-known Napa wines come from its valley floor, both the rich river floor that produces lush wines and the bench lands or piedmont than tends to produce more elegant wines.

Napa Valley is divided into 16 American Viticultural Areas or AVAs by the federal government after application by local vintners and growers. This section looks at the major AVAs in the heart of the valley, and the next looks at the outlying regions that fewer tourists visit.

Note that Napa County requires all wineries established since 1990 to require visitors to make appointments so they don't do it because they're trying to be difficult. Some wineries do have to restrict visitors, however, particularly for tours and special tastings and programs. Some wineries are a bit lax on this, but in any case, you'll likely get better treatment if you call ahead, and in some cases, you can't even get in a locked gate without one! That's particularly true in remote areas where your cell phone may not even work to call them to open the gate.

One hint on visiting wineries on Highway 29: Left turns are difficult in busy times, both off and into the highway. It's convenient to visit wineries on the right (east) when driving north, on the west when coming south.

Oak Knoll AVA

Oak Knoll is the area between Napa and Yountville in the southern part of Napa Valley.

Though no one seems positive, the knoll in contention appears to be on the west side of the valley, hidden from view and off a little-used road. Now the biggest landmark is Oak Knoll Road, one of the few roads that crosses Napa Valley, taking a short jog as it does.

Oak Knoll has been described as the sweet spot for grapes in Napa Valley. It's warm enough to ripen heat-loving grapes such as Cabernet and Zinfandel, yet cooled by San Francisco Bay for delicate Riesling and Pinot Noir. The AVA includes 8,300 acres, about 3,500 acres of vineyards. There are 12 wineries and about 40 vineyard owners in the region.

It suffers a bit in image since a divided highway zooms through it, but it's worth getting off the main road to explore its wineries.

Trefethen Vineyards

The largest vineyard property in Oak Knoll belongs to the Trefethen family, which bought it in 1968. The Trefethens sell some of their crop to other wineries including for sparkling wines, but keep much to make their own wines, some of my favorites.

The cool climate lets them produce excellent cool-climate wines from Riesling, Chardonnay and Pinot Noir, but the area is also warm enough to produce excellent Cabernet and other Bordeaux varieties. They have a delicate hand so none of the wines are over-oaked, over-ripe or over-alcoholic.

The winery is only accessible from Oak Knoll Road, but it's worth the short detour, both to see the historic property and to taste some excellent wines.

The winery is a large old redwood barn, one of the few authentic old Napa models, the other being stone buildings and farmhouses, all using local building materials.

Other notable wineries in Oak Knoll are on Highway 29, Silverado Trail or Big Ranch Road in the middle of the Valley.

Laird Family Estates and Silenus Vineyard are across from Trefethen. The Laird family are primarily growers, and their 2,000 acres of vines make them Napa Valley's largest. They also own a modern winery where many Napa Valley winemakers make their wine – and the Lairds make a little to sell under its name.

Andretti Winery, established by racing legend Mario Andretti and Joe Antonini, and the Corley Family's Monticello Vineyard are on Big Ranch Road. Monticello has a replica of Monticello on site.

Luna Vineyards lies on the Silverado Trail just north of the city of Napa. Luna farms mostly Italian varietals organically.

Van Der Heyden is just north, as is kosher Hagafen Vineyards, which makes wines similar to other Napa Valley wines, not syrupy Concord wines.

One special treat is Judd's Hill Winery just north of Napa on the Silverado Trail. Aside from making fine wines, they have a lot of fun, and throw frequent parties, many featuring Judd Finkelstein and his ukulele. They also have chickens to entertain the kids.

Darioush's homage to Persia

Napa Valley contains many wineries that reflect the cultures of Europe, including Spanish-styled missions, Greek monasteries and temples, Tuscan villas, French chateaux and German houses, but little prepares the visitor for the sight of a Persian palace.

But that's just what Darioush Khaledi, who founded Darioush Estate in 1997, constructed on the Silverado Trail north of Napa. Khaledi grew up in Iran's Shiraz region, a wine-growing region until the Islamic revolution. His father made wine as a hobby, and as a boy, Khaledi used to sneak sips from the barrel. As an adult, he became a devoted collector of fine wines.

Khaledi was trained as a civil engineer, but fled Iran in the late 1970's. He emigrated to Southern California where he and his brother-in-law purchased a failing grocery store in Los Angeles and now 30 years later operate one of the most successful independently owned grocery businesses in the United States.

As his business grew, Khaledi desired to transform from a collector to creating fine wines. In the early 1990's he began a search for the ultimate vineyard estate, and Darioush Estate is the result.

Darioush Estate's 63 acres are planted to Cabernet Sauvignon, Shiraz, Merlot, Malbec, Petit Verdot, Chardonnay and Viognier.

Winemaker/vineyard manager Steve Devitt makes handcrafted red Bordeaux varietals and small lots of Chardonnay, Viognier and Shiraz employing minimal intervention techniques such as hand harvesting and hand-sorting of grape clusters, small-lot whole cluster pressing, extended maceration and barrel-to-barrel racking and bottling without filtration.

The 22,000-sq.-ft. winery, the first in America to highlight Persian culture, provides a unique experience. Reminiscent of the great noble architecture that once existed, Darioush evokes Persepolis, the capital of ancient Persia.

Khaledi's heritage is the inspiration for the winery designed by architects Ardeshir and Roshan Nozari. It incorporates clean, contemporary lines with historical references to Persia's ancient capital city.

Among the design features 16 monumental freestanding 18-ft. columns with capital bulls that act as stone trees at the entrance of the winery. Richly textured travertine-stone cladding quarried near Persepolis surrounds the entire building. Additional Persian design features include pre-cast moldings, furniture, fireplaces, ironwork, lighting, cellars, and an amphitheatre for performances and events.

One of the most important aspects of the Persian culture is hospitality, and the winery is designed to create a welcoming environment for guests who visit its tasting room to taste the excellent wines.

Stags Leap District

The Stags Leap District is tucked into the eastern side of Napa Valley below and around a constriction in the valley that keeps most cool air south. The area has optimum soils and climate to produce some of Napa Valley's most-famed Cabernet Sauvignon and other wines.

Two wineries borrow the district's name, Stag's Leap Wine Cellars and Stags' Leap Winery. They fought over the names until a judge said both could use it since it's the name of a geographic formation high above both, but separated them by placement of their apostrophes.

Stag's Leap Wine Cellars is best known. Its founder and winemaker, Warren Winiarski, made the Cabernet that beat the best of Bordeaux in the famous Paris Tasting of 1976, an occasion that catapulted California wines into the top tier.

Winiarski has since sold the winery to Ste. Michelle Wine Estates of Washington plus famed vintner Piero Antinori of Tuscany. Ste. Michelle owns 85 percent, but they share equally in winemaking and continue to make excellent wine.

The nearby Stags' Leap Winery now owned by Treasury Wine Estates occupies a historic building. It is famed for Petite Sirah as well as Cabernet, a legacy of former owner Carl Doumani, who now owns quirky Quixote Winery nearby. It is a most exotic building and suggests its designer was smoking, not drinking.

One of the most famous wineries in Stags Leap District is Shafer Vineyards, one of the few moderate-size wineries that enjoys cult status for its Hillside Select Cabernet.

Other notable wineries nearby by are Chimney Rock, Clos du Val, Regusci, Hartwell, Silverado Vineyards (with the best views in southern Napa Valley; it's owned by Walt Disney's daughter Diane Miller and her husband).

Chimney Rock's winemaking is under the direction of Doug Fletcher, one of the most insightful in his trade. Clos du Val has a strong French flavor though owned by an American, and Regusci occupies a magnificent restored barn. It supplies grapes to many other wineries, too.

Sinskey Vineyards ia a bit of an anomaly. Though in the Stags Leap District, it specializes in Pinot Noir from Carneros vineyards. Rob Sinskey's wife Maria is a chef who pairs tasty bites with wine.

Cliff Lede Winery, which really should be in the Yountville AVA, contains a commercial art gallery. Lede is a big builder, and also owns the exclusive Poetry Inn nearby.

Yountville AVA

The Yountville AVA doesn't get much attention, but the area is a great place to grow both cool- and warm-climate grapes like Oak Knoll just to the south.

The Yountville Hills, sometimes called the Pelissa Hills after the venerable family that owns them, define the cooler south part of the Napa Valley. Combined with the constriction of the mountain ranges and Wappo Hill, the knoll where Robert Mondavi built his home, they keep the cold air from the bay from travelling north.

The hills are almost completely undeveloped. The Pelissa family could have made a fortune developing it at one time – now county regulations would restrict what can be done – but they're happy to let it pasture a few cattle.

Family patriarch Andy Hoxsey is one of the valley's good guys; he farms 600 acres organically and is very sensitive to the community and environment. His family owns the Napa Wine Company just north in Oakville.

The best-known winery in Yountville is Domaine Chandon, which makes excellent sparkling wines and less-known still wines. It is the only winery in Napa Valley with a full-blown restaurant, having either been grandfathered in or being within Yountville or both; it's hard to get the story straight.

The restaurant, Étoile, is excellent and expensive, perfect for a splurge. The Domaine Chandon tasting salon next door has an inviting deck for warm afternoons.

The impressive Dominus Winery is not open to the public, by the way, but the modest Bell winery south of town is worth visiting. It's owned by jocks, and Carmen Policy, the former president of the San Francisco 49ers, owns Casa Piena Winery, though it doesn't have a tasting room. In fact, a number of athletes have wineries in Napa Valley.

Though short on wineries, the tiny town of Yountville is filled with wine tasting venues:

- Beau Vigne. 6795 Washington St., Yountville. (707) 947-7058. www.beauvigne.com

- Cornerstone Cellars. 6505 Washington St., Yountville. (707) 945-0388. www.cornerstonecellars.com

- Girard Winery. 6795 Washington St.. Yountville. (707) 968-9297. www.girardwinery.com

- Hill Family Estate. 6512 Washington St., Yountville. 707 944-9580. www.hillfamilyestate.com

- Hope & Grace. 6540 Washington St. Yountville. (707) 944-2500. www.hopeandgracewines.com
- Jessup Cellars. 6740 Washington St., Yountville. (707) 944-5620. www.jessupcellars.com
- Ma(i)sonry. Multi-winery tasting room poring wines from Blackbird Vineyards, Captûre Wines, Casa Piena, Fisher Vineyards, Husic Vineyards, Juslyn Vineyards, Kristine Ashe Vineyards, Lail Vineyards, Ma(i)sonry Napa Valley, Pedras Wine Company, Pott Wine, R.A. Harrison Family Cellars, Recuerdo Wines, Renteria Wines, Skipstone, Tor Kenward Family Wines, and Uvaggio. 6711 Washington St., Yountville. (707) 944-0889. www.maisonry.com
- NapaStyle Lifestyle store contains winetasting bar featuring Chiarello Wines and others. In V Marketplace, 6525 Washington St., Yountville. (707) 945-1050. www.napastyle.com
- Page Wine Cellars & Revolver Wine Co. 6505 Washington St., Yountville. (707) 944-2339. www.pagewinecellars.com
- Somerston Wine Co. 6490 Washington St., Yountville. (707) 967-8414. www.somerstonwineco.com
- V Wine Cellar Retail store and tasting venue with outside seating. In V Marketplace, 6525 Washington St., Yountville. (707) 531-7053. www.vwinecellar.com

Oakville AVA

Two AVAs are the most famous in America, Oakville and Rutherford. Oakville's fame is largely due to one individual, Robert Mondavi, while Rutherford boasts two legendary wineries.

The wine districts, appellations or AVAs in this part of Napa Valley were defined by the local towns or townships, and stretch from east to west across the valley.

Ironically, the eastern bench and the western bench of each have more in common with their neighboring AVAs than with each other, and the alluvial valley floor is quite distinct.

In a nutshell, the benches or piedmont grows the best grapes. The valley floor, which has very deep rich soil, would have be planted to vegetables or grain in Italy, for it contains deep, rich soil. Grape vines do best in poor soil, and the grapevines would be on the poorer hillsides.

However, the valley floor produces rich wines Americans tend to like, and anyway, it's very valuable.

Fortunately, growers have been able to compensate for the deep soil with its high water table by severely pruning, hedging and basically abusing the vines so they produce good grapes. Nevertheless, the best wines come from the benches, and the attractive vines around some famed properties like Opus One may not contribute much to their exalted wine.

The Oakville appellation starts north of the Yountville Hills, and Cosentino Winery and Napa Wine Cellars/Folie a Deux/Menage a Trois, which is owned by the Trinchero family (of which more later in St. Helena), are the first wineries you encounter. Napa Wine Cellars allows picnics, one of the few wineries along Highway 29 than can do so and does.

Napa Wine Company lies at the intersection of Highway 29 and Oakville Road. It's so old that it's the only winery in California with a single-digit bond number (4). Now the sprawling winery is a "custom crush winery," providing a home for more than 50 wineries that don't have their own facilities or have outgrown theirs.

The winery is rather ramshackle and not the place for a tour, but its tasting room features a rotating selection of wines made at the winery, some very hard to find elsewhere.

The Oakville Grocery, which has just been completely renovated, carries an excellent selection of local wines, again, some obscure. It also provides the makings for great picnics and even has tables and chairs to eat.

Just beyond are famed Opus One, formed as a joint venture by elegant Baron Philippe de Rothschild and rustic Robert Mondavi. Like the Paris tasting of 1976, this partnership helped establish Napa Valley's reputation, and especially Mondavi's.

The winery is modern and striking, and a tour is worthwhile, as is a tasting. One hint: The winery makes a "second" label called Overture that's a bargain compared to the pricy Opus One.

Nearby are lovely Far Niente with its stereotypical rich Napa wines and an amazing car collection, and the same company's Nickel and Nickel, which focuses on single-vineyard wines rather than blends. Far Niente also produces Dolce, America's best-know luxury dessert wine.

Next is the most famous winery in Oakville if not the whole valley, Robert Mondavi Winery.

Robert Mondavi Winery

The story has been told many times about how Bob Mondavi got into a fight with his strong-willed mother Rosa and brother Peter at the family's Charles Krug winery, and was thrown out of the business.

At 55, he and his son Michael created Robert Mondavi Winery with backing of Rainier Brewery, which for some reason sold its shares back to Mondavi later.

His Mission-style winery has become an icon of Napa Valley even though there were no missions here – the closest was in Sonoma – and they did everything right: make great wine, innovate in winemaking, offer tours and tastings, food program and concerts.

Most of all, Bob was a tireless promoter of not only his winery but Napa Valley, California wines and wine as part of a gracious lifestyle.

Though Bob is gone, and the winery is now owned by giant Constellation Brands, the management at Constellation is not dumb. After paying $1.3 billion for the company, they haven't changed anything important for the worse.

If anyone comes to Napa Valley and can only visit one winery, this is the one to choose. No winery has better or more educational programs and tours that Robert Mondavi Winery. They range from simple tasting to 1½-hour vineyard and winery tours and even lunches with wines. 7801 St. Helena Hwy., Oakville, CA 94562. (707) 226-1395. www.robertmondavi.com

Not far away is Swanson Vineyards, which specializes in excellent Merlot and has a number of interesting tasting alternatives.

Nearby is St. Supéry Wines and Vineyards, which is owned by a French family. It has excellent tours including a demonstration vineyard and an art gallery. It's even friendly to pooches – at least on its patio.

Peju is fun, and Turnbull has a fine art photography museum, but the Cakebread Winery is especially important.

Founded by a photographer and garage owner (!), Jack Cakebread and his wife Dolores, Cakebread not only made good wine, but followed Dolores' instinct to promote its wines with food. In the American Harvest Workshops it has held each fall since 1986, the winery has educated upcoming chefs to pairing wine with locally sourced produce, and that message has now pervaded American cuisine.

One result has been that Cakebread is one of the top wines in restaurants all over America, but another is that America's cuisine is far superior to what it was before they started,

Sons Bruce and Dennis continue the tradition.

A couple of impressive wineries lie on Oakville Crossroad between Highway 29 and the Silverado Trail. PlumpJack is owned by California Lieutenant Governor and former San Francisco Mayor Gavin Newsom and Gorgon Getty, while Gargiulo is owned is a talented guitarist with tight connections to the entertainment world, which often results in interesting events.

The east side of the Oakville AVA includes famed Screaming Eagle, which doesn't allow visitors to see where its $750 wines are made, Rudd Estate, Oakville Ranch, Miner Family, Della Valle and sleeper Tierra Roja.

Rutherford AVA

Until Robert Mondavi built his winery, Rutherford was America's Grand Cru. The home of Inglenook and Beaulieu Vineyards (BV locally), its wines were famous before Prohibition and peaked in the '40s and '50s.

Famed Russian Francophile winemaker André Tchelistcheff at BV had immense influence on winemaking in Napa Valley. He coined the term "Rutherford Dust," for the special quality he recognized in the wines.

Both venerable wineries went through downturns, but now Beaulieu is owned by spirits giant Diageo, which recognizes its treasure. It regular and reserve tasting rooms in the huge old winery are worth visiting.

Just across the road from BV is Inglenook, which screen writer and director Francis Ford Coppola has lovingly (and expensively) restored to its earlier dimensions, quality and name, even tearing down an ugly warehouse that hid its beautiful façade. He recovered the old name at great cost to complete his restoration of the famed estate.

Though sometimes faulted for its large gift shop unrelated to the wine – as well as all the film memorabilia – Inglenook, formerly Rubicon, is worth visiting.

Elizabeth Spencer Wines has a tasting room in "downtown" Rutherford at 1165 Rutherford Road, and Round Pond Estates with an impressive tasting room and olive oil mill lie beyond on the way to the Silverado Trail. Honig is one of my favorites, making elegant Sauvignon Blanc and Cabernet Sauvignon.

Another gem is Frog's Leap Winery, owned by one of the valley's good guys. John Williams, who was trained as a dairyman and cheesemaker, raised grapes the old way with no chemicals nor irrigation, making exceptional wines if not the type of blockbusters that overwhelm critics. He also has a quirky sense of humor, as evidenced by the winery's name, and has a lot of fun.

Caymus Vineyards, one of the valley's long-term best producers, is nearby.

Along the Silverado Trail nearby are venerable ZD Wines, best known for Pinot Noir and Chardonnay, and Mumm Napa, one of the valley's big sparkling wine producers. It has an impressive gallery of art photography, many by famed artist Ansel Adams.

Also there is Conn Creek Vineyards, whose exhibits include a room with a barrel of wine from each appellation in Napa Valley, available for tastings and blending, and Rutherford Ranch tucked under Auberge du Soleil.

Above Auberge is Rutherford Hill Winery, which has great views and a picnic ground as well as fine wine.

Quintessa is a most remarkable estate. When the Huneeus family bought 280 acres to create Quintessa in 1989, they planted Biodynamic vineyards on the last major estate available for development in Rutherford. The tour explains how the gravity-fed winery works and ends with a sit-down tasting of two vintages of Quintessa wines with local cheese.

Back to Highway 29, you find Grgich-Hills Winery. Miljelk "Mike" Grgich, who fled Communist Yugoslavia (now Croatia) as a youth, made the Chateau Montelena Chardonnay that won the Paris Tasting of 1976. He started his own winery and the company continues to make exceptional wines with his nephew Ivo and daughter Violet. The winery has wholeheartedly adopted Biodynamic farming, with 600 acres under the regime.

Staglin Family Vineyards lies off Highway 29 against the western hills. It sponsors the yearly Music Festival for Mental Health, and was also the site of the second version of the Parent Trap when Lesley Lohan was a nice young teenager.

Nearby is Alpha Omega, which is oriented toward customers who visit the winery instead of buying in retails stores. Needless to say, they make visits memorable.

Across the street, Diageo's Provenance makes solid wines.

Franciscan Vineyards is a large and impressive complex featuring the wines of Franciscan, Mt. Veeder and other brands owned by Constellation.

White Hall Lanes and Rutherford Grove are here, too, as is Sullivan Vineyards behind Franciscan on Galleron Lane.

Del Dotto's second locations (the other is at Silverado) is gaudy and emphasizes tasting wine from lots of barrels. It's really a barrel tasting more than a wine tasting! Many people love it, but I consider a wine in which the flavor of oak is apparent (as opposed to its subtle impact) flawed, so it's not my thing.

The real find here, however, is Raymond Vineyards.

Raymond Vineyards and Jean-Charles Boisset

Raymond Vineyards used to be a sleeper, but that changed when it was acquired by French Jean-Charles Boisset's Boisset Family Estates.

The charming Frenchman has upgraded the vineyards and wines but especially its visitors' center to explain Biodynamic grapegrowing and offer experiences unique in Napa Valley and perhaps anywhere.

Raymond has a venerable history. It was founded in 1971 by Roy Raymond, Sr., a descendent of the Beringer family, and his sons Roy and Walter.

The winery was known locally for good values. It also produced excellent wines but seemed to escape the attention garnered by some local wineries. It wasn't seen as a destination like Mondavi or Beringer.

The location didn't help. It is not on busy Highway 29, but on Zinfandel Lane, not an obvious route for tourists.

As soon as Boisset bought the place in 2010, he contracted with famed wine consultant Philippe Melka to help with the first harvest after he bought the winey, then hired well-regarded winemaker Stephanie Putnam from Far Niente Winery.

They've started replanting some vineyards as well as converting 100 acres to Biodynamic growing to start with, and Boisset has made a big investment in the winemaking. They've acquired new equipment including sorting tables, and smaller tanks and presses for more small-lot winemaking.

"Raymond was making good and fair wines," says Boisset. "My intention is to take it to the next level."

He continues, "A lot of Napa Valley wines are heavy and tannic. We want to bring in a level of elegance."

Raymond had a friendly but subdued tasting room. Charismatic and infectious Boisset, who is married to Gina Gallo of the Gallo wine empire, planted a demonstration vineyard and garden to herbs associated with Biodynamic farming as well as other favored crops like sunflowers, lavender and corn.

Boisset has also planted a demonstration garden of cover crops, as well as adding the goats, chickens, sheep and bees specified in the Biodynamic farming regime as well as equipment for producing the homeopathic "potions" used in vineyards.

The infamous cow horns stuffed with manure and other materials and used to produce some of the preparations are buried in the middle of the herb garden – which is aligned with a round "moon" window on the main winery.

Placards will explain everything. "We want to show how nature affects wine and why the lunar calendar is important, for example," Boisset notes.

Boisset has planted many trees around the visitor center, including a fruit orchard, and generally upgraded the visitor facilities.

Inside the tasting facilities, he created a wine education center, a blending room like a high-school chemistry lab for visitors, the Baccarat-filled crystal tasting room, a barrel room for tasting and comparison of different Napa Valley appellations and even different oak barrels plus an extensive arrays of devices to illustrate wine smells, tastes and even textures like silky or leathery.

Topping it all is the gaudy but fun Red Room that would be at home in an 1890 New Orleans Bordello – or Las Vegas today.

It's a great place to visit. 849 Zinfandel Ln., St Helena. (707) 963-3141. www.raymondvineyards.com

St. Helena AVA

St. Helena is well recognized at the heart of the Napa Valley winemaking business, and the town is a major tourist magnet, but until recently, few wineries mentioned that they were in the St. Helena AVA. Yet St. Helena contains some of Napa Valley's most prominent and important wineries.

St. Helena is home to three of Napa Valley's most venerable wineries, two now owned by outside companies but one still family owned (as are most wineries in Napa Valley).

The Peter Mondavi family's Charles Krug Winery

German Charles Krug lays claim to being the oldest commercial winery in Napa Valley that's still operating. It was founded in 1861 by Krug, and contains two magnificent historic structures that have been lovingly restored in recent years by the present owners, the Peter Mondavi family.

The Mondavis bought Krug in 1943. Peter's brother Bob left in 1966 to start his own winery.

Peter Mondavi, Sr. is an innovative winemaker who introduced many modern practices to Napa Valley. Still going strong at close to 100, he leaves most of the management to his sons Peter, Jr. and Marc.

While Bob long overshadowed Peter, he remains a valley legend, and restoration and investment has turned his winery into one of the valley's stars.

A visit to Krug is a must, and it will become more some as the family installs a new tasting room, museum of Napa Valley wine, and a picnic area and deli – the only one at a winery in Napa Valley other than that at V. Sattui. 2800 Main St., St. Helena. (707) 967-2200. www.charleskrug.com

Almost across the street from Krug is Beringer Vineyards. Beringer Vineyards is one of Napa Valley's oldest and most historic wineries. It was founded by the German Beringer brothers in 1868 at a time when many of the immigrant winemakers came from Germany.

The Beringers dug caves for wine storage, and built the Rhine House to remind them of home, starting a tradition that continues to this days with chateaux, castles and temples.

The winery is now owned by Treasury Wine Estates, a spin off from giant Fosters Brewery, but continues to make excellent wine and its tours are well worthwhile.

And yes, that huge complex across from Beringer is where they make the wine, including lakes of white Zinfandel. 2000 Main St., St. Helena. (866) 708-9463. www.beringer.com

Louis M. Martini winery was formed just after Prohibition and has long made great wines at reasonable prices. Though now the winery is owned by giant E. & J. Gallo, Mike Martini remains the winemaker and Gallo has invested to upgrade the facilities and improve the wines. It has a picnic area as a bonus. 254 St. Helena Hwy., St. Helena. (707) 963-2736. www.louismartini.com

V. Sattui is one of the most visited wineries in Napa Valley, and for good reason: It has been the only one with a deli and picnic ground. A very good deli, too, and a wide selection of wines from sweet wines popular with many visitors to Napa Valley who can't find those they love, to sparkling wine and serious Cabernets.

The winery is exceptionally customer oriented, but don't even think of bringing in food, wine or beer from other places to eat on its tables! Owner Daio Sattui has dungeons and a torture chamber at his Castello di Amorosa in Calistoga... 1111 White Ln., St. Helena. (707) 963-7774. www.vsattui.com.

One of Napa's oldest postwar wineries, Joseph Phelps Vineyards is known for its Rhône varietal wines and California's pioneering Bordeaux-style wine blend, Insignia. Views of bucolic Spring Valley are amazing, and the seated tastings are expertly run. 200 Taplin Rd., St. Helena. (800) 707-5789. www.jpvwines.com

Spring Mountain Vineyard was once best-known for the Victorian mansion that served as the symbol of the 1980's soap opera Falcon Crest, but it's well worth visiting for its wine and setting as well.

The tour includes a visit to the caves, vineyards where a variety of grapes are grown for educational purposes and a horse barn filled with winemaking artifacts, then ends with a tasting at the mansion. 2805 Spring Mtn. Rd., St. Helena. (707) 967-4188. www.springmountainvineyard.com

Long Meadow Ranch – a tenuta in California

Many wineries in Napa Valley have their own estate vineyards, but few showcase the enlightened approach to farming of Long Meadow Ranch.

The historic 650-acre ranch lies high above St. Helena and Rutherford in the Mayacamas Mountains that define the western edge of the Napa Valley. Here Ted and Laddie Hall have created an almost self-contained farm like the great estates of Tuscany – or the family farms of yesterday.

They produce not only wine and olive oils but grass-fed beef, eggs and heirloom fruits and vegetables. They even breed and work their own horses.

The Halls bought Long Meadow Ranch in 1989, and set about restoring vineyards first planted in the 1870s. They also discovered long-overgrown olive orchards, and now produce both wine and olive oil using sustainable, organic farming methods.

Their farming is a marriage of the old and the new: Horses and cattle eat the natural organic grass while their manure contributes to the compost piles of grape pomace and spent plants that fertilizes the vines.

Their commitment to the environment extends beyond farming. Their winery and olive oil frantoio occupy a building formed of earth and recycled timbers and it and the adjacent caves allow the Halls to dispense with air conditioning. The ranch's solar panel arrays generate electricity to supply its needs and it employs biodiesel fuels in its farm equipment.

The Halls have also placed their property in the Napa Valley Land Trust, assuring that the land will provide a unique rural environment rich with wildlife for future generations.

Long Meadow Ranch is a special place, well worth a visit. It's not open for casual tasting, but does offer educational tours.

The family opened a tasting room and Farmstead Restaurant in downtown St. Helena to provide wider access and showcase their products, from eggs and produce to beef, oil and wine. 1775 Whitehall Ln., St. Helena. (707) 963-4555. www.longmeadowranch.com

Just to confuse things, another set of Halls have a winery in St. Helena (plus a little one in Rutherford).

Craig and Kathryn Hall bought the decrepit Napa Valley Co-op Winery and tore down the ramshackle building, uncovering and restoring the old stone winery inside while building modern winemaking facilities nearby.

They have a nice tasting room showcasing some of their contemporary art and even a few picnic tables. 401 St. Helena Hwy., St. Helena. (707) 967-2626. www.hallwines.com

Not far away, tiny Milat Vineyards is a bit of a throwback to the days of modest family wineries, and a delightful place to visit. It even has two rare rooms to rent among the vines. Cathy Corison makes wines the old-fashioned way and has gained a following for just that. 1091 St. Helena Hwy., St. Helena. (707) 963-0758. www.milat.com

Flora Springs wines shouldn't be judged by the bizarre tasting room, all swoops and stripes. It has a tasting area on the roof so you can overlook the valley. 677 St. Helena Hwy., St. Helena. (707) 967-8032. www.florasprings.com

Heitz Vineyards was once very prominent, having one of the early cult wines, Martha's Vineyard Cabernet. Of late, the Staglin Family has taken over the grapes from that famed vineyard. Heitz is noteworthy for its rare wines of Grignolino grapes. 436 St. Helena Hwy., St. Helena. (707) 963-3542. www.heitzcellars.com

Merryvale is right in town by Tra Vigne restaurant; it was once owned by the Mondavi family before they bought Krug. 1000 Main St., St. Helena. (707) 252-8001. www.merryvale.com

Spottswoode is one of Napa Valley's top small producers; all organic, it's also notable that the owners are the women of the Novak family. 1902 Madrona Ave., St. Helena. (707) 963-0134. www.spottswoode.com

North of town is St. Clement Vineyards, owned by Treasury like Beringer. It has a nice spot for picnics up the hill overlooking Napa Valley. 2867 St. Helena Hwy., St. Helena. (707) 963-7221. www.stclement.com

Markham has a great art photography gallery, of late featuring Baron Wolman, the photographer who took many memorable shots of mostly dead rock stars for the cover of *Rolling Stone* magazine. 2812 St. Helena Hwy., St. Helena. (707) 963-5292. www.markhamvineyards.com

Morlet across the street is in a restored stone winery; its winemaker Luc Morlet is one of the many talented French winemakers in the valley. 2825 St. Helena Hwy. N., St. Helena. (707) 967-8690. www.morletwines.com

Even farther north is venerable Freemark Abbey, which offers an extensive library of old wines. Its first winemaker was a widow, and the stone building is quite old. The current owner is Jackson Family Wines, headed by Barbara Banker, the widow of Jess Jackson. 3022 St. Helena Hwy., St. Helena. (707) 963-9694. www.freemarkabbey.com

Benessere is in the middle of the valley and specializes in Italian varieties. 1010 Big Tree Rd., St. Helena. (707) 963-5853. www.benesserevineyards.com

Across Lodi Lane on the Silverado Trail is Duckhorn Vineyards. Duckhorn helped to make quality Merlot popular in America, but now also makes a lot of Cabernet, too. Its second label is Decoy. The tasting room replicates an old Napa farmhouse. 1000 Lodi Ln., St. Helena. (707) 963-7108. www.duckhorn.com

The amazing Trinchero family

Though they're little known outside the wine industry and their home in Napa Valley, the Trinchero family has been some of the most innovative and successful players in American wine.

The story is often told how Louis "Bob' Trinchero of Sutter Home Winery invented white Zinfandel wine almost by accident.

Trying to create more intense (red) Zinfandel, he drained off some of the juice early in fermentation – you'll recall that most red grapes have clear juice; the color comes from soaking in the skins – hoping to concentrate the flavor in the red wine.

It's not known whether that worked, but he fermented the almost clear juice he drained off and made a dry "white" wine. It had a slight pinkish color, as many "white" Zins do today.

The technique of making white wine from red grapes is not new. It's used to make Champagne, and Pinot Grigio grapes are pinkish.

The wine wasn't very popular, but when Bob tried it another year, the fermentation "stuck" leaving a bit of residual sugar in the wine. After some hassling with the government, he labeled it "white Zinfandel," and it became an instant success.

One reason was the sweetness. Though Americans say they like dry (unsweet) wines, in truth many prefer a little sugar in their wine; after all, they're raised on Cokes and ice cream!

Other makers jumped on the bandwagon, notably Beringer, which is also based in St. Helena, and for years, white Zin has been the fourth most popular wine sold in America (After Chardonnay, Cabernet and Merlot. It's probably the highest-volume variety of wine produced in Napa Valley, but all of the grapes come from elsewhere, and nobody likes to talk about this in the land of expensive Cabernet.

White Zinfandel has declined a bit in popularity of late, but remains fifth latest variety sold in America.

The Trincheros aren't very concerned about the slow decline in white Zin. They were ready. They've been pioneers in popularizing sweetish Muscat wines (labeled Moscato) under the Sutter Home label, though Gallo's Barefoot brand is the biggest producer. These wines have been immensely popular, particularly with independent young drinkers who don't care that critics tell them that only dry wines are chic.

In addition, a few years ago, they bought small Folie a Deux winery in St. Helena to build a new home for their premium Trinchero Family Estates brand. That winery made a wine with the double entendre Menage a Trois (blend of three), a blend of three red grapes – Zinfandel, Merlot and Cabernet. It's also sweetish and easy to drink alone as well as with barbeques and other casual food. Folie a Deux now features Sonoma wines.

It's a bit more expensive than the Sutter Home brand, good business for the Trincheros, who have extensive holdings of vineyards and efficient production wineries.

It quickly became the top selling red wine sold in the United States, and the Trincheros followed with white (Chardonnay, Chenin Blanc, Moscato) and rosé (Merlot, Syrah, Gewürztraminer) blends, which soon topped their categories.

Seeing a good thing, they introduced varietal wines in the line, all using grapes from three different growing regions: Chardonnay in 2009 and Moscato in fall of 2011, and more recently introduced a Pinot Grigio.

Consumer acceptance has been great. "We're incredibly excited to hear what consumers have to say about the Pinot Grigio," says Bob Torkelson, president and COO of Trinchero Family Estates. The Pinot Grigio is designed to capture what many consumers want in wine: delicious on its own and wonderfully versatile with food, fruit-forward, essentially the perfect way to end the day.

The 2010 Pinot Grigio is cold-fermented in steel tanks, avoiding malolactic fermentation resulting in a wine with zesty tropical fruit aromas, vivid fruit flavors balanced by mouth-watering acidity. It's a Pinot Grigio to appeal to all palates with its balance of acidity and fruit.

Trinchero Family Estates is wholly owned and operated by the Trinchero family, Napa Valley vintners since 1947. They make a lot more than Sutter Home and Menage a Trois wines, however.

The company produces more than 28 brands of wine including Trinchero Napa Valley, Main Street, Napa Cellars, Terra d'Oro, Montevina, Seaglass, Trinity Oaks, and alcohol-removed Fre.

The company also imports Angove Family Winemakers from Australia, Doña Paula wines of Argentina, Carmen wines of Chile and markets the Three Thieves and Joel Gott brands.

In Napa Valley, 95 percent of the wineries are owned by families, but the Trincheros are by far the biggest (followed by the Peter Mondavi family with Charles Krug and CK Mondavi Wines).

The Trinchero family's success has allowed them to follow their dream of producing top wines under their own name, from a small winery north of St. Helena too. They are also exceptionally generous in quietly supporting local good causes. To learn more visit www.tfewines.com.

And their demand for grapes for white Zinfandel has an unexpected side effect – saving large tracts of old Zinfandel vines that would have otherwise been replaced with other, more popular varieties like Chardonnay and Merlot.

Much of those old Zinfandel grapes now go into Old Vine Zinfandel, one of California's treasures, with the demand for white Zin met by new, high-production vines in other locations. Aside from the Trinchero tasting room at 3070 St. Helena Hwy. N., St. Helena. (707) 603-6400. www.tfewines.com, Sutter Home has a visitor center south of town. Almost uniquely in today's Napa Valley, you can taste wines for free. 277 St. Helena Hwy., St. Helena. (707) 963-3104. www.sutterhome.com

St. Helena also boasts a number of tasting rooms:

- A Dozen Vintners, north of town. 3000 St. Helena Hwy., St. Helena. (707) 967-0666. www.adozenvintners.com

- Bello Family tasting room. 929 Main St., St. Helena. (707) 967-8833. www.bellofamilyvineyards.com

- Materra Vineyards tasting room next to the Wydown Hotel at 1424 Main St., St. Helena. (707) 244-4600. www.materrawines.com

- Salon St. Helena features the wines of Jones Family Vineyards and Harris Estate Vineyards, both made by Thomas Rivers Brown. 1118 Hunt Ave., St. Helena. (707) 963-3193. www.salonsthelena.com

- Savour St. Helena with Areté, Houdini, Richard Partridge Wine and Burly Wine, Spotted Owl Vineyards, Terroir Napa Valley and Veedercrest Estates. 649 Main St., St. Helena. (707) 968-5445. www.savoursthelena.com

- Tamber Bey Vineyards. 1234 Adams St., St Helena. (707) 968-5345. www.tamberbey.com

- Velo Vino for Clif Family wines (and Clif Bars and bicycles!) 709 Main St., St. Helena. (707) 968-0625. www.vinovelonapavalley.com

- St. Helena Wine Center is a retail store that offers tasting. 1321 Main St., St. Helena (707) 963-1313. www.shwc.com

The Franco-Swiss ghost winery

It's not really in St. Helena but east down long dead-end Conn Valley Road that now ends at Lake Hennessy lies the large ruin of an old winery awaiting better economic times so the owners Leslie and Richard Mansfield can restore it.

They already own Mansfield Winery, which produces wine at a custom facility, but have approval to restore the 1876 stone "Ghost Winery," once G. Crochat and Company's Franco-Swiss winery.

The site is only 3½ miles east of St. Helena, but down a long, dead-end country road in secluded Conn Valley.

The building was once one of Napa County's largest wineries and produced 100,000 gallons of wine on its 640 acres of land, 150 planted in vines. It also had a still to produce brandy.

Like other wineries of the time, the Franco-Swiss Winery took advantage of gravity and was built on a slope, with fermentation tanks accessible on the second floor via a direct entrance on the eastern side of the building. On the ground floor, large oval casks were positioned to take advantage of the natural gravity flow that the site afforded.

Large keystone-arched doors and windows offered ideal light and ventilation to the fermentation rooms and the thick stone walls provided insulation during the hot summer months to cool and protect the young wines.

The Franco-Swiss winery is one of the largest unrestored wineries in the county. It was also the site of an infamous murder, but was later a perlite plant after phylloxera, the earthquake of 1906 and Prohibition took their toll on the winemaking.

The Mansfields want to restore the old building on Conn Valley Road into a working 8,000-case winery.

They have hired architect Juliana Inman, who specializes in historic renovation, to plan the project. She is a former member of the Napa County Planning Commission and now a councilmember of the city of Napa. The contractor chosen, Andrews Thornley, is an expert in rebuilding historic wineries.

Juliana Inman believes the building has a good chance to be included in the National Registry of Historic Places!

Richard Mansfield has been a winemaker for 28 years, while Leslie is a chef and author of 18 cookbooks. Mansfield holds Master's degrees in Viticultural and Enological Engineering from Germany's University at Geisenheim as well as a Bachelors of Science in Chemistry from the University of Oregon.

Following eight years of formal training in the vineyards of northern Europe, Mansfield founded Callahan Ridge winery in his native Oregon, then sold his winery and moved to Napa Valley. There he worked at Stags' Leap Winery, Bradford Mountain Winery and Palmaz Vineyards, before he left to concentrate on his Mansfield Winery label. He consults for several wineries.

The Mansfields have an extensive history of the winery they will share. Email richard@mansfieldwinery.com. See www.mansfieldwinery.com for more information.

Nearby is Anderson's Conn Valley Winery.

Calistoga AVA

Amazingly, Calistoga only became an American Viticultural Area in 2010 though it had long been recognized as a distinct wine region. Calistoga is one of the warmest parts of Napa Valley, though it does get a little relief from cooling breezes coming through a gap in the mountains in the late afternoon.

It's a fairly long drive up the valley, but it contains five of Napa Valley's top destination wineries.

Chateau Montelena

Its most famous winery is Chateau Montelena north of town, which made the Chardonnay that beat the best white Burgundies in the famous tasting in Paris in 1976. That event is described somewhat fancifully in the 2008 movie *Bottle Shock*.

Montelena occupies an old "castle" built by Alfred Tubbs in 1882 on a knoll. It stopped making wine at Prohibition, and the family sold the property to Chinese electrical engineer Yort Wing Frank, who built the Chinese-style lake below.

The Barrett family and partners bought the winery in 1968 and son Bo joined as a winemaker in 1972. He remains there today.

Today, Montelena specializes in Cabernet, but you can taste its Chardonnay, still made in a "Burgundian," not Napa style. 1429 Tubbs Ln., Calistoga. (707) 942-5105. www.montelena.com

Schramsberg – America's top sparkling producer

As well known now is Schramsberg, America's royalty of sparkling wine. The story has often been told of how Jamie and Jack Davies left corporate life in Los Angeles in 1965, buying the long-abandoned winery and property built by German Jacob Schram a century earlier.

The property was a mess, but the Davies recognized its significance with its deep caves and possibilities, and decided to make America's first premium sparkling wine.

People thought they were crazy, but they persevered, perhaps gaining their greatest coup when then-President Nixon served it to celebrate the 'opening' of China.

In those days, the grapes for the wine came primarily from Schramsberg's Diamond Mountain property. Now Diamond Mountain is recognized as one of the best places in the world to grow Cabernet, but then a variety of grapes were grown there, including Riesling, Chardonnay and Gewurztraminer for nearby Stony Hill, perhaps America's first 'cult' wine.

The grapes did well because of the altitude, soil conditions and exposure, but over time, Schramsberg has replanted the vineyards to more appropriate Bordeaux varieties, and buys grapes for its sparkling wines from cooler climates. (It also makes still J. Davies Cabernet wines from the property.)

Hugh Davies has taken over as general manager and head winemaker. Before joining his family's winery as enologist (in Napa, that job is primarily a scientist working in the lab), Hugh got a master's degree in enology at the University of California at Davis, then worked at Petaluma Winery in the Adelaide Hills of South Australia.

During the respective 1994 and 1995 vintages, Hugh worked at Mumm Napa Valley and at Moët Chandon in Champagne. Being fluent in both Spanish and French enabled him to travel easily throughout the world. He spent time through the years working with Schramsberg's sparkling wine project in Portugal and at Remy Martin Cognac in France. He also in Peru.

Hugh now gets grapes from 60 different vineyards, some as tiny as less than an acre. They include many in southern Napa County, especially Carneros, other in cooler and coastal areas of Sonoma, in Anderson Valley in Mendocino County and even from parts of Marin County only a few miles from the cold Pacific Ocean. They lease the vineyards in Anderson Valley but don't own vineyard property other than around their winery.

Schramsberg makes three levels of wines with different characteristics and flavors, and the 'best' grapes naturally head of the top of the line.

You need an appointment to visit Schramsberg ((707) 942-2414). It's a wonderful experience, both the tour of the old caves, and tasting the wines. 1400 Schramsberg Rd., Calistoga. (707) 942-4558. www.schramsberg.com

Castello di Amorosa

One of Napa Valley's top attractions is new, but it looks as if its' been there for seven centuries.

Castello di Amorosa is Dario Sattui's vision of a 13th century castle built on a hill overlooking Napa Valley.

The castle has a moat, towers, walls, a Florentine-style great room, four stories above ground and four levels of cellars, even a dungeon.

The dramatic exterior, however, hides a state-of-the-art winery where a dedicated team turns out a variety of Italian-inspired wines for every taste from sweet Moscato to intense Cabernet Sauvignon.

Sattui's story is a legend in Napa Valley. Arriving here with few resources, he opened a wine-tasting room in a commercially zoned building south of St. Helena. There he sold wine he bought in bulk from other producers and bottled. He named the operation V. Sattui Winery after his grandfather's business in San Francisco before Prohibition. In the early days, he slept in his van to save money.

Over time, his commercial zoning allowed him to add a delicatessen – the only one in Napa Valley at a winery until Charles Krug's opens next year. (County ordinances prohibit such operations; Krug is in St. Helena and governed by that city's rules.)

The success of his winery allowed him to pursue his life-long dream – build a castle like those from his ancestral home.

The Castello opened in 2007 after 14 years of construction and a reputed cost of $35 million. Sattui built it in homage to his Italian ancestors, and he imported expert stone masons from Europe to construct the edifice and train local workers. He also bought buildings in Europe, dismantled them and imported the materials.

The castle appears authentic to anyone who's visited ancient castles in Italy. Sattui even knocked down some parts after construction and rebuilt them in different styles, as is typical in old castles.

Among its 107 room are the aforementioned, Florentine-style Great Room and a chapel that boasted traditional Latin masses each Sunday until the county nixed church services.

Though a tour of the magical castle is a must even for teetotalers, its modern winery produces sweet and dessert wines as well as excellent dry wines from the steep hillside vineyards surrounding the castle and Sattui's other extensive holdings, many dedicated to the local Land Trust.

Appointments are required, and the cost of the tour includes an extensive winetasting with juice for the kids. My 9-year-old grandson's only complaint, in fact, was, "Too much wine; not enough castle." He especially enjoyed the replica of a torture chamber. Reassuringly, all the devices are reproductions – they claim. 4045 St. Helena Hwy., Calistoga. (707) 967-6272. www.castellodiamarosa.com

Clos Pegase

As impressive as Castello di Amorosa in its own way is Clos Pegase, Napa Valley's temple of wine. While many wineries in Napa Valley contain art, Clos Pegase is art – as well as being filled with it.

Jan Shrem, who made a fortune as a businessman and property owner in Japan, held a competition to design his winery, and famed architect Michael Graves won.

The winery's most famous sculpture is probably the giant thumb emerging from a vineyard, but works by Picasso, Henry Moore and Matisse await visitors, too.

The wine is excellent, too, and occasional concerts occur in the special cave theater. Owner Jan Shrem also gives an entertaining talk "Bacchus the Rascal"about the history of wine and art that's definitely worth attending. 1060 Dunaweal Ln., Calistoga. (707) 942-4981. www.clospegase.com

Sterling Vineyards

Though many other impressive wineries have been built in Napa Valley, including Castello di Amorosa nearby, none can match the setting and visual impact of Sterling Vineyards.

The massive white structure tops a knoll like an ancient monastery on a Greek isle, and you have to reach the winery via a gondola suspended from a cable.

The tour is self guided, and passes the patio on the south end of the complex offers incomparable views of Napa Valley.

The tasting room is friendly and offers sit-down tastings, and even provides juice for kids. You do have to pay for the visit, which includes tasting, and if you're afraid of heights, they will speed you up the hill in a van. 1111 Dunaweal Ln. Calistoga. (707) 942-3300. www.sterlingvineyards.com

There are many other vineyards in Calistoga, some on Diamond Mountain, and a few tasting rooms in town.

Off the Beaten Path

Anyone who visits Napa Valley quickly learns that the Valley is 30 miles from north to south and 1 to 3 miles wide over most of its length.

Legally, however, the Napa Valley American Viticultural Area, or appellation, is much larger. It includes the mountains rising on either side of the valley and a large, mostly mountainous area to the east.

Napa County, in fact, contains many valleys and canyons – 129 with names by one count, and grapes from most can legally be labeled "Napa *Valley* AVA."

A few parts of Napa County that aren't in the Napa Valley AVA can be legally labeled "Napa County," too.

In addition to the many valleys outside Napa Valley itself, the two mountain ranges that create the valley, the Mayacamas Range to the west and the Vaca Range to the east, are topped with many important wine regions with their own identities. These are included in the Napa Valley AVA, too. This section explores these less-traveled regions.

Los Carneros AVA

'Carneros' means sheep in Spanish, and the area was used primarily for grazing until about 20 years ago but the wine region in southern Napa County called Los Carneros contains much of interest to wine lovers – with a few non-vinous treats as well.

The Napa part of Carneros (the region extends into Sonoma) is unique in the larger Napa Valley appellation: It's quite cool, being fanned by breezes from San Pablo Bay, the northern arm of San Francisco Bay.

The gentling rolling hills are well drained, ideal for growing quality grapes – as long as their vines are irrigated since rainfall isn't enough to sustain vines in the fast-draining soil, much less nourish good crops.

The area is quite varied, with some sunny southwestern-facing slopes suitable for heat-loving vines such as Cabernet, but much of the region has become a natural home for cool-climate grapes such as Chardonnay and Pinot Noir. Its Merlots and Syrahs, though not as well known, are some of the best in America.

Most of Napa's Chardonnay and Pinot are planted in Carneros. Many were originally intended for sparkling wines before local vintners realized that the grapes could excel for still wines in the cool region.

Carneros is primarily a land of vineyards, not wineries, but a few of its wineries welcome visitors to taste and buy their wines.

Three wineries lie right on highway 12, the main route into Napa Valley from the Golden Gate Bridge.

They couldn't be more different.

Madonna Estates is a rustic winery that harkens back to the early days of Napa. It's a friendly, low-key winery just up the road at the Old Sonoma Road turnoff. It's one of the few wineries that grows its grapes without irrigation (dry farmed), and makes a variety of nice wines even if the setting isn't very fancy. Don't be put off by the tour busses that sometimes stop but visit when there aren't any in the lot to avoid the crowds. 5400 Old Sonoma Rd., Napa. (707) 255-8864. www.madonnaestate.com

You can continue up old Sonoma Road, and turn left on Dealy Lane to head up bucolic Carneros Valley.

North of the highway are three wineries worth visiting, Michael Mondavi's Folio Wine Estates at 1285 Dealy Ln., Napa. (707) 256-2757. www.michaelmondavifamilyestate, Artesa and Truchard, the last requiring appointments.

Artesa Winery is the dramatic winery owned by the Codorniu wine empire of Spain. A pyramid that almost disappears into its hilltop site, it's one of the most attractive winery buildings in Napa County.

The winery once specialized in sparkling wine, but now focuses on still wines and produces a variety of excellent offerings from vineyards all over wine country. I love its views, its wines and its museum featuring the Carneros region. 1345 Henry Rd., Napa. (707) 224-1668. www.artesawinery.com

The road up Carneros Valley ends in land that is owned by Dario Sattui, who owns the amazing Castello di Amorosa winery in Calistoga and V. Sattui Winery, a tremendously popular winery in St. Helena.

Dario is leaving much of the property in its natural and grazing state, though it would be great for growing more vines, too.

One of the most interesting wineries in all Napa County is Truchard Vineyards. Truchard makes excellent Merlot and other unexpected varieties from the location in hills north of north of Highway 12. They are just a little warmer than the part of the Carneros Region south of Highway 12, but still cool enough to prove the adage: "The best wines come from regions where the grapes can just ripen fully." 3234 Old Sonoma Rd., Napa. (707) 253-7153. www.truchardvineyards.com

The most visible winery from the highway is Domaine Carneros, a faux chateau based on the home of its owners, the Taittinger family of Champagne. Domaine Carneros produces elegant sparkling wine and Pinot Noir.

If the weather is nice, I always sit on the patio at Domaine Carneros and enjoy the sparkling wine, some of the best made anywhere. The winery also serves nibbles, and its still wines are excellent, too. 1240 Duhig Rd., Napa. (707) 257-0101. www.domainecarneros.com

Across the highway from Domaine Carneros is the di Rosa Preserve, an amazing art museum featuring contemporary paintings, sculpture and other art scattered across the landscape and in numerous buildings. It's a must for any art lover.

South of the highway, a few wineries are open by appointment.

The emphasis at Acacia Vineyard is on Pinot Noir and Chardonnay from Carneros. It's a good place for a picnic. 2750 Las Amigas Rd., Napa. (707) 226-9991. www.acaciavineyard.com. Appointments are required.

Bouchaine Vineyards offers tasting at 1075 Buchli Station Rd., Napa.(800) 654-9463 or (707) 252-9065. www.bouchaine.com. You can enjoy a picnic on the deck there.

Pinot Noir specialist Saintsbury requires appointments at 1500 Los Carneros Ave., Napa. (707) 252-0592. www.saintsbury.com. Etude Wines on Cuttings Wharf Road has taken over the old RMS Brandy facility, and is open by appointment. 1250 Cuttings Wharf Rd., Napa. (707) 257-5300. www.etudewines.com

Ceja Vineyards is a favorite. Amelia and Pedro are some of the nicest vintners you'll ever meet and the wines are excellent. Call (877) 633-3954 or (707) 255-3954. It has a tasting room in downtown Napa.

There aren't many other visitors' facilities in Carneros. Head south on Cuttings Wharf Road at the sign that points to Napa River Resorts (There aren't any, by the way) and you find Moore's Landing on the Napa River. It's is a funky place that serves Mexican food and burgers with casual service. You can enjoy your modest but tasty meal on the patio by the river in good weather, or inside at other times. Check to make sure they're open, however, since the schedule sometimes changes. 6 Cuttings Wharf Rd., Napa. (707) 253-7038. www.mooreslanding.com

There's an unexpected marina just down the river from Moore's, but you have to backtrack to get there. You can follow the road to its end at a wildlife preserve to walk off lunch. The area seems more like Louisiana than Napa, with both grand and run-down homes clustered behind a levee that contains the Napa River.

The Boon Fly Café at the upscale Carneros Inn serves classic American food in a casual atmosphere and the Farm Restaurant is more upscale. There's also a small store and deli at the inn. The inn is the only lodging in the area, but its luxurious cottages, private restaurant and spa have made it a new favorite for visitors. 4048 Sonoma Hwy., Napa. (707) 299-4900. www.thecarnerosinn.com.

Off by itself and not in Carneros is Reata Winery on Jameson Canyon Road on the way to (or from) Sacramento and Solano County. It has a pleasant tasting room and picnic grounds. 1 Kirkland Ranch Road Napa (707) 254-8673 www.reatawines.com

Coombsville AVA and east of Napa

Most visitors to Napa Valley naturally focus on the Valley itself, the area that stretches about 30 miles from just north of the city of Napa to just north of Calistoga, but many of the area's most interesting visits lie a bit out of the way.

One such treasure is the area east of Napa, and in fact, east of the ridge that dominates the city's eastern boundary, Alta Heights.

Between this ridge and the steep Vaca mountains lies Coombsville with a number of notable wineries and just north is large Silverado Resort with its 36-hole golf course and surrounding community.

The area is cooler than the northern part of Napa Valley, making it ideal for many grapes including Chardonnay, Merlot and Syrah.

Local growers and wineries succeeded in making the area its own American Viticultural Area as a "sub-appellation" of Napa Valley.

Numerous vineyards and a few wineries are in the area, but many aren't open to the public because of county restrictions or simply because they're too small to receive visitors, such as Dr. Ernie Bates' Black Coyote Wines. Among the wineries in the area that you can visit are Farella-Park and Jarvis.

One of the most interesting wineries in all of Napa Valley, if not the world, was developed by Dr. Julio Palmaz, a cardiologist who invented the heart stent. On the site of the old Hagen Winery against the mountains, the winery occupies caves dug into the side of Mount George and stretches the equivalent of 14 floors from top to bottom.

The winery is wholly underground. It includes a remarkable, 5-story-high dome incorporating 23 fermentation vats rotating on a giant carousel as well as many other tunnels and caves. They're offset and incorporate sizable gaps to maintain the integrity of the hillside.

The winery is open by appointment. 4029 Hagen Rd., Napa. (707) 226-5587. www.palmazvineyards.com

All the roads that head east from Napa into Coombsville end up against or on Mount George, but they provide interesting views of a truly out-of-the-way area of busy Napa Valley.

Just north of there, Monticello Road goes go over the hills to Solano County and the little-known Wooden Valley, part of Napa County with a few vineyards and wineries, too.

Also dramatic is William Jarvis' winery nearby (but not in the Coombsville AVA), itself a remarkable achievement. Here again, the whole winery is underground, which helps maintain the ideal temperature for winemaking as well as restricting the impact on the environment.

The entire winery – including the destemmer/crusher, press, barrel room, aging cellar and tasting room – lie in a huge, doughnut-shaped cave, complete with underground stream and waterfall. The tour also includes access to hidden rooms that display the family's collection of giant cut amethyst geodes. 2970 Monticello Rd., Napa. (707) 255-5280. www.jarviswines.com

Nearby is the Silverado Resort and Spa and a large planned community.

Silverado Resort has two 18-hole golf course, a strong tennis program and both a casual and fancy restaurant as well as suites. 1600 Atlas Peak Rd., Napa. (707) 257-0200. www.silveradoresort.com

Near the entrance to Silverado are Del Dotto Vineyards, Whetstone Wine Cellars at 1075 Atlas Peak Rd., Napa. (707) 254-0660. www.whetstonewinecellars.com and William Hill Estate Winery at 1761 Atlas Peak Rd., Napa. (707) 224-4477. www.williamhillestate.com

If you're interested in the impact of different types of barrels on wine, Del Dotto offers a virtual laboratory in which to taste examples. At most places, you taste wine from barrels to see the impact on the wine, but at Del Dotto, you virtually taste the barrels themselves. 1055 Atlas Peak Rd., Napa. (707) 963-2134. www.deldottovineyards.com

There are few other commercial establishments in this area, one being Monticello Deli and another Jessel Art Gallery.

Mt. Veeder AVA

Mount Veeder occupies the southern tip of the Mayacamas Mountains that define Napa Valley's western edge. Being both high in altitude and near Carneros, it's relatively cool.

The area contains many vineyards and some tiny wineries, including Mayacamas Vineyards, one of California's earliest "cult" wineries, which still makes wine in the same traditional manner.

Even Mount Veeder Winery, now owned by Constellation Brands, makes its wines and offers tastes at the large Franciscan Winery building in Rutherford. Many other noted Napa Valley wineries use valued Mount Veeder grapes, too.

The area does have one gem: The Hess Collection. Occupying a former monastery, the Hess Collection is owned by a wealthy Swiss, Donald Hess. It makes excellent wines, but a big draw is part of Hess' amazing collection of modern art, on view for free with no obligation to taste wines.

The most famous piece is an immense painting called Johanna, but the other contemporary paintings and sculpture are also fascinating. You can sign up for an art tour as well as a winery tour, too.

The Mount Veeder wine association holds annual tastings at Hess. It's the only way to taste many of the wines from the mountain, in fact. 4411 Redwood Rd., Napa. (707) 255-1144. www.hesscollection.com

Next door to Hess is a Christian Brothers retreat, where individuals can stay and share dinner with the retired brothers if it's not filled with a conference. Needless to say, they serve wine with dinner!

Spring Mountain AVA

Ever visitor to Napa Valley has visited the well-known wineries along Highway 29, but some of the wineries that are most fun to visit are little known and off the beaten track. All require appointments but that small effort will certainly reward the visitor.

Some of the most intriguing are on Spring Mountain west of St. Helena on twisty Spring Mountain Road (by the way, there is no Spring Mountain. The name refers to all the springs in the area, part of the Mayacamas range that separate Sonoma from Napa Counties.)

Spring Mountain District was officially established as an American Viticultural Area in 1991. It encompasses about 8,600 acres, and 1,000 acres are planted to vines.

Most of the vineyards lie on steep hillsides between the ridgeline and the 400-foot contour considered the dividing line between hillside and valley vineyards in Napa Valley. Elevations range to 2,600 feet, with a predominantly eastern exposure.

Spring Mountain boasts a more moderate temperature range than the Valley floor with cooler days and warmer nights and it boasts an unusually long growing season. Bud break occurs in mid-March, with harvest from mid-September even into November.

The appellation was among the first locations in Napa Valley to receive recognition as a prime grape growing region with the first documented planting by Charles Lemme at La Perla Vineyard in 1874.

Frenchman Fortune Chevalier planted 25 acres and built a stone winery and San Francisco banker Tiburcio Parrott established a vineyard and built a Victorian-style home that became famous as the face of Falcon Crest, an evening soap opera of the '70's.

It, La Perla and Chevalier are now part of the Spring Mountain Winery estate.

About 80 percent of the vineyards on Spring Mountain are planted to red varieties, particularly Cabernet Sauvignon and Merlot, but some white grapes also do well.

The Spring Mountain area came to life again in 1946, when Fred and Eleanor McCrea planted a small vineyard and founded Stony Hill Winery, California's first cult winery that sold wine only by a restricted mailing list.

Stony Hill Winery remains famous for its long-lasting Chardonnays, though it recently started producing a red wine, while Smith-Madrone produces one of California's rare fine Rieslings. Stony Hill and Trefethen also make excellent Rieslings.

About 20 wineries make wine on Spring Mountain, all small operations that produce excellent wines. Among those open to the public – by appointment only – are Cain Vineyard, Pride Mountain, Smith-Madrone, Terra Valentine, Fantesca, Juslyn, Schweiger, Domaine Charbay and Spring Mountain Vineyard. Other smaller wineries may be open, too. Visit their website or call.

- Cain Vineyards. 3800 Langtry Rd., St. Helena. (707) 963-1616. www.cainfive.com

- Domaine Charbay. 4001 Spring Mtn. Rd., St. Helena. (707) 963-9327. www.charbay.com

- Fantesca Estate & Winery. 2920 Spring Mtn. Rd., St. Helena. (707) 968-9229. www.fantesca.com

- Juslyn Vineyards. 2900 Spring Mtn. Rd., St. Helena. (707) 265-1804. www.juslynvineyards.com

- Pride Mountain. 4026 Spring Mtn. Rd., St. Helena. (707) 963-4949. www.pridewines.com

- Schweiger Vineyards. 4015 Spring Mtn. Rd., St. Helena. (707) 963-4882. www.schweigervineyards.com

- Smith-Madrone Vineyards. 4022 Spring Mtn. Rd., St. Helena. (707) 963-2283. www.smithmadrone.com

- Spring Mountain Vineyard. 2805 Spring Mtn. Rd., St. Helena. (707) 967-4188. www.springmountainvineyard.com

- Terra Valentine. 3787 Spring Mtn. Rd., St. Helena. (707) 967-8340. www.terravalentine.com

Diamond Mountain AVA

The Diamond Mountain District is an American Viticultural Area in the Mayacamas Mountains in the northeastern part of above Napa Valley.

It's higher in elevation than most Napa Valley wine regions, but above the fog line with higher exposure to sunlight. The entire AVA lies above 400 feet, which helps to cool it compared to the nearby valley floor. The result is warm days and cool nights, ideal for the Cabernet Sauvignon it's best know for.

The soil of the Diamond Mountain District is volcanic and drains well, and includes small bits of volcanic glass that give the area its name.

The AVA is defined by the Napa-Sonoma county line to the west, Mark West-Petrified Forest Road on the north, the 400-foot line of altitude running parallel to Route 29 on the east, and the Spring Mountain District to the south. Ironically, most of the mountain including its peak lie in Sonoma County but are not in the appellation.

Diamond Mountain's first vines were planted by Jacob Schram on the Napa side of the mountain in the mid 1800s. By 1892, he owned 100 acres, including underground cellars dug by hand by Chinese laborers for aging and storing wine. Robert Louis Stevenson wrote about visiting him in his famed "Silverado Squatters." His property is now known as

All wineries on the mountain require appointments:

- Diamond Creek Vineyards. 1500 Diamond Mtn. Rd., Calistoga. (707) 942-6926. www.diamondcreekvineyards.com

- Dyer Vineyard. 1501 Diamond Mtn. Rd., Calistoga. (707) 942-5502. www.dyerwine.com

- Constant Diamond Mountain Vineyard. 2121 Diamond Mtn. Rd., Calistoga. (707) 942-0707. www.constantwine.com

- Von Strasser Winery. 1510 Diamond Mtn. Rd., Calistoga. (707) 942-0930. www.vonstrasser.com

Pritchard Hill

Though Napa County is split into more than a dozen separate American Viticultural Areas – informally called appellations –one of its top locations doesn't have a formal status. It's Pritchard Hill east of Rutherford. The *Wine Spectator* calls Pritchard Hill "the home to profound Cabernets," and "Napa's new Grand Cru."

That magazine was referring to newcomers such as Colgin, Bryant Family, Ovid, Tim Mondavi's Continuum and David Arthur, but Pritchard Hill has been home of the Chappellet family since 1967.

Their winery was the second major winery founded after Prohibition (Mondavi was a year earlier). They were joined by Bob and Zelma Long in 1978, and more recently by top small producers.

Though Pritchard Hill overlooks Napa Valley, you reach it via a winding two-lane highway 128 that curls around man-made Lake Hennessey.

Donn and Molly Chappellet early recognized that mountain vines would produce superior wine, following the advice of legendary winemaker André Tchelistcheff. The Chappellets were the first winery owners to plant vineyards exclusively on high elevation hillsides and their wines proved their belief. Though best known for their Cabernet Sauvignon, they also produce other wines including one of the few Chenin Blancs still made in Napa Valley.

Because of its remoteness and mountaintop location, Chappellet is open only by appointment. It occupies a unique wooden pyramid structure, still one of the most striking wineries in Napa County. 1581 Sage Canyon Rd., St. Helena. (707) 286-4219. www.chappellet.com

Cloud View and Girard are also on the hill, but some of the tiny newcomers in the area seem to garner most of the attention with their cult-like wines with lofty prices. None are generally open to the public, and in fact, sell their wines primarily through tight mailing lists. You can find some at local restaurants, however.

Atlas Peak AVA

The Atlas Peak AVA encompasses a "hanging bowl," an elevated valley near 2,900-ft. Atlas Peak in the Vaca Mountain Range that creates Napa Valley's eastern border.

The region ranges in elevation from 760 to 2,663 feet. The actual appellation is primarily within Soda Canyon and Foss Valley above the Stags Leap District.

You access it only on two dead-end roads, Soda Canyon Road and Atlas Peak Road, that end eight to 10 miles from the Silverado Trail tantalizingly close to each other, but aren't connected

Likewise, it almost abuts Pritchard Hill, but deep canyons and lack of roads prevent a connection.

The Atlas Peak Appellation has cool, wet winters and warm, dry summers with temperatures 4 to 10 degrees cooler than the Napa Valley floor. Usually above the fog line, the region gets full sunlight throughout the day, with big nighttime drops in temperature.

Partly in the AVA is large Stagecoach vineyards, which sells grapes to many top producers.

The area contains few wineries, and most aren't open to visitors.

The role of the Antinoris

Poor Italian immigrants and Italian-American winemakers have a long history of overcoming adversity to succeed in Napa Valley, and an Italian nobleman has done the same.

Marchese Piero Antinori, scion of one of Tuscany's oldest and most respected wine dynasties, has owned the 1,200-acre Atlas Peak Vineyards property in the rocky volcanic eastern hills of the Vaca Mountains since 1993, but existing contract and relationships prevented him from making wines there for more than 15 years.

Now, Antinori has taken over the property and is helping put the rugged Atlas Peak appellation on the map. Using the Antica label, it's making superb Cabernet and Chardonnay as well as selling grapes to other wineries.

The Antinoris were early investors in the Atlas Peak property, which confusingly is also the largest vineyard in the Atlas Peak Viticultural Area, but the 500 acres of vineyards have been managed by a series of owners. The brand-name Atlas Peak Vineyards has bounced around among various owners, the last producing wines with the strange labels, "Atlas Peak Vineyards Howell Mountain," and similar names.

In the meantime, the Antinoris bought an adjoining 40-acre parcel in 1998 and built a decidedly un-Tuscan house on the larger property. Antinori also owns 15 percent of venerable Stag's Leap Wine Cellars, and shares winemaking responsibility with majority owner Ste. Michelle Estates.

The Marchese has three daughters, Allegra, Alessia, and Albiera, who all work in the company; winemaker and president Renzo Cotarella, brother of famed winemaking consultant Riccardo Cotarella, helps make the wines.

It took the family a while to accept that Cabernet was their destiny in Napa. They early helped nurture Sangiovese, the regal grape of their home in Tuscany, but found it was challenging to tame in the unfamiliar location. They finally succeeded, but found little market for the grape or wine made here and great demand for the vineyard's Cabernet. They still grow a small amount of Sangiovese, but sell it to others. They figure if you want Sangiovese, they make plenty in Tuscany.

Astrale e Terre Winery is nearby.

Elan Vineyards

Elan Vineyards, which lies at the end of Atlas Peak Road past the Bubbling Well Pet Memorial Park satirized in the cult favorite movie *Gates of Heaven*. Elan could not be more different than Antica, though it's a short distance away – if you're a bird.

From the property, the view is toward the southern end of Lake Berryessa to the east, not towards Napa Valley.

Patrick and Linda Elliott-Smith own the winery, which Patrick bought in 1979 and tended admittedly almost as a hippie.

The 42 acres (13 acres in vines plus 12 acres of vines adjacent leased to Elan) are planted on rocky slopes at 1,700 feet above sea level. The vines receive exceptional sun exposure during the growing season, but without the high temperatures that sometimes occur in Napa Valley due to cooling breezes that sneak up from the San Francisco Bay.

The vines are primarily Cabernet Franc, with some Merlot and Cabernet Franc, which are blended into a single wine.

Winemaker Patrick Elliott-Smith was born in the United States to an American father and a French mother who taught Patrick to appreciate fine wines at a young age.

The location precludes a tasting room or visitors, and they sell only direct. Elan's phone number is (707)-252-3339.

Also on Atlas Peak Road are tiny VinRoc (707) 265-0943. www.vinrocnapa.com, and Jocelyn Lonen Winery. 4400 Atlas Peak Rd., Napa. (707) 257-2821.www.lonenwinery.com

Howell Mountain AVA

One of Napa Valley's most exalted wine-growing appellations is flat-topped Howell Mountain, otherwise most noted locally as the home of a community of teetotaling Seventh Day Adventists: Some of America's most renowned wines grow alongside a college that expects abstinence. The hamlet's stores and even the post office are closed Saturday out of deference to the sect's beliefs, and the store doesn't sell products containing caffeine or meat (other than pet food), much less alcohol.

Yet Howell Mountain has been home to vineyards for more than a century. Jean Adolph Brun and Jean V. Chaix planted hundreds of acres of vineyards at what is now Ladera Vineyards. Other growers founded Liparita Vineyards and another stone winery known as La Jota today.

By 1900, there were more than 600 acres of wine grapes planted on the mountain, and the vineyards on Howell Mountain have developed an excellent reputation for their powerful wines.

Unlike most American Viticultural Areas, however, today's Howell Mountain is defined by height, not rivers or political boundaries. All property above 1400 ft. on the mountain is included; the intersection of Deer Park and Howell Mountain Road lies at that height. Other "mountain" appellations in Napa Valley start at 400 ft. As a result, many famed wineries such as Burgess and Viader are on the mountain but not in the appellation. They're equally worth visiting.

Perhaps the most distinctive feature of the mountain – other than the altitude that tempers Valley heat – is that it is above the fog. When the fog rolls off the ocean and San Francisco Bay into Napa Valley, Howell Mountain generally remains sunny. Because of the altitude and lack of fog, evening temperatures are generally warmer and daytime temperatures are cooler than in the Valley below. Cool spring temperatures lead to later bud break than at lower altitudes, and warm summer nights produce balanced fruit.

Soil can have as much effect on the grapes as the weather. The mountain top gets nearly twice as much rainfall as the Valley below, but the rocky, porous soil drains well. Howell Mountain is composed of two main soil types. The first is decomposed volcanic ash, or "tufa," the second red clay high in iron. Both soil types are poor in nutrients, so they stress the vines, producing small clusters and berries that produce intense wines.

To visit Howell Mountain, drive up Deer Park Road just north of St. Helena. It's a steep and winding path that eventually arrives at the high valley containing Pacific Union College, the small shopping center closed Saturday, and little more. Continue down the road and you drop into Pope Valley, but that's another story.

All the wineries on Howell Mountain are small and require appointments, but it's worth the effort to taste their rare and intense flavors. Being small, they're also more interesting to visit than the giant wineries of Napa Valley proper – though it should be noted that many famed Valley wineries such as Beringer, Charles Krug and Cakebread use Howell Mountain fruit as well.

Two larger properties that do welcome visitors by appointment are Cade and Ladera. Cade, which is owned by the same owners as PlumpJack Winery including Lt. Gov. Gavin Newsom and Gordon Getty, is ultramodern and environmentally pristine, while Ladera is a resurrected "ghost" winery.

For more information, go to the website of the Howell Mountain Vintners & Growers Association: www.howellmountain.org.

Cade Winery. 360 Howell Mtn. Rd., South Angwin, (707) 965-2746. www.cadewinery.com

Ladera Vineyards. 150 White Cottage Rd., South Angwin. (707) 965-2445. www.laderavineyards.com

East of Eden – Across the Eastern Range

The Napa Valley Vintners claim that Napa Valley is "Eden for grapevines." Two valleys east of geographic Napa Valley therefore are 'east of Eden,' and they contain numerous vineyards, interesting wineries and other attractions.

To reach Pope Valley, you drive east from St. Helena over Howell Mountain and descend to the large valley below.

As prices have risen for land in Napa Valley itself, many wineries and growers have turned to the Pope Valley for both vineyards and grapes. Though it's not part of Napa Valley geographically, being over a mountain range and draining into Putah Creek toward Lake Berryessa, the area was gerrymandered into the Napa Valley American Viticultural Area by smart landowners and wineries and its grapes qualify for inclusion in expensive Napa Valley wines.

That doesn't mean there's anything wrong with the grapes, by the way. Many are excellent. Higher in altitude and warmer than Napa during the day, the Pope Valley cools off more at night, making it ideal for many wines, particularly Bordeaux and Rhône varieties.

You can visit Aetna Springs and Pope Valley, but be sure to call ahead. There are no facilities in the valley except a tiny store in a where Howell Mountain Road meets Pope Valley Road.

South of Pope Valley is even smaller and higher Chiles Valley. It produces some of Napa County's best grapes. You can visit Green and Red and RustRidge with appointments.

RustRidge has one of very few B&Bs in Napa's back country – or at any winery, for that matter. 2910 Lower Chiles Valley Rd., St. Helena. (707) 965-9353. www.rustridge.com

There's no winery at the Volker Eisele Family Estate, but you can visit this historic estate. 3080 Lower Chiles Valley Rd., St. Helena. (707) 965-9485. www.volkereiselefamilyestate.com.

At the end of Lower Chiles Valley Road, you can turn right onto Chiles & Pope Valley Road, but you might want to take a look at the historical plaque above the road on the left. It commemorates an early mill; it's difficult to believe, but this was a prime route to the Bay Area in 49er days.

The Green & Red Winery lies up the hill just beyond. 3208 Chiles Pope Valley Rd., St. Helena. (707) 965-2346. greenandred.com

Nichelini Winery

Just outside of the Valley on highway 128 back to Rutherford is historic Nichelini Winery, still run by the Swiss-Italian family who settled there in 1884. It's a great place for a picnic, too.

The winery was founded by Anton and Caterina Nichelini, who were the first Swiss to settle in Chiles Valley, then known as Napa's "High Valley."

They immigrated from the Alpine village of Verscio in Ticino, the Italian-speaking southern part of Switzerland. They homesteaded 160 acres and later acquired a total of 540 acres of land in Sage Canyon, built a small home up the hill from the present site in 1888, and planted 30 acres of grapes as well as other crops.

The original tiny cabin where four children were born has been moved down the hill to a site near the winery and awaits restoration. In 1895, Anton built the larger home still hanging on the side of the mountain as in his native land.

The basement of the seven-bedroom house – he had 12 children – served as the wine cellar, and he used an ancient Roman press that is still on display, but long abandoned for more convenient presses.

Anton actually met Caterina in San Francisco, even though she was also from Ticino in Switzerland. She largely ran the vineyard and winery as Anton worked as a stonemason.

Like most wine-making families, they made wine and sold it during Prohibition. They sold sacramental wine, which was legal, and also made regular deliveries to Oakland and other places with wine hidden under the floorboards of a 1924 Lincoln that once belonged to the mayor of San Francisco.

Caterina also served meals to rare passers by; the steep and rough road was only paved in the early '40s and electricity came in 1947.

Family legend says Caterina accidentally sold wine to treasury agents during Prohibition, but since they didn't then jail women, Anton had to serve her sentence, though only on weekends so he could work.

Skip ahead to the present, and about 15 of his descendents from the third, fourth and fifth generations are involved in operating the winery.

Doug Patterson is the oldest of the fourth generation, while winemaker Aimée Sunseri is from the fifth. She's also the seventh winemaker in the winery's history.

Sunseri became winemaker in 2009 after getting her degree in winemaking at UC Davis and working at New Clairvaux Vineyard, part of the Abbey of New Clairvaux, a community of Cistercian or "Trappist" monks in Vina, Calif., between Redding and Chico in the northern Sacramento Valley.

She also worked at Boeger Winery in Placerville; Greg Boeger was the grandson of Anton Nichelini.

Nichelini has 75 acres of vineyards in nearby Chiles Valley at about 1,000 ft. altitude, but only produces 2,500 cases of wine per year, selling the rest of the grapes. The vines range in age as far back at 1928 for zinfandel and 1946 for the Muscadelle. No grapes grow around the winery, but the family is considering planting some in their historical locations.

The winery produces a number of wines, but may be best know for its Zinfandel/Primitivo as well as its Muscadelle de Bordelais, which the winery previously called Sauvignon Vert, though that name is more correctly applied to another grape, the Sauvignonasse found in Chile and called Friulano in northern Italy.

Muscadelle de Bordelais is the 'third' white grape of Bordeaux, and is allowed in white Meritage wines. It's not related to Muscat or Muscato wines, and certainly not to Muscatel.

Nichelini also produces excellent Cabernet Sauvignon and Petite Sirah, and has recently started making Sauvignon Blanc. It offers some other wines at the tasting room.

The winery remains picturesque but has recently been upgraded, and Patterson says, "Now we have a smooth concrete floor and can wash everything!"

It also has added modern equipment and replaced all of its ancient redwood tanks with modern stainless and oak barrels.

In addition, the first floor of the old house has been turned into a tasting area to supplement the space in the cellar, and they've added a stairway so guests don't have to navigate the steep driveway or treacherous old stairs. The rest of the home is offices.

Though parking is tight (and scary), the winery can accommodate plenty of cars at an area just past it.

Nichelini is open Saturday and Sunday and by appointment. 2950 Sage Canyon Rd., St. Helena. (707) 963-0717 . www.nicheliniwinery.com

Just out of Chiles Valley on the way to Lake Berryessa lie Brown Family Estate and Somerston wineries.

Brown makes superb Zinfandel and Cabernet, while Somerston is an ambitious operation with sheep as well as grapes and plans for more amenities.

Brown Estate Vineyards

Brown Estate began in 1981, when physician Dr. Bassett Brown, who was originally from Jamaica, and his wife Marcela, originally from Panama, bought a run-down ranch on rolling hills in an isolated part of Napa County. The property was covered with walnut groves and oak trees and contained a dilapidated hundred-year old Victorian home.

After restoring the house, the family –including two daughters and a son – planted its first 10 acres of hillside Zinfandel in 1985.

Five years later, they planted more vines and now have 40 acres including 8.5 acres of Cabernet Sauvignon, 4.5 acres of Chardonnay, and 27 acres of Zinfandel.

The area has hot days during the summer, with evening fog providing dramatic nighttime temperature drops.

The soil is moderately fertile silt loam on alluvial fans with gentle slopes leading to a series of creeks that facilitate natural surface and subterranean drainage.

For 10 years the family farmed the vines, selling the fruit to wineries in Napa Valley as they learned more and more about producing superb fruit. The grapes received increasing praise from winemakers and the wine-loving public, and in 1996 the family released its first Zinfandel under the Brown Estate Vineyards label.

David Brown, who lives on the property, manages the grape growing and makes the wine with help from respected consultant Duane Dappen. His sister Carol handles promotion and sales while Celia Deneen Brown is in charge of marketing and distribution.

They make the wine in a recently restored old stone barn, and have a cave to store their barrels of wine and give them more room for other winery operations.

The wines are exceptional. The cool nights seem to slow sugar development and maintain acidity, so the wines have full flavors but are not overdone.

You can buy Brown Estate wines at a few select wine stores, but it's really a treat to visit the winery. Needless to say, you should call first and make an appointment and get directions. A hint: They have a nice place for picnics and you're not likely to find other visitors. 3233 Sage Canyon Rd., St. Helena. (707) 963-2435. www.brownestate.com

Napa's Hot Winemakers

Any serious wine lover knows of today's superstars of cult winemakers: Heidi Peterson Barrett, Mia Klein, Helen Turley, but there's another group making waves in Napa Valley. Some of the new breed include Philippe Melka, Mark Aubert, Luc Morlet and Bob Levy, who make the next cult wines, those destined to join Screaming Eagle, Shafer Hillside Select, Grace Family and Bryant at the top of every collector's wish list.

Perhaps the most visible is Philippe Melka, the French-born soil-scientist turned winemaker consulting to a dozen upscale boutique wineries in Napa Valley.

Among his clients are Bryant Family, Caldwell, Gemstone, Hundred Acre, Lail Vineyards and Vineyard 29. He gained special notice when he took over Bryant after the owner had an explosive falling-out with Helen Turley.

Melka was chosen by Agustin Huneuus, the proprietor of Quintessa, where he once made the wine, to produce Pirouette Bordeaux blend for Washington's prestigious Long Shadows, and he also makes his own Métisse proprietary red wine and CJ Cabernet Sauvignon.

Melka may seem a piker compared to his fellow Frenchman, Michel Rolland, however. Rolland admits to having about 100 clients worldwide and many in Napa Valley. He serves as a consultant, however, and doesn't actually make the wine for most of these companies.

Some of the American winemakers do the same, but the details of their relationships are often hidden by vintners who want to appear as their wineries' main focus.

Among the other consulting winemakers who make Napa Valley wines that are candidates for culthood are Charles Hendricks, who produces wines for Bacio Divino, Barnett, Mendelson, Paoletti and Regusci.

Bob Levy is the winemaker for Harlan Estates, Napa Valley Reserve and Bond, three wine ventures of Bill Harlan, who also is a major owner of Meadowood Estate.

Mark Aubert produces Colgin, already a cult wine, and formerly made wine for Peter Michael. He also makes wine under his own label, Aubert.

And Mark Herold, formerly of Napa's Joseph Phelps winery, has his own upscale brand, Merus, and makes wines for Kamen Estate, the Mount Veeder wine operation owned by screenwriter Robert

Mark Kamen, who wrote *The Karate Kid, The Fifth Element* and, suitably, *A Walk in the Clouds*.

Celia Welch might not be considered up-and-coming as she's arrived, but certainly belongs among the group.

There are dozens of others making superb wines, however, and sometimes it's only luck which wine gets elevated into the heights.

Winetasting in Downtown Napa and Nearby

Though only a few wineries actually make wine in the city of Napa, it offers plenty of opportunities to taste wine from wineries all over the Valley.

More than 20 wine-tasting rooms, wines stores offering tasting, wine bars and wine-oriented cafés are clustered within a few blocks of First and Main, and others continue to join them.

Downtown Napa probably has the densest concentration of wine tasting venues in California.

These popular sites arose both because of Napa's overall renaissance and for very practical reasons: Many local wineries can't host their own tasting rooms or find it impractical or prohibitive. They may not have a physical winery building but make their wines at someone else's winery or a "custom crush" facility. The county may prohibit them from offering tasting or restrict it significantly. Their winery may be remote or difficult to reach. Or their production may be too small to justify their own building and staff.

By law, every winery is allowed to open a "second" tasting room away from its primary site (even if it doesn't have a primary site!), and a number of the venues act as remote sites for one or more wineries, including Vintners Collective, which hosts a number of wineries.

A number of the tasting rooms are basically wine retail stores that offer tasting, including Back Room Wines, at First and Main and 1313 Main. Back Room sells cheese and charcuterie, too.

The Bounty Hunter and Oxbow Wine Merchants are retailers, but have active wine bars. The Bounty Hunter also offers prepared food.

ZuZu and Carpe Diem are classic wine bars, offering tastes of interesting wines with tapas, small plates and full meals but don't sell wine by the bottle.

And we shouldn't overlook the restaurants, which often serve interesting wines — some tastes — at their bars.

For visitors to Napa Valley, there's little question that going to a winery, getting a tour and meeting with the winemaker or owner is a special treat, but those of us who live here realize that most of the wineries simply have staffers — often very entertaining and knowledgeable, admittedly — pouring wines.

As one who's seen more than his share of wineries and their tanks and bottling lines, I won't say, "You've seen one, you've seen them all," but most wineries tend to be the same after a while.

There are advantages to visiting the downtown tasting rooms. You can taste and compare a number of wines from different producers and you don't offend the owner or winemaker by not buying a bottle. Just pay a small fee and that's the end of the obligation.

In addition, you can walk to all of these sites from nearby downtown inns and hotels. No designated driver is needed.

Naturally, all charge for tastes, but the $25 Napa Downtown Wine Tasting Card lets you try the first wine at many tasting rooms for only 10 cents each. You can buy the card at any tasting room that accepts it, the Visitors' Center in the Riverfront or www.donapa.com.

The tasting rooms that recently participate include 1313 Main, Bounty Hunter Wine Bar & Smokin' BBQ, Ca' Momi Winery & Enoteca, Mason Cellars, Napa General Store, Napa Tourist Information Center, Silo's at The Napa River Inn, Stonehedge Winery, Taste at Oxbow, TopFlight closed, Uncorked at Oxbow and Vintage Sweet Shoppe.

In addition, there are many wineries in the industrial area and business parks south of Napa, including Bourassa Vineyards at the Napa Smith Brewery tasting room, and vineyards in the southeastern part of the county along Jameson Canyon, the main route east. These areas have a cool climate similar to Carneros.

Some vineyards intertwine among the tees and greens at Chardonnay and Eagle Vines Golf Courses, while others fill the hills and line Highway 29.

The most prominent winery is Reata Winery, the former Kirkland Ranch Winery, on Jameson Canyon Road. It welcomes visitors and even has a picnic area.

Real wineries in Napa

Two wineries actually make wine in downtown Napa, and others may join them.

Vinoce and 20 Rows Winery is at 880 Vallejo St., Napa. (707) 265-7750. www.twentyrows.com. It offers wine tasting; a tour would be very short.

Marketta Fourmeaux, the former winemaker at Chateau Potelle, has a tiny commercial winery, Marketta Winery & Vineyards, in her basement near downtown. She can't formally host tastings, but you might give her a call at(707) 226-5944. www.markettawinery.com

St. Clair Brown Winery plans an ambitious winery, microbrewery and café close to Vinoce.

Hyde de Villaine, while not in Napa (it's across Trancas) produces some of Napa Valley's best wines, not surprising as it's a joint venture between one of the area's best growers, Larry Hyde, and the manager of Domaine de la Romanée Conte, one of the most famous wineries in the world.

Wine bars and tasting rooms in downtown Napa

Tasting rooms pour and sell wine from only one or a few wineries, as legally they're outposts of those wineries. Wine bars can offer wines from anywhere they choose. Some also sell wines by the glass and most sells bottles at retail.

1313 Main

1313 Main Wine is a welcoming wine bar, tasting room and retail wine sales that also serves snacks. 1313 Main St., Napa. (707) 258-1313. www.1313main.com

Back Room Wines

Back Room Wines is a wine shop and wine bar. It features special tasting programs Thursday and Friday nights plus cheese and charcuterie. It's a top choice for hard-to-find local wines but also carries a lot of imports. It's very popular with locals. 1000 Main St. Shop 120, Napa. (707) 226-1378. www.backroomwines.com

Bounty Hunter Wine Bar & Smokin' BBQ

Bounty Hunter Wine Bar & Smokin' BBQ is a wine bar and retail shop but is also a café with excellent food. It also now has selected cocktails. It's a popular hangout for young patrons. 975 First St., Napa.(707) 226- 3976. www.bountyhunterwinebar.com

Ca' Momi Winery & Enoteca

Ca' Momi Winery & Enoteca is an Italian café that also pours and sells its inexpensive wines. It boasts the best prices for bottles of wine in Napa – including Napa wines for about $12. 644 First St., Napa. (707) 257-4992. www.camomienoteca.com

Carpe Diem Wine Bar

Carpe Diem Wine Bar is a wine bar and restaurant that specializes in small plates. Very friendly, mostly young local patrons, many from the wine business. Always busy. 1001 Second St. #185, Napa. (707) 224-0800. www. carpediemwinebar.com

Ceja Vineyards

Ceja Vineyards is a wine tasting salon with artisan cheese in a lounge atmosphere and art gallery of by local artists. 1248 First St., Napa. (707) 255-3954. www.cejavineyards.com

District 4 Wines

District 4 Wines is a tasting room for X Winery, Amicus Cellars and others. Comfortable lounge atmosphere. It offers unique blending to make your own wine. Wine lounge atmosphere. 1405 Second St., Napa. (707) 204-9522. www.district4wine.com

GustavoThrace

GustavoThrace Tasting Room pours GustavoThrace wines. It welcomes visitors to bring in food from Oxbow Market across the street and enjoy it in the salon. 1021 McKinstry St., Napa. (707) 257-6796. www.gustavothrace.com

John Anthony

John Anthony Tasting room is really more like an upscale wine bar than a tasting room. It is owned by John Anthony Truchard of the same family that owns separate Truchard Vineyards. 1440 First St.,t Napa. (707) 265-7711. www.javwine.com

Mark Herold

Mark Herold Tasting room is next to Taste at Oxbow. 710 First St., Napa. (707) 256-3111. www.markheroldwines.com

Mason Cellars

Mason Cellars Oxbow Tasting Room pours and sells wines, including its inexpensive Pomelo Sauvignon Blanc. 714 First St., Napa. (707) 255-0658. www.masoncellars.com

Napa General Store

Napa General Store Napa is a café and gift store with a stand-up wine bar. 540 Main St., Napa. (707) 259-0762. www.napageneralstore.com

Olabisi and Trahan

Olabisi Wines shares a tasting room with Trahan Winery 974 Franklin St., Napa. (707) 257-7477. www.trahanwinery.com www.olabisiwines.com

Oxbow Wine Merchant

Oxbow Wine Merchant & Wine Bar in Oxbow Public Market sells tastes, glasses, carafes and bottles plus charcuterie and probably the best selection of cheese in Napa Valley. Oxbow Public Market. 610 First St., Napa. (707) 257-5200. oxbowwinemerchant.com

PureCru Wine Experience

PureCru is Mitch Cosentino's new brand in Napa Square behind Gordon Huether Galley. 463 First St., Napa. (707) 226-3046. www.purecruwines.com

Robert Craig

Robert Craig Winery Tasting Room pours wine from his mountain vineyards. 625 Imperial Way # 1, Napa. (707) 252-2250. www.robertcraigwine.com

Stonehedge

Stonehedge Winery Tasting Room & Gift Shop. 1004 Clinton St., Napa. (707) 256-4444. stonehedgewinery.com

Square One at the Tourist Information Center

New is the tasting bar Square One at the Tourist Information Center at First and Franklin in the hot West End of Napa. It pours tastes and glasses and sell bottles of wines from Raymond Vineyards and the Treasury (Beringer, St. Clement, Etude) family at very reasonable prices (for Napa). It also has salume and cheese to take back to your hotel and is open until at least 9 p.m. nightly.

Taste at Oxbow

Taste at Oxbow Wines pours wines from Waterstone Winery, and sells snacks and bottles. It even has music Friday nights. 708 First St., Napa (at McKinstry St.) (707) 265-9600. www.tasteatoxbow.com

Uncorked at Oxbow

Uncorked at Oxbow Tasting Room pours Ahnfeldt and Carducci wine. 605 First St., Napa. (707) 927-5864. www.uncorked-at-oxbow.com

Vintage Sweet Shoppe

Vintage Sweet Shoppe. 530 Main St. # B, Napa. (707) 224-2986. www.vintagesweetshoppe.com

Vintner's Collective

Vintner's Collective is a multi-winery co-op tasting room with many renowned Napa boutique wines in the historic Pfeiffer Building, the oldest stone building in Napa. 1245 Main St., Napa. (707) 255-7150. www.vintnerscollective.com.

ZuZu

ZuZu is a popular tapas and paella restaurant with many interesting wines by the glass. 829 Main St., Napa. (707) 224-8555. www.zuzunapa.com

There are also wine bars and tasting rooms in Yountville, St. Helena and Calistoga that will be covered in the sections on those cities.

Hidden Retailers Sell Rare Wines

Walk into a shop painted like a cave in Calistoga and you're transported to a world most wine lovers can only dream about: A store that sells wines normally available only to those who've climbed from the waiting list for the waiting list at a cult winery to get onto the real waiting list.

Enoteca Wine Shop is one of a number of wine stores in Napa Valley that sell the wines you can't find elsewhere – even at the wineries making the wines.

Many visitors to Napa Valley are surprised to learn that they can't find wines they'd like to buy at the wineries that make them. In fact, they may not be able to find the wineries. Some don't welcome visitors, or aren't allowed to by the county, while others actually make their wine at other locations including large custom wineries that provide space, equipment and services to many wineries.

That means you can only buy some wines at collective tasting rooms or retailers, some offering tastes as well as sales.

Enoteca is one of the retailers. Proprietor Margaux Singleton, a charming and knowledgeable legend in the valley, sells much of her rare stock to an e-mail list of special customers, but also offers wines at her store in Calistoga to walk-in customers.

Other interesting retailers include Acme Fine Wines, 750 Wines, the St. Helena Wine Center, Dean & Deluca and Sunshine Market in St. Helena; V Wine Cellar in Yountville; Oakville Grocery, and Back Room Wines, the Bounty Hunter, Napa General Store and 1313 Main in Napa.

Many offer tasting, too. Back Room Wines also conducts themed wine tastings each week, and the Bounty Hunter has a popular wine bar and limited-menu restaurant as well as retail sales.

In the last few years, Napa Valley has also spawned a number of collective tasting rooms where you can taste a variety of wines from small producers and buy them, too. Some feature wines that are in great demand, and it's always surprising to find them for sale at these facilities.

Food and Restaurants

A Passion for Food

Napa Valley may be best known for wine, but its residents are some of the most food-oriented people in America.

Beside supporting world-class restaurants, they flock to food-oriented events, and they patronize gourmet shops and cookware stores equal to those found only in very large cities.

That's why it's fitting that one of America's most important shrines to food – The Culinary Institute of America – lies in the Valley.

A St. Helena campus of New York's prestigious Culinary Institute of America, the CIA as it's called locally, offers education for trained chefs and wine professionals. Some classes are open to amateurs – and those considering a career in food and wine.

The CIA also offers daily cooking demonstrations, and its Campus Store is a comprehensive cookware store and bookshop aimed at hobbyists as well as professionals.

Napa Valley also has three other interesting cookware stores. One is Dean & Deluca in St. Helena, which also features an amazing assortment of gourmet food. In downtown St. Helena, Steves Hardware combines an old-fashioned hardware store with a wide selection of items for cooking and serving food.

Most impressive of all, however, is Shackford's, an unimposing kitchenware store in downtown Napa piled high with products for both the world-class chefs who practice in the valley and ordinary home cooks. The selection and prices surpass some of the famous chain cookware stores, but you may have to ask for help finding what you want in the crowded aisles.

The Valley also teems with exceptional markets and food shops. Three, Dean & Deluca in St. Helena, Genova Deli in Napa and Oakville Grocery, are clearly gourmet shops that also include delis for picnics, while V. Sattui Winery is the only winery in Napa Valley with a deli – and it's a treat. A local favorite is funky Napa Valley Olive Oil Manufacturing Company, which is owned by a family from Lucca in Tuscany and stocks amazing treasures as well as bargain extra virgin and regular olive oil. It's opening in Napa, too.

Some of the local supermarkets are equally tempting. Sunshine Market in St. Helena, Brown's Valley and the Vallerga's Market in Napa and CalMart in Calistoga have real butchers, delis and many gourmet produce and specialty cheeses and foods.

The food of Napa Valley

The food of Napa Valley has evolved based on local ingredients and wine. In simple terms, Napa Valley is most famous for Cabernet

Sauvignon. That hearty, tannic red wine goes perfectly with big beef, though it also well matches lamb or duck.

The ultimate big beef is probably the Porterhouse, the enormous Fiorentina of Tuscany. You'll find no better combination than Cab and beef. Local vintners often try to match their Cabernet with pork, chicken or even fish, but they're trying too hard.

Of course, Napa Valley's cuisine has been heavily influenced by the ingredients we have, and almost everything grows here or in nearby counties where the land is cheaper. The patron saint of our food, and wine country, even California, food is Alice Waters, who preached the gospel of using fresh, local ingredients handled with care.

Locally, one of her most influential apostles was Cindy Pawlcyn, who, along with John Ash in Sonoma, created the wine country cuisine we know and love today.

Look closely, however, you'll see that we have basically a Mediterranean cuisine, which is suitable as we live in a Mediterranean climate and Med vegetables and fruits grow so well here.

Look even closer, and you'll see that we basically eat Italian food adapted to out local ingredients. That doesn't mean heavy tomato sauces from Naples, but lighter food, much handed down from the Ligurian immigrants who populated North Beach of San Francisco.

In later times, we adopted other Italian traditions like those of Tuscany, Venice and Emilia-Romagna, even Rome. We also embraced Spanish and southern French food, but Italian food rules.

Napa Valley's Favorite Restaurants

Most people who live in Napa Valley obviously don't eat very often at famous restaurants such as the French Laundry and La Toque, but they don't flock to chain restaurants, either. Instead, they eat at local favorites that offer excellent food, friendly services, recognition, reasonable prices – and often, flexibility about corkage charges for wine.

There's a lot of good wine in Napa, often free or highly discounted to people who work in the industry, and to attract business, many restaurants waive corkage for winery employees who can refer patrons, but others forgive it for everyone. The restaurant still has to serve good food, however. People in Napa have become a bit spoiled and expect excellence even with bargain prices.

No matter the type of restaurant, unless it's Asian or Latin, you'll see Italian touches, from pasta to pizzas and flatbreads, as well as an emphasis on healthy fruits, vegetables and grains rather than meat. That creates a dichotomy with the famous Napa Cabernets, which aren't typically at their best with fresh vegetables. Chefs work to overcome this conflict, often adding acid citrus, salt or savory ingredients full of umami to bridge the gap.

Still, in spite of the appreciation for healthy Med-based food, Napans and tourists alike love greasy short ribs, steaks and burgers perfect with Cabernet.

So here's a rundown on the restaurants locals love. Some are off the tourist track, others right in the middle, so they can be very busy at peak times.

In St. Helena, Market is a local favorite for dinner and Gott's, formerly Taylor's, Refresher drive-in, is packed at lunch; it may be the only such drive-in in America to sell fine wine, in fact. Cindy's Backstreet Kitchen off the main drag is another local hangout, particularly for the exotic mixed drinks and comforting global-tinged food. New French Blue, owned by vintner, restaurateur and deli-ateur (? Dean & DeLuca and Oakville Grocery) Leslie Rudd and architect Howard Backen, has become an instant local favorite. Rutherford Grill in Rutherford doesn't charge corkage, and that's helped make it the favorite spot for many winery employees. Nearby La Luna Market reportedly has the best tacos in the valley.

Mustards has been a local as well as tourist favorite for decades and in Yountville, Hurley's Restaurant and Bar is a local favorite.

Everyone also loves very French Bistro Jeanty and Bouchon Bistro accepting the firm corkage charges and stiffer prices for the exceptional French food.

Many locals claim that overall, Bistro Don Giovanni is the best place to eat in the valley, though waits can be long and everyone pays corkage. It's certainly one of the best.

Less known to tourists but very popular with locals is Fumé Bistro on the freeway frontage road in Napa.

Downtown Napa now has many local favorites even if the visitors are finding their way to them. Modest Uva Trattoria has excellent Italian food, including half portions, reasonable prices, music most nights – and friendly camaraderie.

The tapas bar ZuZu is filled with people from other restaurants, a sign of quality, and Angèle on the river is where Napans go for a special time out – or to sit at the bar and enjoy Mac 'n' cheese with wine. Carpe Diem and Pearl Restaurant are two other downtown favorites, though neither is on First or Main Streets, the prime destinations.

And Michael Gyetvan's Azzurro Pizzeria and Norman Rose Tavern are always full of Napans enjoying great food at reasonable prices.

Soda Canyon Store deserves special notice. It's the only place to get a bite or a drink on the 27 miles of Silverado Trail between Napa and Calistoga. It has fine sandwiches, burritos and other food as well as plenty of beverages and a few other basics.

A Peek Inside the CIA

The Culinary Institute of America's campus in the old Greystone Cellars in St. Helena is like a Disneyland for food lovers. Though its prime function is educating food and wine professionals, it also has many attractions of interest to casual or serious food lovers.

You can visit much of the campus alone, but a good way to start your exploration is with a 30-minute tour of the campus, which are offered three times a day (11:45 a.m., 2:45 p.m. and 5 p.m.) for $10.

The tour includes the historic Greystone building including the Brother Timothy Corkscrew Collection, the Breitstein Collection, the Rudd Center for Professional Wine Studies, the herb garden, the Vintners Hall of Fame and a view of the CIA Teaching Kitchen. The tour doesn't enter the teaching kitchen since that would intrude on student classes.

Of course, for many people, the most obvious draw is the Wine Spectator Greystone Restaurant. *Wine Spectator* magazine gave a large donation to the restaurant, but is not involved in its operation. The restaurant is open daily, with a patio offering a panoramic view of upper Napa Valley as well as seating inside surrounding the open kitchen and bar.

The meals are prepared by professionals as well as students under the direction of executive chef and chef instructor, Almir DaFonseca. DaFonseca emphasizes fresh, sustainable ingredients, with most of the produce coming from the school's 2-acre student garden. He has also implemented programs for teaching the art of butchery, and in-house practices for dry-aging beef, curing bacon, making charcuterie, cheese, and other ingredients featured on the menu.

The restaurant offers lunch and dinner prix fixe menus that change and vary weekly. These range between $30 and $50, with wine pairings available for an additional $20 to $30.

Another special is Five Bites: Five bites of food plus a glass of wine for $10, served between 4:30 and 6:30 p.m., Monday through Thursday. You can also enjoy "nonstop" tasting flights of wine with meals.

The restaurant offers the unique Olive To Live super-premium olive oil tasting for only $9 for two people.

A second big attraction at the CIA is the Spice Islands Market place, the school's 'campus store' and then some. This 'culinary toy store' has recently been remodeled and expanded and includes top-of-the-line amateur and professional cookware, more than 1,700 cookbook titles including many by local authors and CIA graduates, locally made specialty foods, and Greystone Cellars wines made by nearby Markham Vineyards.

Also new in the Marketplace is the new Flavor Bar that offers chocolate tasting, super-premium olive oil tasting, a demonstration of how to pair wine with cheese, and a course that teaches how to taste like a chef. The tastings are on the hour and half hour between 11 a.m. and 5 p.m. The price is $10 or $15, depending on the tasting.

Handmade chocolates made by students under the direction of a baking and pastry degree graduate are also for sale, and visitors can take a peek inside the new Chocolate Room to watch students at work.

The CIA, as it's called locally to visitors' confusion, offers 1-hour cooking demonstrations at 1:30 p.m. on Saturdays and Sundays. They cost $20 and include a taste of the food plus a glass of wine for guests over 21 years old.

For the more curious, the CIA offers many different food and wine classes for enthusiasts. They range in scope from 2 hours to a full day, or a full week of Boot Camp.

Taste of CIA Cookbooks are one-day, hands-on cooking classes inspired by the school's popular cookbooks. From Italian and Asian cuisine to grilling to artisan bread baking, you'll find a class to match your interest and you'll take the cookbook home.

CIA Samplings are two-hour cooking classes where California and world cuisine come alive. Enjoy a demonstration, do a little hands-on cooking, and savor the results expertly paired with wine.

Wine Explorations are the perfect complement to cooking classes. In two hours of discussion and tastings, you'll learn about the wonderful world of wine.

CIA Culinary Boot Camps are for serious food lovers who really want to learn to cook, and have fun doing it. You'll learn to cook and bake like a professional with the guidance of CIA chef-instructors. Students are assigned recipes, learn about ingredients and techniques, and eat great food. Boot camps range from 2 to 5 days, and each course covers a range of topics from basic skill development, grilling, bread baking and flavors of the wine country.

Wine Lover's Boot Camps are also available where students stroll the lush vineyards with expert instructors, taste and analyze wines in the CIA's professional tasting classrooms, and return home understanding more about wine than you ever dreamed possible.

Among other attractions at the CIA are the Vintners Hall of Fame celebrating the men and women responsible for the growth and worldwide prestige of the California wine industry. Bronze sculptures of the inductees are displayed on the 2,200-gallon redwood wine barrels in the former Christian Brothers' Barrel Room.

Visitors will also find the Breitstein Wine Collection, an exhibit that documents the rich history of the California wine industry as told through unopened bottles and informational placards. The exhibit is on permanent loan from wine collectors David and Judy Breitstein and open to the public.

Get more information or make your reservation for any of these programs online at www.ciachef.edu/california or telephone at (707) 967-2320.

Hot Chefs, Hot Restaurants

Food is hardly second to wine to residents and visitors to Napa Valley, and the relatively small valley has both attracted talented chefs from elsewhere and spawned home-grown talent.

It's so difficult to pick the top 10 than we decided to list a dozen. Masuharu Morimoto is a top draws, but doesn't live here though he has a popular restaurant in the Riverfront development in downtown Napa and is sometimes there.

All of these restaurants are busy and getting a reservation can be challenging. Your hotel concierge or innkeeper can help and suggest alternatives, including eating mid-afternoon, European style.

Thomas Keller (The French Laundry, Bouchon, Bouchon Bakery, Ad Hoc, Addendum)

Any list of top chefs in Napa Valley – or the United States – must start with Thomas Keller. His French Laundry, and its counterpart in New York Per Se, are generally considered two of the best restaurants in the country, and both have been awarded three stars by Michelin.

The French Laundry serves exquisite multi-course prix fixe meals in an almost reverential atmosphere.

Keller's French bistro Bouchon is a favorite, too, as are his Bouchon Bakery and Ad Hoc, the once-temporary prix fixe restaurant that's so popular that it's being expanded – and recently spun off a take-out arm, Addendum. All are in Yountville, the "per capita" food capital of America.

Keller is also known for his extensive gardens, which lie across the street from the French Laundry. They provide much of the produce used in the restaurant. 6640 Washington St., Yountville. (707) 944-2380. www.frenchlaundry.com

Michael Chiarello (Bottega)

A close second in renown is Michael Chiarello. His Bottega Ristorante in Yountville features lusty food inspired by his roots in Calabria merged with California ingredients.

Chiarello first gained fame as the founding chef of Tra Vigne, once Napa Valley's hottest restaurant, but then he took time out to star in TV series that made him a familiar face, most recently on *Top Chef Masters* on the Bravo Channel.

Chiarello also created the NapaStyle brand and retail and Internet stores, and has written a number of cookbooks. The NapaStyle store next to Bottega makes fine panini and other light eats.

He owns Chiarello Family Vineyards, which makes Cabernet, old vine Petite Sirah and Zinfandel. 6525 Washington St., Yountville. (707) 945-1050. www.botteganapavalley.com

Cindy Pawlcyn (Mustards Grill, Cindy's Backstreet Kitchen and Cindy Pawlcyn's Wood Grill and Wine Bar)

Cindy Pawlcyn is generally credited with creating the iconic Napa Valley cuisine based on local, sustainable meats and produce with Mediterranean inspiration with her Mustards Grill in Yountville, which she founded in 1983. 7399 St. Helena Hwy., Napa. (707) 944-2424. www.mustardsgrill.com

She later started Cindy's Backstreet Kitchen in St. Helena at 1327 Railroad Ave., St. Helena. (707) 963-1200. www.cindysbackstreetkitchen.com, which serves globally influenced fusion food , and more recently, Cindy Pawlcyn's Wood Fire and Wine Bar with wine country cuisines. 641 Main St., St. Helena. (707) 963-0700. She is the partner chef of famed Monterey Aquarium.

Like a number of other top chefs in Napa Valley, Pawlcyn maintains an extensive garden at Mustards.

Ken Frank (La Toque)

Ken Frank is proprietor/chef of La Toque Restaurant attached to the Westin Verasa Hotel in Napa. He's gained a fervent fan base for his innovative creations and especially pairings with wine; it's one of the few restaurants where it's better to let them choose the wine for each course, though La Toque has an impressive list, thanks partly to its many vintner investors.

Frank is especially noted for his truffle preparations, and offers whole menus devoted to them in January, also time of the Napa Valley Truffle Festival.

Frank also supervises Bank Café and Bar in the lobby of the Westin Verasa, which serves more casual food – plus three-course menu of food from different regions of France nightly for $34.

He was a pioneer with other downtown chefs in tending the once-abandoned kitchen gardens at the former Copia center to grow produce that feeds his seasonal cuisine. 1314 McKinstry St., Napa. (707) 257-5157. www.latoque.com

Christopher Kostow (The Restaurant at Meadowood)

Christopher Kostow is the chef at The Restaurant at Meadowood, which shares with the French Laundry in being one of two three Michelin star restaurants in the Bay Area.

The Restaurant at Meadowood offers a casually elegant dining experience featuring a modern approach to Napa Valley cuisine. He says that it's approachable, dynamic, evocative – not provocative –

and playful, but not scary. 900 Meadowood Ln., St. Helena. (707) 963-3646. www.therestaurantatmeadowood.com

Robert Curry (The Restaurant at Auberge du Soleil)

Robert Curry is chef at The Restaurant at Auberge du Soleil, which boasts the best views of any restaurant in Napa Valley.

As part of the tony resort, Curry prepares exquisite prix fixe menus for celebrities and the well heeled, but the adjoining Bistro and Bar offers reasonably priced smaller meals of high quality – including on the same deck as the restaurant. 180 Rutherford Hill Rd., Rutherford. (707) 963-1211. www.aubergedusoleil.com

Brandon Sharp (Solbar at Solage)

Brandon Sharp is the chef at Solbar at Solage, the sister resort to Auberge du Soleil and Calistoga Ranch (whose restaurant is only for guests and members). He prepares creative "California Soul Food," inventive new twists on time-honored soul food inspired by the freshest locally grown, seasonal ingredients. The result is flavorful cuisine that showcases the best organic, sustainably farmed elements for both indulgent and healthful selections. 755 Silverado Trail, Calistoga. 707) 226-0850. www.solbarnv.com

Perry Hoffman (Étoile at Domaine Chandon)

Perry Hoffman is the young but celebrated chef at étoile at Domaine Chandon, the only restaurant at a winery in Napa Valley. Étoile was the first luxury restaurant in Napa Valley under chef Philippe Jeanty, but later lost its cachet. Hoffman has restored the glory and prepares meals suitable for pairing with the restaurant's excellence sparkling wines as well as its less-known still Pinots and Chardonnays. 1 California Dr., Yountville. (888) 242-6366. chandon.com

Tyler Rodde and Curtis Di Fede (Oenotri)

Tyler Rodde and Curtis Di Fede created a big stir when they opened Oenotri in downtown Napa featuring food based on their southern Italian roots. Traveling regularly to Sicily and the southern 'boot' for inspiration, they create traditional dishes with local ingredients. The food ranges from innovative pizzas to full meals, all excellent. 1425 First St., Napa. (707) 252-1022. www.oenotri.com

Masuharu Morimoto (Morimoto Napa)

When Iron Chef Masuharu Morimoto chose downtown Napa as the site for his first west coast restaurant, it was a sign that Napa had arrived. Morimoto Napa is a booming hot spot with Japanese-influenced modern décor, superb sushi and sashimi, and fusion foods the chef is known for.

Morimoto has become a major draw for hip young patrons from San Francisco, who hang out at the bar and in the lounge as well as outside along the river, but it's also a favorite of locals who appreciate the food as well as the weeknight bargains each day from 4 to 6 p.m. 610 Main St., Napa. (707) 252-1600. www.morimotonapa.com

Bob Hurley (Hurley's Restaurant and Bar)

Bob Hurley is one of Napa Valley's favorite chefs and people. In addition to serving up popular Mediterranean-inspired food at his popular restaurant in Yountville, he seems to contribute to every charity event and festival in the valley. 6518 Washington St., Yountville. (707) 944-2345. www.hurleysrestaurant.com

Greg Cole (Cole's Chop House, Celadon)

Greg Cole was a pioneer in downtown Napa before the flood-control project tamed the wild river. He started his Celadon featuring intriguing global fusion comfort food in a tiny space behind the then-closed Napa Valley Opera House, then expanded to the Napa Mill development. 500 Main St., Napa. (707) 254-9690. www.celadonnapa.com

Cole's Chop House, is a classic steak restaurant serving huge portions of exquisite beef and other meat. It's been voted the best steak house in the whole Bay Area by Zagat reviewers, and that's no small achievement for a restaurant in a small city dwarfed by San Francisco, Oakland and San Jose. 1122 Main St., Napa. (707) 224-6328. www.coleschophouse.com

Todd Humphries (Kitchen Door)

Todd Humphries, a native of Saskatchewan who loves fungi, gained his name in Napa Valley as the chef at the Martini House in St. Helena. He now runs the well-regarded Kitchen Door, a casual restaurant in the Oxbow Public Market serving simpler presentations of fine food at reasonable prices. 610 First St., Napa. (707) 226-1560. www.kitchendoornapa.com

Caterers

A small note: Because Napa Valley has so many events and meetings, it's developed a cadre of superb caterers. You won't find rubber chicken at local benefits or winery meals, but first class food lovingly prepared.

Among the top caterers are Elaine Bell, Morgan Robinson (Smoke Catering), Melissa Teaff, Oak Avenue Catering (Formerly Knickerbocker) and Piper Johnson but many restaurants plus gourmet markets like Dean & Deluca also prepare fine meals.

Elaine Bell. 254 1st St., East Sonoma. (707) 996-5226. www.elainebellcatering.com

Morgan Robinson (Smoke Catering). Cant find info

Melissa Teaff. 101 S. Coombs St., Napa. (707) 254-8160. www.mtcatering.com

Oak Avenue Catering (Formerly Knickerbocker). 1314 Oak Ave., St. Helena. (707) 963-9278. oakavenuecatering.com

Piper Johnson. 2450 Foothill Blvd., Calistoga. (707) 942-5432. www.piperjohnsoncatering.com

Dean & Deluca. 607 St. Helena Hwy., St. Helena. (707) 967-9980. www.deandeluca.com.

Gardens Fuel Meals at Local Restaurants

Napa Valley is best known for its wines, but its food is a close second. And while its vineyards are renowned, many people don't realize that many restaurants in the valley have a secret ally in preparing great food – their gardens.

Top chefs in Napa Valley are passionate about using fresh local ingredients, and what better way to ensure their produce is fresh from the garden than to pick it themselves? So while most also procure fruit, vegetables and meats from local producers, many have their own gardens and all garden organically without chemicals.

The gardens may be highly visible and attractions in themselves, like those at the French Laundry, Farmstead, Brix and Mustards, or they may be offsite or out of view.

"Our garden has become a gathering place for visitors and our neighbors," says chef Thomas Keller of the gardens across the street from his famed French Laundry restaurant. "Guests love to visit the gardens."

Keller says he's always had gardens, and the restaurant had gardens when he bought it. "It's a big part of the history of this restaurant," he says.

Keller tended the space even before he bought the property in 1999 and it now supplies 10 to 15 percent of the vegetables on the menu in season at his French Laundry and Bouchon. At his Ad Hoc, which plans meals based on what's ripe in the garden, the portion is even higher.

He says that growing produce isn't about saving money but the image and education for staff and patrons. "The fava beans may not actually be better, but they seem to taste that way!" he says.

It's not practical to have gardens at his other restaurants in Manhattan, Las Vegas and Beverly Hills, but Keller sometimes ships produce to Per Se, highlighting their origins at the French Laundry in Napa Valley.

He also notes that what he's doing wouldn't seem unusual in much of the world, and his French mentor and teacher Roland Henin agrees. "It's the way it used to be; we're going back to our roots," Henin says. "Every hotel had a backyard garden where they grew at least herbs."

Ken Frank of La Toque in downtown Napa's Westin Verasa Hotel doesn't have a garden on site, but he persuaded the owners of nearby closed Copia center to allow him and other chefs to replant the neglected kitchen gardens there. Now he and about eight other chefs are tending kitchen gardens and using the produce.

Franks says it was a natural for him. "My gardening goes way back to the early '80s in Los Angeles. I used to sell a plate of homegrown tomatoes from my back yard for $5," he laughs.

He even paid his son a nickel for every snail he collected, which Frank purged and served in his restaurant.

When Frank moved to Napa Valley, he depended on Farmers Markets and local purveyors, but always gardened at home. "This valley is a wonderland for gardeners," he says.

His wife Sherylle was the original gardener at Brix, and she assists in the garden at Copia.

They tend about 4,000 sq.ft. in raised beds. "It's a lot of work, but also a lot of fun. We grew every cucumber we needed for pickles," he notes, and also grew padrón and espelette peppers, sunchokes and many more common vegetables.

Frank also buys a lot of local produce, including from Long Meadow Ranch, which supplies him grass-fed beef. But in the summer, he has half a dozen items from the gardens on his menus.

Other downtown restaurants that farm at Copia include Bank Café and Bar, Ca' Momi, Carpe Diem, Fish Story, Hog Island, Kitchen Door, Oenotri, The Thomas/Fagiani and ZuZu,

The Fish Story plot was originated by Mark Dommen of One Market in the Lark Creek chain that owns the Napa seafood restaurant, but Leslye Deller, wife of Lark Creek CEO Michael Deller prepared the garden. "It was full of weeds – and potatoes," she says.

The chefs have also erected a 60-seat table by the Napa River that is used for community dinners.

Cindy Pawlcyn likes to grow vegetables that are hard to find. She was a pioneer in planting gardens next to the restaurant when she opened Mustards, the classic Napa Valley roadhouse, almost 30 years ago. "We planted gardens when we started, but they've grown over the years," she notes.

Pawlcyn says that during the peak of the summer, 80 percent of Mustards' produce is from her gardens and trees. At her Wood Grill, she has small gardens but many fruit trees including 36 heritage apple varieties.

She doesn't have space for a garden at Cindy's Backstreet Kitchen, but does grow produce at home and uses it in the restaurant.

Even during the winter, she gets lettuce, carrots, potatoes and other greens from the garden; they put covers over the gardens to protect them.

She also buys from local producers including Forni Brown, the long-established Calistoga supplier to restaurants, famed vineyard Hudson Ranch, which supplies meat and poultry, and Dollarhide Ranch, St. Supéry Vineyard's property in remote Pope Valley.

Almost next door to Mustards is Brix, which has some of the most appealing culinary gardens in Napa Valley. The whole property is almost a garden, in fact, with fruit trees and potted herbs scattered about along with impressive flowers, some edible.

But the showcase is the large garden that stretches behind the extensive he lawn behind the restaurant's patio. Property manager Guillermo 'Memo' Rodriguez tends the gardens. He says that 95 percent of the vegetables in season come from the garden.

The property also includes 11 acres of owner Valerie Kelleher Herzog's vineyards used for Kelleher wines.

Rodriguez starts plants in a greenhouse next to the restaurant, which allows him to grow plants that are hard to find as seedlings.

Brix' garden is often used for events including weddings, too, and many patrons stroll through the gardens when they eat at the restaurant.

Sous chef Rob Hurd says that he changes menus based on the produce that's available; when tomatoes arrive later in the summer, the menu is filled with them.

Not far from Brix in Yountville is Bardessono, one of three environmentally pristine Platinum LEED hotels in the world. Everything on the property is organic, including gardens where they even grow artichokes, a crop usually planted in cooler regions than Napa Valley, but Yountville lies in the cooler part of the valley.

They grow herbs, naturally, as well as citrus, berries and more, but also depend on nearby Hill Family Farms for produce as well as tending their gardens. Fully 30 percent of the menu comes from the garden during the summer.

As hinted before, Napa Valley wineries and wine grape growers are also getting into commercial produce gardening. Many have gardens for their own use as well as for their staff, but some are now supplying produce and more to local restaurants.

Besides St. Supéry Vineyards and Hudson Ranch, Frog's Leap supplies produce, and the wineries that offer their own olive oil and condiments is lengthy.

None, however, can compare with Long Meadow Ranch. Ted and Laddie Hall, who come from farm families, established their winery property in the Mayacamas Mountains as a virtual self-contained estate like the great tenutas of Tuscany.

Aside from grapes and olives, they raise grass-red longhorn cattle for meat, chickens, eggs, vegetables and fruit. And if that weren't enough, they bought prime property on Highway 29 in Rutherford and raise a wide variety of vegetables and fruit, not Cabernet Sauvignon grapes.

They also raise Red Wattle pigs, a heritage variety, and get honey from their own bees.

Napa County doesn't allow restaurants at wineries outside cities, so the Halls created Farmstead Restaurant in St. Helena to showcase the products from their farms.

Aside from the restaurant and a tasting room that also offers food pairings, the site contains extensive demonstration gardens.

All of the beef is from the ranch, and 30 to 40 percent of ingredients overall during the summer, 10 to 15 percent during the winter.

Farmstead itself grows heritage and less common vegetables.

One concern some have is about the safety of produce, but Napa County has developed systems to monitor culinary gardens at restaurants so patrons can enjoy the benefits of fresh food.

Ironically, California's Alcoholic Beverage Control board restricts the amount of Long Meadow Ranch wines that can be sold in the restaurant, a leftover from Prohibition, but the Halls would undoubtedly offer other local wines anyway. Their house wines are an exceptional value, and very popular.

No visitor would go to Bordeaux and buy Italian wine or drink French wine in Florence, and many Napa Valley restaurants serve not only local produce, but locally produced wine. They're a perfect pair, and make visiting or living in Napa Valley even more special.

Should Napa Restaurants Feature Napa Wine?

Visit a restaurant in Bordeaux, and you won't find any Napa wines. In fact, you're unlikely to find any wines from anywhere outside that famed wine region.

The same is true in Burgundy, Tuscany or Piedmont. That's especially true of the finest restaurants, which proudly serve the area's best wines.

That's not true in Napa Valley. Though this wine region is arguably on a par with those areas, many local restaurants pride themselves on serving wines from all over the world, not just from Napa Valley.

It's a situation that annoys many local winery owners, and certainly the Napa Valley Vintners, which deserves a lot of credit for making people everywhere else appreciate Napa wines.

The Vintners even posts a web page listing the Napa restaurants that support local wines, and has extended that support to San Francisco and New York (albeit at a realistic lower level).

The web page says, "Thinking local when choosing wine at a restaurant helps, too. The Napa Valley wine industry generates 40,000 jobs and more than $1 billion in local tax revenues. And the diversity of varieties, styles and price of Napa Valley wines means that when you dine here, you can find choices that fit your taste— and budget — while helping ensure that the local economy remains strong."

The Vintners offer more than a web page to support restaurants that feature Napa wines here and elsewhere. This includes programs during Napa wine month each January and California wine month in September.

It also sends trade visitors during Premiere Napa Valley and all during the year to supporting restaurants. Winery tasting room staff know which restaurants sell their wines, too.

Not on the list

The vintners don't expect restaurants to forgo all other wines. By its definition, restaurants with Napa wines making up 50 percent or more of the list are supporting the valley.

Missing from the list are some of the valley's top names: The French Laundry, Redd and La Toque, and a few surprises like farm-to-table-oriented Farmstead – owned by a local vintner.

But included are other top restaurants like Auberge, étoile, Meadowood and Solbar, as well as some international restaurants that might be forgiven for looking elsewhere like Angèle, Bottega and Morimoto.

Of course, the percentages of wines on the list don't tell the whole story. The French Laundry has a huge wine list, with many rare treasures that are rarely ordered. Probably many patrons order local wines.

Farmstead's general manager Adam Kim says 75 percent of its actual volume sold is Napa wine, and another 18 percent comes from places that most people would consider local like Sonoma County even if they're not in Napa County.

"We focus on locally produced seasonal food (including wine) sourced directly from the farm to table. Consequently, our wine program features Long Meadow Ranch wines (in bottle and on draft) and other neighbor Napa Valley wineries," says Kim.

"In addition, we offer wines from other appellations around the world which we believe are excellent pairings with food. In most cases, these wines are produced by family friends of the Halls and/or are produced using sustainable farming methods. We look for wines that are balanced and are appropriate as food."

Farmstead also has winemakers' dinners feature a different Napa Valley winemaker on the third Tuesday of every month.

Its Corkage for Community program with a fee of just $2 per bottle results in many local producers (in addition to regular guests) eating there to show off their wares.

He also feels that the Vintners' approach to only count the number of listings on a wine list is a weak indicator of an establishment's wine focus and of relative wine volume, especially because of the role of by-the-glass wine.

Jessica Pinzon, the head sommelier at Bouchon, says, "As for our Bouchon wine list, our program is structured to be about 50/50 French to domestic wines. A large percentage of our list offerings come from all over Napa Valley and our reserve list is dominated by Napa Valley wines. We love giving guests the opportunity to purchase a French wine that they might see in a Lyonnais bistro in France, but also enjoy introducing our guests to all of the wonderful local wineries that we support and have relationships with."

Perhaps no restaurant lists such a high percentage of Napa wines as Press in St. Helena, and it recently added a large number of older local wines to its list. The list is all Napa – except for a few Champagnes and Chateau d'Yquem.

"We want to be the leading restaurant in the country for Napa wines," says owner Leslie Rudd, who also owns Rudd Winery and has interests in other local wineries. "I think people come to Napa Valley to drink Napa wine."

Alluding to the situation in other wine regions, he says, "I'm unclear on why other restaurants don't also focus on local wines."

He acknowledges that Napa is best known for its Cabernets, a perfect complement for the beef specialties of Press, but notes that the valley supplies plenty of other good choices including Pinots and Chardonnays.

Terry Hall from the Vintners expands on that thought: "We have varieties from Albariño to Zinfandel."

It's hardly surprising that Cindy Pawlcyn is a big supporter of local wines; her Mustards was a pioneer in serving local ingredients, and the list at her eclectic Cindy's Backstreet Kitchen also emphasizes Napa wines. Her third restaurant, Cindy Pawlcyn's Wood Grill and Wine Bar, that emphasizes Napa offerings.

Managing partner Sean Knight says, "Tourists are here to drink Napa wines," but admits that some local wines are expensive, and the restaurants offer alternatives. Still, the majority of the wine volume at all of the restaurants is from Napa.

He adds another reason for the restaurants' policy. "Cindy and I have always looked at the restaurants as part of the community. They support us and we support them."

The Napa Valley Wine Train is also a big supporter of local wines. More than 65 percent of its list is Napan, and sales volume is even higher as the 'house' wine is local Raymond. "People who come to Napa Valley really come to taste Napa Valley," notes Melodie Hilton, the Train's director of marketing. Chef Kelly Macdonald adds, "We're in one of the world's most important wine regions and we like to celebrate that."

One of the restaurants that might be expected to emphasize other wines is Bottega, which features Michael Chiarello's California version of Southern Italian foods, but he's a big supporter of local wines. "Our food is adjusted to the American palate, and our local wines are, too."

Chiarello says that 75 to 80 percent of its wines sales are Napa wines, including his own label.

Knowing that Napa wines can be expensive, Chiarello adjusts his prices to make them attractive, charging closer to twice wholesale than the usual three times.

"Satisfied guests return often," he says, adding that they're also more flexible in eating times at the busy restaurant.

Another restaurant that might easily highlight international wines due to its eclectic fusion cuisine is Terra, but it also focuses on Napa wines.

Partner Lissa Doumani says the restaurant started out buying and selling only Napa wines in 1988. She says the restaurant was once berated for offering only Napa wines, in fact.

One result of laying in all these wines, however, is that the restaurant has an excellent selection of older Cabs. She notes that they are less tannic and alcoholic, and pair better with some of Terra's Asian-tinged food than many aggressive young Cabernets. She's happy to see recent vintages in Napa more in this style, largely due to cool weather.

Over time, she added some other wines – "intruders" they once jokingly called them – to offer locals and visiting young chefs more affordable choices. Napa Valley also provides more varieties now, too.

With all the arguments for emphasizing Napa wines, even the Vintners don't expect restaurants to forgo other wines. One strong argument for serving "other" wines is that locals, many of them in the wine business, like to try other regions' wines.

That's a message heard in many local restaurants and wine stores: "Tourists buy Napa wines; locals buy others," says one leading wine merchant in Napa. Part of that is due to curiosity and a s desire to educate their palates, and part, frankly, to price.

The recent recession – and wine glut – has made many Napa wines more affordable, and spawned the introduction of some new, lower-cost brands, but that doesn't seem to have had much impact at restaurants where prices keep rising. A return to better times and tighter wine supplies may maintain the status quo.

Don't expect the French Laundry to change its policy of emphasizing international wines, but other restaurants might if they see a benefit.

Corkage at Napa Valley Restaurants

Corkage charges at Napa restaurants are a very big deal to locals. Many want to drink their own wines – or ones they've acquired inexpensively – and don't think they should have to pay a lot for a bottle of wine or charges for corkage.

By contrast, most restaurateurs seem to assume their patrons rarely eat out, and so there's willing to pay plenty for a great bottle of wine.

Many of us enjoy an exceptional bottle of wine with a fine meal, and are willing to pay for it. But if you eat out a lot, as many people now do, you may not be looking for a mystical experience when you taste the wine. You may just want a nice complement for dinner (and rare lunches with wine).

Many restaurants don't accept that. They charge huge markups – especially on wine by the glass, a notorious rip off. It's no wonder people want to take wines to restaurants. But they should expect to pay to do so.

All restaurants in Napa Valley except a wine shop or two allow you to bring in bottles of wine if it's not on their list.

Most restaurants charge corkage, typically $10 to $20, but as much as $75 at the French Laundry. Many have dropped corkage some or all days to attract customers, however, particularly early and mid week.

Most also forgive the corkage on a bottle if you buy one, which is ideal if you want to start with a white or sparkler they have chilled, then segue to a red wine.

Personally, I don't take wine to a restaurant unless there's a good reason. I'd rather they have reasonable wine prices. Then everyone wins.

It's like taking in a steak and expecting them to cook it for you. It's not easy to make a living running a restaurant anyway, and selling wines is as much a part of their business as preparing the food. Many patrons don't really appreciate the cost of the glassware, labor and breakage, too. One local restaurant spends $300 per month in glasses and decanters, though that sounds high.

Most restaurants have a wide range of wines and many have some wines in the $20s, which is reasonable for casual places and meals. A few places have poor lists or grossly overpriced wines, however, and I don't hesitate to take wines there.

Wine prices should be in line with the food, however. If most people order pastas or pizzas for under $10 or $12, for example, there should be glasses for $5 or $6, and some decent bottles for no more than $20 or so. After all, you can buy perfectly acceptable wines at retail for $5 to $10 per bottle.

Wine pairings are becoming increasingly common for special meals, and they're appealing unless you have enough people to buy a number of different wines. Ken Frank says that two-thirds of his customers at La Toque choose pairings.

It's also appropriate to take a special bottle to a restaurant, but never one on a wine list.

Most people find markups high on bottles, however, though some restaurants set limits. Market charges $14 over standard retail; the Wine Train adds $15. Bistro Fumé and Brix charge twice their cost rather than the typical three times, Hurley's 2.5 times, sometime 1.5 times. Carneros Inn charges 1.7 times wholesale on selected wines. More typical is three times wholesale, which is about double retail. Most cut that for more expensive wines, however.

The real rip-off is wines by the glass, for many restaurants may charge the retail price of a cheap bottle for one glass – five times mark up! It's often worth the corkage charge to avoid paying $12 for a glass of wine as an aperitif, and surely for two.

One real lack in Napa Valley is good, inexpensive house wines such as those you find in Europe. Some excellent house-type wine is now becoming available in kegs, and some is sold in 3-liter boxes, but apparently many restaurants would rather not sell wine than offer a reasonable choice.

Free corkage

Some restaurants waive corkage all the time, while others do on quiet nights during the week to encourage local patronage. It's appropriate to take your wine in this case, and some places really encourage it.

A few places that waive corkage aren't really wine oriented, but some are fine places serving food as good as other restaurants in the valley.

In most cases, they find their cocktail, appetizer and dessert sales rise when people bring in a bottle of wine.

At Rutherford Grill, for example, general manager Don Wetherell says the table tab is actually higher when the patrons bring a bottle.

So feel free to take wine to places that offer free corkage, and especially patronize the places that have special no-corkage nights rather than staying home.

But don't take wine unless it's special to other places just to save a few bucks. Expect them to snicker if you take in Two Buck Chuck.

Some places, like Redd and Bistro Jeanty, really don't want you to bring in bottles, but if you can't find a wine you like there, you should probably be eating elsewhere – like Applebee's.

Here are restaurants that don't charge corkage at least on the first bottle (These are all subject to change, so check with the restaurant if it's important.) If I'm going to take a wine to a restaurant, I like to buy a bottle of bubbly or white wine for the first course or appetizer, then bring a bottle of something special:

- Barolo. 1475 Lincoln Ave., Calistoga. (707) 942-9900. www.barolocalistoga.com
- Bistro Sabor. 1126 First St., Napa. (707) 252-0555. www.bistrosabor.com
- Brannan's Calistoga. 1374 Lincoln St., Calistoga. (707) 942-2233. www.brannansgrill.com
- Checkers. 1414 Lincoln St., Calistoga. (707) 942-9300. www.checkerscalistoga.com
- Compadres Rio Grille. 505 Lincoln Ave., Napa. (707) 253-1111. www.compadresriogrille.com
- Cucina Italiana. 4310 Berryessa Knoxville Rd., Lake Berryessa. (707) 966-2433. www.cucinaitaliana.com
- Cuvée. 1650 Soscol Ave., Napa. (707) 224-2330. www.cuveenapa.com
- Downtown Joe's. 902 Main St., Napa. (707) 258-2337. www.downtownjoes.com
- Firewood Café. 3824 Bel Aire Plaza, Napa. (707) 224-9660. www.firewoodcafe.com
- Hurley's. 6518 Washington St., Yountville. (707) 944-2345. www.hurleysrestaurant.com
- Kitchen Door. 610 First St., Napa. (707) 226-1560. www.kitchendoornapa.com
- Market. 1347 Main St., St. Helena. (707) 963-3799. www.marketsthelena.com
- Pizzeria Tra Vigne. 1016 Main St., St. Helena. (707) 967-9999. www.travignerestaurant.com
- Rutherford Grill. 1180 Rutherford Rd., Rutherford. (707) 963-1792. www.rutherfordgrill.com
- Sushi Mambo. 1202 First St., Napa. (707) 257-6604. www.sushimambonapa.com
- Tra Vigne. 1050 Charter Oak Ave., St. Helena. (707) 963-4444. www.travignerestaurant.com

- Uva Trattoria. 1040 Clinton St., Napa. (707) 255-6646. www.uvatrattoria.com
- Vercelli. 1146 Main St., St. Helena. (707) 963-3371. www.vercelliristorante.com
- VINeleven at the Marriott. 3425 Solano Ave., Napa. (707) 253-8600. www.napavalleymarriott.com

Some free corkage

Napa Valley restaurants offering free corkage under some conditions:

- Allegria Napa waives Monday night
- Boon Fly Café Napa waives Thursday
- Fumé Bistro Napa waives Tuesday night
- Napa General Store Napa Local if they ask.
- Napa Valley Wine Train Napa waives for Napa County residents for first bottle
- Royal Oak at Silverado Resort Napa Free corkage Thursday
- Siena at Meritage Resort Napa Free corkage for locals Sunday through Tuesday
- Brix Yountville waives for locals
- Étoile at Domaine Chandon Yountville waives on Sunday
- Cc Blue St. Helena waives Wednesday for locals.
- Press St. Helena waives Wednesday
- Wine Spectator Greystone Restaurant St. Helena waives for 'regulars.'
- Solbar at Solage Calistoga waives Wednesday

Restaurant	City	Corkage for 750 ml bottle	* Waive corkage if buy bottle
A Taste of Himalaya	Napa		
Ad Hoc	Yountville	$20 (limit 2)	
Alex	Rutherford		
All Seasons	Calistoga	$10	* (No fee for wines from Castello di Amorosa)
Allegria Ristorante	Napa	$10	* Waive Monday night
Angéle	Napa	$20	* even halves

			and carafes
Auberge du Soleil	Rutherford	$30 (limit 2)	*
Avia /Arnaz	Napa	$15	Corkage free of locals 'if they ask.'
Azzurro Pizzeria e Enoteca	Napa	$15	*
Bank at the Westin Verasa	Napa	$20	*
BarBersQ	Napa	$15 up to 2	
Bardessono restaurant	Yountville	$20 (two maximum)	Waive for "locals"
Barolo	Calistoga	$15	* Waive on first bottle for locals
Bistro Don Giovanni	Napa	$20	* maximum 6 bottles
Bistro Jeanty	Yountville	$20 for first 2 bottles, then $25	*
Bistro Sabor	Napa	none	
Boon Fly Café at Carneros Inn	Napa	$15	* Waive Thursday
Bosko's	Calistoga	$10	
Bottega	Yountville	$25	*
Bouchon	Yountville	$20 (limit 2)	
Bounty Hunter	Napa	Not allowed	
Brannan's	Calistoga	**$15**	* Waive for locals on first
Brix	Yountville	$20 up to 2	Waive for locals..
Bui Vietnamese Bistro	Napa		
C Casa	Napa		
Ca' Momi	Napa	$10	*
Calistoga Inn	Calistoga	$15	*
Carpe Diem	Napa	$15	*
Celadon	Napa	$15	*
Checkers	Calistoga	**$15**	* Waive for locals and Wednesday
Cielito Lindo	Napa		
Cindy's Backstreet Kitchen	St. Helena	$15	*
Cindy Pawlcyn's Wood Grill & Wine	St. Helena	$15	

Bar			
Cole's Chop House	Napa	$25	* (including halves)
Compadres Rio Grille	Napa	none	
Cook	St. Helena	$15	*
Cucina Italiana	Lake Berryessa	none	
Cuvée	Napa	none	
Downtown Joe's	Napa	none for 1, then $10	
Eiko's	Napa	$10	None on Napa wines
Emmy Lou ('Pasta Prego' at night	Napa		
Étoile at Domaine Chandon	Yountville	$35 (1st) $50 (2nd) $75 (3rd) $50 (magnums)	*
Farm at Carneros Inn	Napa	$25	$15 industry corkage
Farmstead	St. Helena	$2	Fee donated to charity
Filippi's	Napa		
Firewood Café	Napa	none	
Fish Story	Napa	$15	*
French Blue	St. Helena	$10	
French Laundry	Yountville	$75 (limit 1 per 2 guests in party)	
Fumé Bistro	Napa	$10	* Waive Tuesday night
Gott's Refresher	Napa and St. Helena	$1	
Grace's Table	Napa	$10	*
Grill at Meadowood	St. Helena	$35	Waive for guests and members of Meadowood
Grill at Silverado Resort	Napa	$10	Waived Sunday
Grille 29 at Embassy Suites	Napa	$10	* Waive if order two entrees and an appetizer
Hog Island Oyster Co.	Napa	$15	*
Hurley's	Yountville	none	

Hydro Bar & Grill	Calistoga	$15	* Waived for Castello di Amorosa wine
JoLe	Calistoga	$15	*
Kitchen Door	Napa	none	
La Condesa	St. Helena		
La Strada	American Canyon	$15	*
La Toque	Napa	$25	* 4 bottles maximum
Market	St. Helena	none	
Mini-Mango Thai Bistro	Napa	$9.50	
Morimoto	Napa	$25	*
Mustard's	Yountville	$15	*
Napa General Store	Napa	$15	*
Napa Valley Wine Train	Napa	$15	* Also waive for Napa County residents for first bottle.
Norman Rose Tavern	Napa	$15	*
Oenotri	Napa	$15 for first, then $25	
Pacific Blues Café	Yountville	$5	*
Pearl	Napa	$12 ($6 donated to Napa Humane)	*
Press Restaurant	St. Helena	$25	*Waive corkage on Wednesdays,
Redd	Yountville	$25 each for 2, then $50	
Redd Wood	Yountville		
Restaurant at Meadowood	St. Helena	$50 (2 maximum) $100 magnum	Waive for members of Meadowood
Royal Oak at Silverado Resort	Napa	$10	
Rutherford Grill	Rutherford	none	*
Siena at Meritage Resort	Napa	$15	* Waive for locals Sunday-Thursday
Silo's Jazz Club	Napa	$30	*
Solbar at Solage	Calistoga	$20	*Waive

			Wednesday
Sushi Haku	Napa		
Sushi Mambo	Napa	none	
Tarla	Napa		
Terra	St. Helena	$20	*
Tra Vigne Restaurant	St. Helena	none	*
Pizzeria Tra Vigne	St. Helena	none	
Tuscany	Napa		
Uva Trattoria	Napa	None for first bottle	No corkage on first bottle, then $10.
Vercelli	St. Helena	none	
Villa Romano	Napa	$13	
VINeleven at Marriott	Napa	**none**	
Wine Spectator Greystone Restaurant	St. Helena	$20	* Waive for 'winemakers and vintners
ZuZu	Napa	$10	*

Enjoy Food with Wine at Wineries

Though it might seem prudent to encourage people tasting wine to pair it with food, county ordinances in Napa Valley – unlike almost every other wine region in the world – prohibit wineries from having restaurants.

That doesn't mean you can't enjoy your wine with food at wineries.

In fact, as everyone in Napa Valley knows, Domaine Chandon has a very nice restaurant called étoile and V. Sattui Winery has an excellent deli, though you have to sit outside on picnic tables. Both were grandfathered in when restaurants were outlawed in the winery definition ordinance passed in 1990.

That ordinance says, "Marketing of Wine – Any activity conducted at the winery shall be limited to members of the wine trade, persons, who have pre-established business or personal relationships with the winery or its owners, or members of a particular group for which the activity is being conducted on a prearranged basis. Marketing of wine is limited to activities for the education and development of the persons or groups listed above with respect to wine which can be sold at the winery on a retail basis and may include food service without charge except to the extent of cost recovery when provided in association with such education and development but shall not include cultural and social events unrelated to such education and development."

The reason for that rule was to force wineries to focus on wine as a product of the agricultural preserve, not ancillary activities such as restaurants, weddings, stores, inns, concerts and other activities.

Naturally, restaurants don't want wineries to have restaurants, either, which they consider unfair competition that might subsidize their food operations to promote their wine.

The winery definition ordinance seems to clearly says that the wineries can only serve food to the trade, existing customers and the like, not the general public. Desirable of not, that's the law.

Wineries in city limits, however, can operate under different rules than those in unincorporated county land. Siena Restaurant at the Meritage can also serve the Trinitas wines of its owner.

Soon, Charles Krug Winery will have a deli, too, a consequence of being in the city of St. Helena, where county rules for unincorporated areas don't apply. Likewise, St. Clair Brown Winery is building a winery and restaurant in Napa. Long Meadow Ranch has a restaurant, but it's not at the winery in the hills but in St. Helena.

It's surprising that no one else has built a winery and restaurant in any other Napa Valley city, in fact, as there are plenty of wineries and vineyards in city limits.

Wineries are allowed to hold marketing dinners including for wine club members, and many produce wine and food classes events well worth attending – but they're usually promoted only to club members or for the trade.

Partly to stand out – and partly to raise more revenue – more and more wineries are offering wine and food pairings to visitors. Many are just cheese and charcuterie, which after all go very well with many wines, but some are more elaborate. The county says you can't make a profit on the food, but I don't know how they enforce that rule. Food may allow you to sell more wine or charge more.

Here are examples of wineries that offer food pairings; the list is not intended to be exhaustive. The number offering food is expanding rapidly, too.

Nevertheless, though wineries (and the county) historically regarded tasting rooms as promotional vehicles for wineries, they are often revenue sources in themselves. "It's a way to generate some cash to support the visitors centers," says Craig Root, an expert of running tasting rooms. Some wineries keep a low profile on this subject because they're walking a fine line on permit issues.

Here are some wineries offering food pairings though these change rapidly, so check with the winery.

Cakebread Cellars

Cakebread Cellars is famous for its wine and food classes, including the annual American Harvest Workshop. It has run for chefs, media and a few consumers for 25 years.

For others, it has a wine and food pairing experience by prior appointment only: Thursday and Friday (and Mondays in peak season) from 11 a.m. to 12:30 p.m. The cost is $20 per wine club member, $40 for others.

It begins with a 30-minute mini-tour of the winery then a 30-minute interactive wine and food pairing featuring four recipes from the Cakebread garden. 8300 St. Helena Hwy., Rutherford. (800) 588-0298. www.cakebread.com

Ceja Vineyards

Since Ceja's tasting room is in the city of Napa, it can serve artisan cheeses and gourmet food items. 1248 First St., Napa. (707) 226-6445. www.cejavineyards.com

Darioush

Darioush offers two food and wine pairings. The 90-minute fine wines and artisan cheese experience offers guests an in-depth tour of the vineyard and production area, then culminates in the private barrel chai where they pair limited production and reserve wines with cheeses from Cowgirl Creamery. It's held daily at 2 p.m. by appointment. The cost is $50 per person.

The other offering is called By Invitation Only. Proprietor Darioush Khaledi pours sample from acclaimed châteaux of Bordeaux and Burgundy, alongside current releases of Darioush Signature wines in his private cellar. Explore, compare and celebrate the expression of terroir in a unique two hour wine experience hosted within Darioush Khaledi's private cellar.

They are served with bites designed by the Khaledis' private chef. By Invitation Only is offered at 11 a.m. on Friday, Saturday and Sunday for $150 per person. 4240 Silverado Trail, Napa. (707) 257-2345. www.darioush.com

Domaine Carneros

At Domaine Carneros, in addition to full meals, you can enjoy table service in the salon or on the terrace with caviar and artisan cheese.

In the tasting room, it offers lighter fare like panini and cheese boards to enjoy and enhance the Carneros wines. 1240 Duhig Rd., Napa. (707) 257-0101. www.domainecarneros.com

Kuleto Estate

Kuleto will offer Tuscan lunches paired with its wines at the winery. It does provide artisan cheese and small snacks such as nuts with tastings. 2470 Sage Canyon Rd., St. Helena. (707) 302-2209. www.kuletoestate.com

Merryvale Vineyards

Merryvale offers a wine and food pairing seminar with a behind-the-scenes tour of the winery and tasting of its wines with small samples of selected foods while discovering guidelines of food and wine pairing.

It is held the fourth weekend of every month from 10:30 a.m. until 12:30 p.m. for $20 per person, free to Profile Club members. 1451 Stanley Ln., Napa. (707) 252-8001. www.merryvale.com

Newton Vineyard

Newton Vineyards' consumer tours, held at 11 a.m. daily except Monday, cost $35 per person which includes a tour of the winery, then a tasting of Newton wines paired with a plate of walnuts, cheese, dried berries to complement the wines. 1 California Dr., Yountville. (707) 963-9000. www.newtonvineyard.com

Patz & Hall

The Patz & Hall Tasting Salon (also in Napa) offers seated, private tastings with six Pinot Noir and Chardonnays, and seasonal gourmet food complements. It costs $40 per person and lasts 60 to 90 minutes. 851 Napa Valley Corporate Way, Napa. (707) 265-7700. www.patzhall.com

Peju

In addition to its normal tasting flight, guests at Peju can try wine and cheese pairings, and wine and tapas pairings.

Wine and cheese pairings occur Thursday and Friday at 11 a.m. for $40 per person and include four artisan cheeses paired with four white/red whites.

Wine and tapas pairings take place Thursday and Friday at 1 p.m. for $60 per person and include four bite-sized tapas plates paired with four reserve/limited production wines.

It can add plates of charcuterie, cheeses, tapas or chocolate truffles that pair with a corresponding wine for groups. 8466 St. Helena Hwy., Rutherford. (707) 963-3600. www.peju.com

St. Clement Vineyards

St. Clement's event manager has a food and wine pairing background and is ramping up its focus on education and food and wine pairing. In addition to the regular $10 tasting, the winery has opened a single vineyard tasting room that allows guests to sit down at a table, customize their wine selections and get one-on-one attention.

The focus wines for this tasting are single vineyard offerings and the cost is $25. They add cheese and chocolate pairings for $10.

The cheeses are all California (Cowgirl Creamery Mt. Tam; Vella Jack from Sonoma; Laura Chenel Goat Cheese; Cypress Grove Humboldt Fog), and the platter includes olives and other local products. The chocolate tasting includes Guittard, Scharffen Berger and Ghiradelli. 2867 St. Helena Hwy., St. Helena. (707) 963-7221. www.stclement.com

St. Supéry Vineyards & Winery

St. Supery occasionally offers food and wine pairing such as pairing four cabernet with hors d'oeuvres prepared by its winery chef or an artisan cheese and wine pairing storage, uses and history. Each is $35 per person. 8440 St. Helena Hwy., Napa. (707) 963-4507. www.stsupery.com

Schramsberg Vineyards

In addition to regular tastings, Schramsberg offers a Sparkling Affair, a canapé and wine pairing with a tour of Schramsberg's historic caves offered only Tuesday through Friday at noon. The fee is $60 for consumers; $25 for Schramsberg Cellar Club members. 1400 Schramsberg Rd., Calistoga. (707) 942-4558. www.schramsberg.com

Robert Sinskey Vineyards

As Maria Sinskey is a world famous chef, it's not surprising that Sinskey offers special wine and food pairing for $20 as part of its regular wine tasting. Like other wineries, she does find the county ordinances restrict the winery's ability to offer food, however. 6320 Silverado Trail, Napa. (707) 944-9090. www.robertsinskey.com

Swanson Vineyards

Swanson offered one of the first elegant salon experiences in Napa Valley. The Jean Lafitte Tasting focuses on the wines Swanson is best known for such as the Swanson Pinot Grigio, Merlot, and Alexis, paired with individual plates of select artisanal cheeses and a signature Alexis Bonbon. It's $30.

Its Harvey Tasting is a bird's eye view of Swanson wines paired with individual plates of Swanson caviar, select artisanal cheeses and the bonbon. The cost is $55 per person including seven wines. 1271 Manley Ln., Rutherford. (707) 967-3500. www.swansonvineyards.com

Viader Vineyards & Winery

Viader offers lunches and dinners arranged in advance, typically for groups. 1120 Deer Park Rd., Deer Park. (707) 963-3816. www.viader.com

Restaurants with vineyards

While wineries in unincorporated parts of Napa County can't have restaurants (or inns, but see that section), some restaurants are surrounded by vines and may even serve their own wine, though not made on premise.

Meritage

The Meritage Resort has vineyards blanking the hill behind it and an unusual tasting room in a cave for its owner's Trinitas Cellars. It also has a number of eating options including Siena Restaurant. 875 Bordeaux Way, Napa. (707) 251-1900. www.themeritageresort.com

Brix

Brix just north of Yountville backs up on gardens and vineyards of the owner's Kelleher wines. It almost seems as if you're in a vineyard. 7377 St. Helena Hwy., Napa. (707) 944-2749. www.brix.com

Outdoor Cooking and Eating

If there's one hallmark of wine country living, it's cooking and eating outdoors. Some home chefs get by with simple gas or charcoal grills, but many others enjoy elaborate outdoor cooking areas. Some are almost as complete as the kitchens inside their homes.

Perfect for the mild climate, outdoor kitchens mirror those throughout the Mediterranean, where few homes have air conditioning to cool hot kitchens and grilled meats and vegetables are daily fare.

I've spent weeks in St. Tropez, Greece and Italy where virtually every lunch and dinner were prepared outside, even in restaurants. A similar trend is occurring in California's wine regions.

The appeal of outdoor cooking isn't just keeping the kitchen cool, however. Grilling food or roasting it in a wood-burning oven lends special flavors that seem particularly compatible with our signature wines. Many food writers find big Chardonnays and Cabernets difficult to match with food, but those reservations vanish with outdoor cooking.

Intense heat enhances and caramelizes sugars in food, and that complements the caramel and vanilla flavors characteristic of wine aged in oak. Likewise, smoky tannins from toasted oak match that from the fire. The subtle sugar in many wines also pairs well with caramelization, as it does with sweet marinades, rubs and sauces.

Even asparagus and artichokes, two vegetables hostile to wine, surrender gracefully when grilled. Other vegetables and fruit are simply better when fire roasted or grilled than steamed or boiled.

Flavors aren't the only appeals of grilling or roasting outside, however.

Outdoor cooking evokes primeval memories of cavemen throwing a pig on a fire. It's axiomatic that men cook outside, providing relief to their wives and helping keep the kitchen clean for at least one night. And guests love to stand around watching and even helping as they nibble on appetizers — perhaps from the grill — and sip wine.

The focus of outdoor cooking is naturally the grill. Many firms produce elaborate self-contained grilling centers, but a built-in barbecue is de rigueur for true outdoor kitchens.

These days, most homeowners opt for gas grills that can be started and controlled as easily as a kitchen range. Fats flaming as they hit hot surfaces and contact with hot grills lend smoky flavors and characteristic grid marks, but real connoisseurs still prefer hotter hardwood charcoal like mesquite. Some homeowners install both gas and charcoal grills for convenience plus authenticity.

Whether they cook with gas or wood, most home chefs add gas side burners so they can cook a whole meal outside and not have to run inside to check on the rice or beans. A rotisserie over a grill is popular for luscious poultry and roasts.

The rest of the kitchen follows naturally. A sink with running water is invaluable, and if you don't have hot water handy, a flash heater works fine — but it needs electric power.

People often include refrigerators, but they're really not necessary unless you're far from the kitchen. What *is* vital is a smooth work surface that can be cleaned easily, plus adequate storage. Often forgotten is a serving area near the grill, a huge convenience.

An outdoor kitchen can be as simple as a cheap throwaway grill or as elaborate as a $30,000 masterpiece, but few home additions return so much to their owners.

Brick Ovens Make Wine Country Memories

I can well remember the first time a wood-fired oven captured me. It was in La Botte, a restaurant in Sirmione, a tiny walled town at the end of a skinny 7-mile-long peninsula jutting into Lake Garda in northern Italy.

It was November and there were no other tourists around, but when I opened its door, the restaurant was loud and lively with animated groups waiting for seats while others enjoyed dinner as only Italians can.

A roaring fire warmed the room, or maybe it was the brick oven used for everything from flatbread and pizzas to casseroles and desserts. Wonderful aromas of roasted garlic and meat and onion and tomatoes filled the room. They even masked the ubiquitous cigarette smoke.

When I sat down, the waiter served wafer-thin rounds of flat bread — you'd call it pizza if there were any sauce on it, but it was just baked with sea salt and Lake Garda's unique green olive oil. Taking a bite, I could taste the soul of the fire, the smoke, the pleasantly bitter burned spots where the hand-formed dough was especially thin.

Pizza wasn't all that came out of that oven. I enjoyed roasted vegetables and homemade bread while people at adjoining tables shared chicken and pork roasted earlier that day, before the staff added wood to bake pizza.

As I watched the cooks, I thought that it seemed the most sensual possible way to cook.

A gift from Italy

Though wood-burning ovens were brought here from Naples to bake authentic pizzas, they also create unique flavors and textures for roasts, poultry, vegetables, bread and desserts.

The ovens have become de rigueur at wine country restaurants, and they're hot for homes, too. "All the high-end estates are installing them," says Jack Chandler, a Napa Valley landscape architect who finally got his own oven after designing them for many customers.

A wood-burning oven not only makes wonderful food, it creates wonderful memories. Whether you're preparing an elaborate benefit dinner for charity or pizzas for the family, a brick oven makes any occasion special. It's also good for family fun. Kids love to get their hands on the pizza dough.

With all their attractions, however, a brick oven is a lot like a vintage Jaguar: It's big, expensive and heavy, and requires a lot of care and feeding. You have to build a fire hours before you can cook, and often have to wait until the oven interior settles to the proper temperature.

You have to add wood regularly to maintain the right temperature: The heat ideal for pizza can incinerate a roast in minutes, yet the ovens are notoriously slow to cool. They can still measure 300 degrees 16 hours later.

In spite of these quirks, wood ovens are becoming fixtures at wine country estates, and it may not be too long before anyone can buy one for the back yard for a few hundred dollars, as in Italy.

For now, homeowners (and restaurants) buy prefabricated oven inserts that are enclosed in masonry shells. Inserts typically consist of a heavy compressed firebrick base fired at 3,000 degrees and a porous cast half-dome cover.

Most inserts come from Italy, and their $3,000 to $5,000 price is just a start. They can cost $25,000 to $35,000 by the time you've paid the architect, the county and the mason. "I call it my $100-per-slice pizza," jokes one owner.

Some people make their own ovens or commission custom versions, but inserts are easy, proven and they work.

Using the oven

Traditional ovens have a single opening for fuel and food as well as air and smoke. The door is used to regulate temperature by restricting oxygen.

The hot oven floor heats from below while the dome radiates energy from above, and if the oven is properly designed, swirling air currents provide natural convection heating that speeds initial heating and reduces cooking times.

Though you build a fire in the oven to heat it for any cooking, they basically operate in two modes: baking pizza, and cooking everything else.

To cook a pizza properly in just a few minutes requires a very hot oven and an open flame sustained by an open door. Under these conditions, the dome surface can reach 900 degrees, the deck 650 to 750 degrees.

For baking and roasting everything else, the door is closed once the oven is hot, then the oven cools to perhaps 550 degrees in an hour or two. The food bakes or roasts with the door closed and no flame.

As the oven cools, it's less finicky. Jack Chandler cooked a whole 57-pound pig in his oven. It was a tight fit, but he started it cooking at 11 at night and it was perfect by 8 the next morning. It remained in the slowly cooling oven until lunch. "It was fork tender and delicious," he says.

Most ovens are constructed outside, but they can also be installed in a kitchen if fire and building regulations are observed. A few people have both, so they can enjoy oven-cooked meals in both summer and winter.

Some localities restrict wood-burning devices to combat pollution; commercial pizza ovens often burn gas, and this may become necessary for homes one day. Even then, however, cooking with a brick oven won't be like using a microwave. Jack Chandler admits that his oven is a lot of trouble to use. "It's a pain in the butt," he says, "but it's a fun pain."

Hints for using brick ovens

The fire

Cook regularly, but heat the oven slowly. Thermal cycles stress the oven.

Start the fire with kindling and Weber odorless Fire Starter cubes, and use a combination of hardwoods. Almond burns fast, walnut poorly, but provides a good bed of coals.

Red oak burns well, leaving good coals. Local Napa oak is cheaper but burns fast. Manzanita is too hot. Don't use resinous pine or eucalyptus, which impart strange odors.

Baking pizzas and foccaccia

Add a small piece of wood to increase flames when cooking pizzas.

Don't use cooked tomato sauce for pizzas. The tomatoes get overcooked. Use fresh or canned San Marzano tomatoes put through food mill.

The finished pizza should have a dry bottom, the cheese should be melted and there should be black blisters on the crust. It should be a flexible, bread-like crust, not like a cracker. If it takes 4 minutes, the oven isn't hot enough.

Other baking and roasting

You can bake bread with the heat left over from making pizzas. Wood fires don't dry food as much as gas does, but inject water when baking bread — a clean garden sprayer is ideal.

To convert recipes, cook at 75 to 100 degrees higher than specified; if the recipe calls for 400 degrees, use the oven at 500 degrees—it will cook in half the times.

Tent poultry and other meat requiring long roasting with aluminum foil until three-quarters done, then remove foil for browning. It will cook faster than in a gas or electric home oven.

You can also cook stews in the oven, or hot-smoke meat by adding wood chips soaked in water to provide flavorful smoke.

Suppliers

Most suppliers focus on commercial applications; Mugnaini Imports is oriented toward home use as well as restaurants, and conducts cooking classes. (888) 887.7206 or (831) 761.1767. www.mugnaini.com.

Forno Bravo made my oven, which I bought from NapaStyle.

Renato Specialty Products Inc., (800) 876.9731 or (972) 864.8800.www.renatos.com.

Cooking Classes in Napa Valley

With all the interest in food in Napa Valley, you would expect plenty of cooking classes, and the valley does host many. However, there's no place that focuses on them. Instead, a number of organizations offer classes for amateurs. Two focus primarily on professionals, but also offer excellent classes for home cooks.

Cakebread Cellars

For more than 39 years, Cakebread Cellars has been committed to promoting the enjoyment of wine with food and the sharing in the pleasures of the table. To promote this, it offers a range of cooking classes throughout the year, held either in its winery kitchen or at its outdoor barbecue area with a wood-burning oven. It is one of the few places in Napa Valley to offer participation (hands-on) classes so that guests cook and learn alongside chefs and other food and wine lovers.

All classes are participation style with a tour of the property, a tasting of Cakebread Cellars wines, the cooking class and a three-course lunch paired with wine. All participants leave with a Cakebread Cellars logo apron, a booklet of the recipes and wine notes from the day, some great memories and quite often, new friends. 8300 St. Helena Hwy., Rutherford. (800) 588-0298. www.cakebread.com

CasaLana Gourmet Retreats

CasaLana in Calistoga offer Gourmet Retreats wine country cooking classes, culinary vacations and cooking vacations that help take your cooking to the next level.

The hands-on cooking classes are taught in CasaLana's professionally equipped kitchen and range in length from 5 hours to 5 full days.

Classes are limited to nine participants. All cooking classes include a multi-course meal of the recipes prepared served with wine. A three-day session is $650. 1316 S. Oak St., Calistoga. (707)942-0615. www.casalana.com

Cedar Gables Inn, Napa

Cedar Gables Inn in Napa hosts regular cooking classes with local chefs, who demonstrate the meal for the students to prepare, then enjoy with paired wine.

The four-hour classes are limited to 12 students and begin at 4 p.m. on Saturday. Any apron and the recipes are included. The cost is about $150

486 Coombs St., Napa. (707) 224-7969. www.cedargablesinn.com

Cooking with Julie

Professional chef Julie Logue-Riordan, who trained in France and formerly ran a cooking school, offers intimate, hands-on cooking classes that showcase the products and wines of the Napa Valley.

Her classes include tours of the Oxbow Public Market or Farmers Market in Napa to choose ingredients followed by a cooking class.

(707) 227-5036. www.cookingwithjulie.com.

Culinary Institute of America at Greystone

The CIA is one of America's top schools for professional chefs. When it opened, St. Helena prohibited classes for consumers for fear of attracting undesired crowds. Over time, the town has relented, and now the CIA offers a wide range of classes for foodies.

Its Food Enthusiast program has classes as short as two hours or as long as five days. Most are limited to 12 students, and they tend to sell out rapidly. The CIA also offers shorter demonstrations.

Two-hour "CIA Samplings" include a lecture and demonstration, followed by preparation of small plates, for $95.

The "Taste of CIA Cookbooks" series are naturally based on consumer cookbooks from the CIA. These classes last five hours with a lecture, hands-on instruction, lunch, a copy of the cookbook and a CIA apron for $250.

Short mini-classes unlock the flavors of chocolate or olive oil in 20 minutes at the institute's Flavor Bar and cost $10 to $15.

2555 Main St., St. Helena. (707) 967-2309. www.ciachef.edu.

Fatted Calf

The Fatted Calf in Napa is an artisanal charcuterie producing a wide range of hand crafted products using high quality, natural ingredients. It also offers a wide range of classes in everything from butchery to making charcuterie.

All classes are from 11 a.m. until 3 p.m. The class includes a morning snack, lunch and a bag of meaty goodies students helped to prepare. Most classes are $175 per person and fill quickly.

644 First St. # C, Napa. (707) 256-3684. To reserve, e-mail contact@fattedcalf.com. www.fattedcalf.com.

NapaStyle Cooking Classes

NapaStyle's Yountville store features cooking classes and demonstrations hosted by seasoned Napa Valley chefs and vintners.

The culinary program at is a celebration of extraordinary meals, entertaining tips, and personal recipe secrets.

V Marketplace, 6526 Washington St., Yountville. (707) 945-1229. www.napastyle.

Napa Valley College Cooking School

Napa Valley College has a professional cooking school at its Upvalley campus in St. Helena, and it also offers many food lover classes in evening and weekend classes.

The classes are taught by chef instructor Laura Lee and the school's executive chef, Barbara Alexander, as well as other experts including local chefs and authors.

Students eat the meals they prepare and receive the recipes.

The school also offers much sought graduation lunches where its students prepare and serve meals with wine.

The classes typically cost $75 to $100.

Upper Valley Campus, 1088 College Ave., St. Helena. (707) 967-2900 to register. www.napavalley.edu for class descriptions

Oenotri

Oenotri, the downtown Napa restaurant specializing in the cuisine of southern Italy, offers cooking classes on select Saturdays.

Chefs Curtis Di Fede and Tyler Rodde show students the secrets to creating pastas and pizzas in their own homes. Each class will focus on a specific food from southern Italy. Each class lasts two to three hours, ending with lunch prepared by class participants.

The cost for each of the classes is $75 per person. Classes fill quickly with a maximum of 16 people per class. 1425 First St., Napa. (707) 252-1022 ext. 1 or visit www.oenotri.com for details.

Silverado Cooking School

New Silverado Cooking School offers hands-on and demonstration cooking classes featuring chef Malcolm de Sieyes. He uses farm-fresh ingredients from his own farm, paired with ingredients from the finest local purveyors and world-class wines from Napa Valley.

Classes culminate with everyone sitting down together to enjoy the meal they've just prepared.

1552 Silverado Trail, Napa. www.silveradocookingschool.com (707) 927-3714

Other cooking classes

Restaurants, wineries and markets offer classes occasionally, as do Farmers Markets and the Napa Chefs' Market during the summer.

Olive Oil in Napa Valley

Though Napa Valley is known for its grapevines, it's also full of olive trees. The climate is perfect for the long-lasting trees, and they keep their leaves during the winter to provide color as well.

Many wineries in Napa Valley also maintain olive trees, either a few as landscaping, or whole orchards.

Olives are harvested after the grape harvest, making them complementary for growers who can use the same workers.

Olive trees, however, don't produce much of their precious oil, so it's a labor of love for most growers and vintners; many make so little oil they keep it for their own or their winery's use, though many sell some as well at their tasting rooms.

A number of stores in Napa Valley offer olive oil tasting, but only two companies – both noted wineries – press their own fruit.

Long Meadow Ranch and Round Pond Estates, both in Rutherford, have both olive orchards and mills or frantoios. Both allow visitors by appointment, and have tasting as well. November and December are generally the best times to see the pressing of the olives.

Long Meadow Ranch

Long Meadow Ranch in the hills above Rutherford has Napa Valley's oldest olive orchards. Abandoned for years, the orchards were hidden from view by new forests that grew over the original sites.

Although aware of a few olive trees when the Ranch was acquired, no one knew of the mysterious treasures to be uncovered.

Owners Ted and Laddie Hall discovered a large olive orchard hidden among much taller trees. This site contained over 250 mature trees that were last cultivated in about 1920.

More trees were found over time, and now the ranch has restored more than eight acres of olives with nearly 1,000 organically farmed mature trees.

Experts have been unable to identify the variety of olives, but they make fine oil.

The Halls propagated cuttings from the original olive trees to grow 1,500 new trees and developed other orchards of traditional Italian cultivars of Frantoio, Leccino, Pendolino and Moraiolo.

Long Meadow Ranch had a traditional stone grinding wheel among its modern olive-processing equipment. They make two organic extra virgin olive oils: Prato Lungo ($49 for 500 ml), the estate oil from Napa Valley's oldest olive orchards and Napa Valley Select ($25 for 375 ml), a blend of organic olive oils it crushes and blends.

Tasting and oils are available at the Long Meadow Ranch tasting room and Farmstead restaurant site in St. Helena. Call about visits to the frantoio.

Longmeadow Ranch and Farmstead Restaurant is at 738 Main St. in St. Helena. (707) 963-4555. www.longmeadowranch.com

Round Pond Estate

Round Pond Estate grows eight distinctive varietals of Italian and Spanish olive trees, each selected for flavors, aromas, superior reputations and compatibility with Napa Valley's climate.

It began importing and planting olive trees in 1998. Today, its olive orchards' 12 acres contains 2,200 trees, some over 100 years old and imported from Spain.

These estate-grown olive trees produce rich and fragrant extra virgin olive oils from the Tuscan-style fruity, green essence of Leccino olives to the rich and buttery flavors of Spanish Sevillano olives.

Each of the four gourmet olive oils is crafted from hand-harvested olives using traditional stone mill techniques with state-of-the-art technology. Traditional stone mill pressing provides less stress to the skins and pits, thereby exuding a smoother, less pungent oil; whereas, the hammer mill perforates the skins and pits of the olives to produce sharper, more robust flavors.

Round Pond makes four varieties of olive oil, Italian Varietal and Spanish Varietal (each $26 for 370 ml), as well as two flavored with citrus crushed with the olive, Blood Orange and Meyer Lemon (each $28). They also sell 50-ml nips for tasting for $7 each.

875 Rutherford Rd., Rutherford. (888) 302-2575. www.roundpond.com

Olive oil stores

In addition to the companies that process olive oil in Napa Valley, a number of stores here specialize in olive oils, some they process elsewhere.

Napa Valley Olive Oil Mfg. Company

Napa Valley Olive Oil Manufacturing Company in St. Helena is a quaint old-fashioned Italian grocery store hidden away on a back street.

It sells authentic Italian food, but olive oil is its specialty. Though it no longer presses the oil on site, some of the equipment is still around. Family owned and operated, the store has been in business since 1931 and its techniques and processes in olive oil making have not been altered.

The extra virgin and regular olive oil are sold by the jug and the prices are reasonable. They're not the peppery stuff, but mellow oil suitable for cooking as well as drizzling on food.

835 Charter Oak Ave., St. Helena. (707) 963-4173. www.oliveoilsthelena.com

Olivier

Established in 1995, Olivier began producing fine gourmet oils and savories for specialty stores. In 1999 it opened a retail store in St Helena. It offers tastes and bulk and packaged oils.

1375 Main St.. St. Helena. (707) 967-8777. www.oliviernapavalley.com

St. Helena Olive Oil Co.

St. Helena Olive Oil Co. in St. Helena has a tasting bar, and sells oils and related products. It's opening an outlet in downtown Napa at First and Franklin Sts.

St. Helena Olive Oil Co. 1351 Main St., St. Helena. (707) 968-9260. www.oliveoilsthelena.com

The Olive Press at Oxbow Public Market

The Olive Press at Oxbow Public Market is a retail arm of the Olive Press at the Jacuzzi Winery in southern Sonoma. The actual pressing is done at that site.

The Olive Press also presses olives for wineries and other olive growers. It, too, offers tastes, packaged and bulk oil.

The Olive Press at Oxbow Public Market.610 First St., Napa. (707) 226-2579. www.theolivepress.com

Many wineries and gourmet markets like Dean & Deluca, Oakville Grocery and Sunshine Market in St. Helena also sell local olive oil.

Grapeseed Oil

In addition to olive oil, Napa Valley produces grapeseed oil.

Though little known or used in America, oil pressed from grape seeds is popular in Europe. It offers a number of advantages over other cooking oils like high levels of antioxidants, low levels of saturated fat, and a high smoking point.

Now a Napa company that has been importing quality European oil is pressing oil from seeds of wine grapes from California's premium north coastal wine regions. Food & Wine, Inc., which uses Salute Santé as its brand name, is offering both blended and varietal oils, and yes, the Syrah oil tastes of Syrah wine, the Chardonnay of that wine as does the Merlot.

The extra-virgin, cold-pressed oils are extracted without heat or chemicals. The oils have the other health benefits of grapeseed oil and natural chlorophyll and lecithin and contain desirably biological active substances.

They have a subtle nutty flavor with the aromas of freshly fermenting wine and a rich buttery feel. Food & Vine's Valentine Humer suggests using the regular Salute Santé oils for most cooking, saving the varietal cold-pressed oil for enhancing foods. They're ideal for drizzling on cheeses, tomatoes and other foods or dipping bread in the way many people use olive oil.

The varietal and regular Salute Santé oils are available at NapaStyle and other retailers in Napa Valley.

They also make the oils sold at Castello di Amorosa.

Gourmet Chocolate in Napa Valley

Though it's unlikely to overtake wine, chocolate is becoming a star attraction in Napa Valley. New luxury artisanal chocolate makers are joining long-time local favorites to provide treats for every taste – and pocketbook.

The newest is Kollar Chocolates in the V Marketplace in Yountville, joining La Fôret in Browns Valley, Woodhouse Chocolate in St. Helena and venerable Vintage Sweet Shop in the Napa Mill and Anette's Chocolates in two locations on First Street.

All have enticing retail shops.

Le Belge Chocolatier, which doesn't have a store, also makes upscale chocolates in Napa. Many restaurants, wineries and stores offer chocolate treats, too.

Why all the activity? For one thing, there's a tremendous interest everywhere in chocolate as studies have shown its bitter polyphenols have many healthful properties. The Aztec rulers knew this, and drank chocolate much as we drink coffer – strong and bitter.

Not many Americans go that route, but wide interest in artisanal food products is fueling part of the activity.

And Napa Valley benefits as its reputation grows as a center for gourmet food ass well as wine.

And there's wine and chocolate. Many consumers love wine with chocolate, and wineries are happy to oblige them with pairings. Others argue that the sweetness of wine conflicts with wine, but that doesn't deter the fans.

Let's take a look at the chocolatiers.

Woodhouse Chocolate

Perhaps the highest visibility chocolatier in the valley is Woodhouse Chocolate in St. Helena. The windows in its upscale shop on Main Street are always filled with chocolate creations – many could easily be called sculptures – and its exquisite and expensive candies are jewel-like, an association reinforced by the Tiffany-like blue packaging materials.

Woodhouse was started almost 8 years ago by John and Tracy Anderson, who sold their family's S. Anderson winery, but wanted to stay in Napa Valley.

Tracy, who is mostly self-taught, makes the chocolates. Many are molded into traditional shapes, and often painstakingly decorated.

John runs the business. Their business is largely retail, much from the shop but also over the Internet. They don't wholesale the products for resale except to Gump's in San Francisco, though they do make chocolates for wineries, restaurants and corporations.

He adds, "Our products are very dear but of high quality. It's nice to have a little something that makes you happy."

They plan to introduce a chocolate club this year for those who like to get a treat in their mail occasionally. 1367 Main St., St. Helena. (707) 963-8413. woodhousechocolate.com

La Fôret

Though Woodhouse has a dozen employees, La Fôret just hired its first two – other than founder Wendy Sherwood and her part-time helper and husband Mark Sherwood (He has a full-time job at Vine Cliff Winery).

Wendy was the chef de partier at the French Laundry for 2 years before starting La Fôret in July 2010; she was previously at Woodhouse and earlier studied in France and worked under France's premier chocolatier.

Sherwood has two restaurant clients – Benu and Morimoto – and a few inn and winery accounts, but otherwise sells her chocolates from her small storefront in the Browns Valley Shopping Center and through an exclusive allocation program that has a waiting list.

She says that she wanted to take the fine dining esthetic to a chocolate shop: "At the French Laundry, no one says, 'It's too costly or too much trouble.' We're not trying to be the low-cost provider. We want clients that buy into our vision."

That's especially an issue now, for all chocolate is expensive, and high-end products like Valrhona especially so.

Sherwood likes to create over-the-top sculpture with her chocolates, too. She admits that most aren't ever eaten, however.

Her obscure location isn't a problem either. People find it on purpose, and few just come in to take a look. 3261 Browns Valley Rd., Napa. (707) 255-1787. www.laforetchocolate.com

Kollar Chocolates

The newest chocolatier in the valley is Kollar Chocolates. It opened only a few months ago.

Chris Kollar was the chef at renowned Peter Michael Winery, and worked at Go Fish, Tra Vigne and étoile at Domaine Chandon with 18 years experience all together.

He makes the chocolates, while Naomi Pasztor, whom he met in Switzerland, runs the business. She has a degree in hospitality and business.

Kollar says his vision is to make modern chocolates; many include unusual, often savory flavors such as fennel pollen and saffron. He uses a lot of colored cocoa butters to enliven the look of the pieces. "Brown, black, white – chocolate looks boring," he says.

A special treat for customers is that they can watch Kollar make the chocolates in his self-described 'fishbowl' in the shop.

He creates custom products for wineries and hotels and sells some chocolates wholesale. They also sell gelato.

V Marketplace, 6525 Washington St., Yountville.

(707) 738-6759. www.kollarchocolates.com

Two venerable chocolate companies shouldn't be overlooked, either.

Vintage Sweet Shoppe

Vintage Sweet Shoppe has been making chocolates for over 30 years, for 16 years in Brown's Valley, and in the Napa Mill for 7 years.

Owner Debbie Dever's 20 varieties of truffles, especially the wine-flavored ones, are very popular, but she's probably best known for the chocolate-covered wine bottles.

The bottles are shrink-wrapped with plastic, then carefully coated with chocolate so the label shows through.

Like the other shops, she makes the chocolates on site, but she alone has a wine and chocolate tasting bar.

The bar offers flights on wine with chocolate, featuring mostly local wines.

The shop also sells ice cream and other candies including toffee.

530 Main St. # B, Napa. (707) 224-2986. www.vintagesweetshoppe.com

Anette's Chocolate

The oldest chocolatier in Napa Valley is Anette's Chocolate, owned by Anette Yazidi and her brother Brent Madsen and his wife Mary Stornetta. They've been making chocolate for 30 years after taking over a confectioner at their present site on First Street near Franklin.

Brent makes the chocolate, Anette runs the retail store at that site and in the Oxbow public Market, and Mary handles wholesale and other sales. "We do a lot of wholesale business," notes Anette.

They also sell on the Internet.

They make a wide range of chocolates and other candies at their crowded factory. Their specialties are innovative brittles, chocolate wine sauces – and chocolates.

Most of the chocolates are sold at retail in their stores and locally, while the wholesale business is largely sauces and brittle.

Customers include upscale retailers like Williams Sonoma and wineries.

Many local wineries buy the sauces made with their wines.

Though it makes old-fashioned candies, Brent says 80 percent of the items are things they've added since they took over the business.

The innovations include chocolates containing salted caramels, Mayan nibs with a dusting of chili and other savory flavors. The most popular are dark chocolate truffles.

Though their chocolates are hand made and elegant, Brent doesn't focus as much on the decoration as do Woodhouse or La Fôret. They're more about eating than looking.

The store also makes its own ice cream, available only at the main location, and also offers coffee drinks and some pastries.

Anette says that business has grown every year but 2008 when it was flat, and the Oxbow location has also grown steadily.

Her brother Brent adds, "When the economy goes down, you sell more chocolate. It's a small luxury people can afford." Main location and factory, 1321 First St., Napa

Oxbow Public Market, 610 First St., Napa.

(707) 252-4228. www.anettes.com

Prepared foods

Beans

Well, they're not really prepared, but Steve Sando's Rancho Gordo beans are the Kobe beef of beans.

Steve has found rare artisanal heirloom native beans all over Mexico, and he grows them in California and Mexico. They're amazing, fantastic beans that don't taste anything like the cheap bags of dried beans in supermarkets. They're also fresh, less than a year old, so they cook up quickly and evenly. Some dried beans are never ready to eat.

Steve also sells hominy (pozole), chiles and chile powder, herbs and spices, amaranth and quinoa, popcorn, Mexican cooking vessels and handmade tortillas on Friday and Saturday.

You can buy Steve's beans in gourmet markets and some stores, but it's most fun to stop by his retail operation at 1924 Yajome St. (south of Lincoln), near downtown Napa. www.ranchogordo.com

Bread and pastry

Many Napa Valley Restaurants bake their own breads, but most buy from some excellent suppliers that also bake and sell pastries.

Be warned that they tend to sell out, so shop early.

Alexis Baking Company

Alexis Baking Company, locally called ABC, is near downtown Napa. Besides pastry – its focus – it also bakes excellent bread. It's very popular for breakfasts and lunches as well. 1517 3rd St., Napa. (707) 258-1827. www.alexisbakingcompany.com

Bouchon Bakery

Thomas Keller's Bouchon Bakery was created to supply his restaurants – the French Laundry, Bouchon and Ad Hoc/Addendum – but is now so popular that it's taken on a life of its own.

During the usual good weather, people enjoy their pastries and coffee at tables next to the bakery. It also serves excellent sandwiches. 6528 Washington St., Yountville. (707) 944-2253. www.bouchonbakery.com

Butter Cream Bakery

Immensely popular with some Napans, Butter Cream Bakery is not a good place for those watching their weight to eat or shop. It also serves popular breakfasts and lunch. 2297 Jefferson St., Napa. (707) 255-6700. www.buttercreambakery.com

Ca Momi

Better known for its authentic Neapolitan pizzas, Ca' Momi Enoteca e Pastecceria in the Oxbow Public Market also bakes exquisite light small pastries from Venice, the home of its owners.

The pastries – pastecceria – will tempt even the most weight-conscious to indulge. 610 First St., Napa. (707) 257-4992. www.camomienoteca.com

Model Bakery

Model Bakery has locations in St. Helena and the Oxbow Public Market in Napa. It bakes a wide variety of excellent bread, and also serves slices of pizzas, sandwiches and other items at both sites.

The store in St. Helena is a favorite hangout of locals, including Rep. Mike Thompson, the local Congressman who's so popular that even conservative Republican vintners support him and the Republican Party doesn't even bother to oppose him in any serious way. 1357 Main St., St. Helena. (707) 963-8192. www.themodelbakery.com

Model Bakery in Napa bakes in the afternoon as well as in the early morning, so you can get a fresh baguette for dinner a la Française if you stop in there. They sell bread at a discount as they approach closing time. 644 First St. # B, Napa. (707) 259-1128. www.themodelbakery.com

Sciambra-Passini French Bakery

Sciambra-Passini French Bakery doesn't have a retail store, but its breads are served at many Napa restaurants and is available in local markets other than the big supermarket chains that now bake their own bread, which is mediocre at best.

Sweetie Pies

As the name suggests, Sweet Pies in the Napa Mill specializes in pastries, but also serves light breakfasts and lunches. 520 Main St., Napa. (707) 257-7280. www.sweetiepies.com

Village Bakery

Calistoga's Village Bakery specialized is sweet pastries. It's popular for breakfast. 1353 Lincoln Ave., Calistoga. (707) 942-1443

Goat cheese

Though neighboring Sonoma is full of excellent cheesemakers, Napa has only one – Goat's Leap Dairy. It has a very small herd – some of its cheeses are named after the goat that produces the milk – but it's exceptional, if hard to find and expensive.

Honey

Many wineries now produce honey, for though grapes don't need pollination, ornamental and food crops that grow around them do.

In addition, funky Marshall Farms processes local honey in American Canyon. Some people swear that honey from local plants helps allergies, and they offer honey from specific areas like Napa County.

They sell retail at the farm and small processing plant.

Sauces, pickles etc.

A number of companies produce prepared sauces, dips, fruit purees and other prepared products labeled with the Napa name, and some are even in Napa Valley. Others just borrow the name like Napa Valley Mustard Company in Beaverton, Ore.

Among those in the valley are Mezzetta, Tulocay's Made in Napa Valley, Napa Valley Products and the Perfect Purée.

They are sold in many stores and winery tasting rooms, some of which offer their own brands of such products. The Napa Valley Traditions store in downtown Napa sells many such products including its own Wine Country Kitchens brand.

Gourmet Shops and Delis in Napa Valley

Napa Valley is the home of many gourmet food markets, some masquerading as supermarkets.

CalMart

CalMart in Calistoga is an independent supermarket blended with a gourmet market and deli. It has a large selection of cheeses, real butchers, a wide selection of items, some you might not even find in other Napa Valley markets (four kinds of kimchi...) It's similar to Sunshine Market in St. Helena, and Vallerga's and Brown's Valley Markets in Napa. 1491 Lincoln Ave., Calistoga. (707) 942-6271. www.calmartnv.com

Dean & Deluca

Dean & Deluca in St. Helena is owned by local resident Lesley Rudd, who also owns the original branches in New York and one in North Carolina. It has almost every gourmet food you can imagine, kitchen tools, a small selection of fresh produce and a huge assortment of Napa Valley and other wines.

It also has a popular deli, though there's no seating in the store. Many people take their sandwiches next door and buy a bottle of Flora Springs Wine to accompany it on the roof patio.

Don't even think of crossing busy Highway 29 to picnic at V. Sattui. Even if you aren't run over, only food from the V. Sattui deli is allowed there. Dean & Deluca. 607 St. Helena Hwy., St. Helena. (707) 967-9980. www.deanandeluca.com

Sunshine Foods Market

Sunshine Market is where people who can shop in St. Helena, though they may buy cat food and paper towels at the large Safeway hidden off Main Street.

It's a combination supermarket and deli, with a real butcher section, sushi made onsite and an amazing assortment of beautiful vegetables and fruit.

It also has a remarkable selection of very good cheeses and will offer samples and cut cheese to order.

Prices tend to be high, but in most cases, that's because of the quality of the products. 1115 Main St., St. Helena. (707) 963-7070. www.sunshinefoodsmarket.com

Giugni's Deli

Guigni's Del in downtown St. Helena reportedly should be spelled Giugni's, but a sign painter got it wrong years ago and they just left it like that.

It sells meat, cheeses, candy and other products, but is primarily known for its excellent sandwiches. It's dingy and crowded, suggestion a place that that's been there a long time – and has been. 1227 Main St., St. Helena. (707) 963-3421.

NapaStyle

Michael Chiarello's NapaStyle features a wide variety of gourmet foods as well as panini made to order, salads and other treats – plus wine. V Marketplace, 6525 Washington St., Yountville. (707) 945-1229. www.napastyle.com

Napa Valley Olive Oil Manufactory

The Napa Valley Olive Oil Manufactory hiding at the end of Charter Oak Ave., the road between Farmstead and Tra Vigne, is a local legend and favorite.

Owned and run by a family from Lucca in Tuscany, it's the place residents send guests if they've had enough pretention.

It no longer crushes and presses the olives on site, but buys olive oil from a source in the Central Valley. It sells both pure olive oil for cooking and a very fruity Extra Virgin oil that tastes like ripe olives. You can buy it in sizes from nips for your picnic to gallons, and at reasonable prices.

Almost everyone in Napa Valley uses the oil, though some like the sharper style that Tuscans have made popular.

The Olive Oil Manufactory also has a large assortment of products imported from Italy and elsewhere, much in bulk.

It also sells cheese cut to order, salumi and is even the local source for bacalao (salt cod).

A few picnic tables among the trees welcome those who want to assemble a rustic picnic, too. 835 Charter Oak Ave., St. Helena. (707) 963-4173. www.oliveoilsainthelena.com

They're opening a branch in the Tourist Information Center in downtown Napa featuring tasting, too.

V. Sattui Winery and Deli

V. Sattui Winery is the only winery in Napa Valley with a deli – at least until Charles Krug completes its deli in2013.

It's a very good deli, too. In addition to making excellent sandwiches, it has a dizzying array of salads, entrees, desserts, cheeses – and wine.

It's best to taste wine first, then choose a wine that complements your food.

You can picnic outside under giant oaks, but no food or beverages other than those bought on site are allowed. 1111 White Ln., St. Helena. (707) 963-7774. www.vsattui.com

Oakville Grocery

Oakville Grocery was once a country market, but it's gone upscale. Especially after a recent renovation to open it up and reduce the crowded jostling to order, and buy food, it's a delight to shop for gourmet items and get sandwiches and salads for a picnic.

It also has a large collection of local wines, and at times, sells produce from a farmstand in the back from owner Lesley Rudd's extensive gardens.

There are picnic tables in the back, and even beer on tap outside during pleasant weather. 7856 St. Helena Hwy., Oakville. (707) 944-8802. www.oakvillegrocery.com

Vallerga's Market

Vallerga's Market is the Napa version of Sunshine, an excellent upscale market that sells superior produce, meat from real butchers who are happy to hack off a chunk from a leg of lamb or clear shellfish on order.

It also has an impressive deli, rolls sushi on site and has an impressive cheese and bread section as well as salad, soup and olive bars.

A few tables offer seating, but it's not very inviting in the busy parking lot at Redwood and Highway 29 (really on Solano Road). 3385 Solano Ave., Napa. (707) 253-8780. www.vallergas.com

Browns Valley Market

Browns Valley Market is in upscale Browns Valley, a semi-isolated enclave of west Napa entered through a gap in the western hills.

Except for no sushi made on site, it offers the same attractions as Sunshine in St. Helena and Vallerga's Market in Napa: excellent produce, cheese, a deli and old-fashion butcher section plus friendly local service.

If you can't find a meat elsewhere in Napa Valley, you can probably get it here – if not today, tomorrow. If you're a hunter, you can even get them to butcher your deer or pig.

You won't find tourists here, just locals. 3263 Browns Valley Rd., Napa. (707) 253-2480. www.brownsvalleymeat.com

Genova Delicatessen

Genova Delicatessen on Trancas St. in north Napa is everyone's vision of a classic Italian deli, except maybe not as cramped.

Though it sells all sorts of foods and beverages imported from Italy, the real draw is the sandwiches and prepared food. A counter lines almost the whole length of the store, and the busy staff prepares every conceivable variety of sandwich and dishes up salads, pasta and desserts.

You can also buy cheese and salume, or get an espresso from the bar. That's also the place to pay for stick food items if you don't want to wait for the sometimes long line of people waiting for sandwiches made to order.

A couple of small tables outside aren't very inviting, though the food prepared certainly is. 1550 Trancas St., Napa. (707) 253-8686. www.genovadeli.net

Whole Foods and Trader Joe's

Just to be complete, we should mention Whole Foods and Trader Joe's almost next to each other in the Bel Aire Plaza at Trancas and Highway 29. They're also good sources of gourmet items, included prepared food and at Whole Foods, sandwiches and other items made to order.

They're very popular with locals and I catch wealthy vintners and chefs shopping there – sheepishly when they're caught, like a celebrity seen at a naughty movie.

If you don't have either where you live – or they can't sell wine there – be sure to mosey around and weep. For that matter, even the local big chain supermarkets have wine sections that put wine stores in many places to shame. Bel Aire Plaza, Trancas Street at Highway 29, Napa.

Oxbow Public Market

The Oxbow Public Market in Napa is in a class by itself with its restaurants and food vendors. See its description on page 52.

Farmers' and Chefs' Markets

We can't overlook the Farmers' Market held during the summer in Napa, St. Helena and Calistoga.

Napa's are on Tuesday and Saturday next to Oxbow Public Market, while St. Helena's is Friday in Crane Park hidden from Highway 29 and Calistoga's Saturday downtown, all to noon.

While their emphasis is on vegetables and fruit to take home and prepare, they also sell many prepared items, too, many ready to eat.

The Chef's Markets Thursday nights during the summer in Napa also have small produce markets but mostly sell food to eat there, some definitely more gourmet than usual street food.

Cookware Stores in Napa Valley

In addition to being a center for wine and food, and increasingly the arts, Napa Valley is home to passionate food lovers, both professional and amateur. They include chefs, food writers, video producers and compulsive home cooks.

They can buy their ingredients from many sources up and down the valley, from the Oxbow Public Market to Cal Mart, from farmers' markets during the summer to Vallergas, Sunshine, Brown's Valley Market, Whole Foods – and even Trader Joe's.

But the valley also boasts some remarkable stores that feature the tools to prepare wonderful food. A few have been magnets for foodies for a long time, but four have undergone significant changes of late, one moving into a large new site downtown.

Let's take a look at these kitchenware stores:

Dean & DeLuca

Unlike the other stores highlighted, Dean & DeLuca just south of St. Helena is also a gourmet food store as much as a kitchenware store, but its selection is wide and impressive.

It leans toward the high end, but don't forget to check put the selection of tableware in the back of the adjoining wine section. Some would be at home in a bistro in Lyon.

While there, you're likely to be seduced buy the incredible selection of food items, especially the cheese and charcuterie. They also prepare foods to enjoy on a picnic and a many local wines. 607 South St. Helena Hwy., St. Helena. (707) 967-9980. www.deandeluca.com

NapaStyle

NapaStyle in Yountville is the retail store of TV star chef, and according to my female friends, heartthrob, Michael Chiarello. It's in back of V Marketplace in Yountville right across from his Bottega restaurant, one of the toughest reservations in Napa Valley.

It sells many unique products, many super stylish and innovative. Quite a few are repurposed antiques and imports from Europe and perfect to live the Napa lifestyle.

The store sells a number of Michael's food gourmet products, too.

And you can also grab a panino or salad there, or taste some wines from Michael's own company. While you're there, you might want to try to get into Bottega; sometimes just showing up works better than trying to reserve.

V Marketplace, 6525 Washington St., Yountville. (707) 945-1229. www.napastyle.com

Shackford's Kitchen Store

Shackford's Kitchen Store is Napa's venerable cooking store. Recalling nothing as much as a crowded old-time hardware store when you have to get help to find many items, Shackford's stocks an incredible variety of equipment for both chefs and home cooks.

Just look for tall John Shackford. He's all business but can help you with anything. I once went in to buy a new $20 carafe for my coffee maker, and he sold me a 75 cent piece of plastic instead.

Its stock of parts for kitchen tools like mixers, food processors and coffee makers is legendary.

When I lived in San Francisco, Sur La Table referred me to Shackford's for parts for my Kitchen Aid mixer.

They have real chef's clothing, too, so you can make like Emeril to impress your guests.

The prices are good, too, and they can get your knives and food processor blades sharpened – bring them in on Thursday.

The store's clerks still write your order in small pads with carbon copies, but they will take credit cards...

Shackford's is on the edge of downtown on Main Street, an easy walk from the center though you'll likely need you car for the treasures you buy.

Shackford's Kitchen Store.1350 Main St., Napa. (707) 226-2132. www.

Spice Islands Marketplace at the CIA at Greystone

The strangely named Spice Islands Marketplace is the campus store at the Culinary Institute of America in the old Greystone Cellars north of St. Helena. The store was recently moved, expanded and upgraded into a destination of its own.

Unfortunately, it's a treacherous snare if you like to cook or bake.

Stylist, utilitarian, developed just for America's top cooking school or sold everywhere, it's likely to be for sale here.

The school has partnered with some leading brands to create special versions with its logo. They're first rate if not bargains.

Many of the other stores mentioned carry cookbooks, but the CIA is in a class of its own. If you can't find a cookbook here, it's probably not in English – or is out of print.

It features books by the many food writers who call Napa Valley home, as well as its own textbooks. and those written by its staff.

If that weren't enough, it has chocolate and olive oil tasting bars, and sells those products, too.

The Culinary Institute of America at Greystone.2555 Main St., (Hwy 29)St. Helena. (707) 967-2309.www.ciastore.com

Steves Kitchenware

Steves (no apostrophe) Hardware has been a staple on St. Helena's impossibly appealing Main Street for ages. Now it's built an adjoining annex filled with every imaginable food–preparation and serving item, from utilitarian cheesecloth to fancy machines and serving dishes.

It has an especially large assortment of innovative and interesting serving ware.

I defy any food nut to leave Steves without buying something useful or desirable. You can also slip next door and buy some nails or a shotgun.

A hint: Park in back.

Steve's Hardware.1370 Main St., St. Helena. (707) 963-3423. www.acehardware.com.

Top Picnic Areas at Napa Valley Wineries

Everybody loves a picnic at a winery except Napa County. Though almost every visitor to Napa Valley, and most of us who live here, imagine nothing could be more fun than enjoying a picnic at a winery while drinking the winery's wines, Napa County bureaucrats prohibit picnicking at most wineries.

In particular, picnicking is prohibited at the places that first come to mind, those wineries with great views such as Sterling, Castello di Amoroso, Viader, Burgess and Silverado, as well as at the "classic" Napa Valley legends, Mondavi, Beringer, Rubicon and Beaulieu. In some cases, it may be the preference of the owners that disallows them rather than law.

In addition, though the state has softened its rules about allows consumption of other than tastes at wineries, Napa County ordinances overrule them. In a nutshell, wineries have to apply for permission for picnics, and to my knowledge, it's no longer granted for new wineries, thought it's difficult for me to imagine how enjoying a winery's agricultural product with a picnic lunch on its property threatens the agricultural preserve.

A number of wineries do allow picnics. A few are in city limits, where different laws apply, and others are grandfathered in. You can get a more extensive list at the website of the Napa Valley Vintners, but remember that a few wineries aren't members (like RustRidge and Nichelini, two prime sites for picnics).

Here are my ten favorite sites for picnics. It was hard to pick them.

It's wise to call to reserve; some places require it. You're expected to buy a bottle or so, and no other alcoholic beverages are allowed.

Charles Krug Winery

Charles Krug Winery is the historic, oldest commercial winery in Napa Valley, and it has a shady picnic grove. Come the end of 2013, it will even have a deli so you can buy your picnic on site. 2800 Main St., St. Helena. (707) 967-2200. www.charleskrug.com

Clos Du Val

Clos Du Val in the Stags Leap District offers a pleasant picnic area not far from Napa. It's far off the highway in a shaded area. 5330 Silverado Trail, Napa. (707) 261-5200. www.closduval.com

Cuvaison

Cuvaison Estate Wines in Calistoga has a picnic area that's not too far off the Silverado Trail, but still offering a nice experience. Note that its winery in Carneros doesn't allow picnics. 4550 Silverado Trail, Calistoga. (707) 942-6266. www.cuvaison.com

Menage a Trois and Napa Cellars

Menage a Trois and Napa Cellars, which share a winery and bizarre geodesic tasting room in Oakville, have a pleasant picnic area under the trees. They offer especially good picnic wines, too. 7481 St. Helena Hwy., Napa. (800) 535-6400. www.folieadeux.com

Frank Family Vineyards

Frank Family Vineyards in Calistoga is one of the premier picnic location on the valley floor.

You can taste at the new tasting room in a restored farm house, then enjoy your picnic at one of the tables on the well-tended ground.

They have sparkling as well as still wines to accompany your picnic. 1091 Larkmead Ln., Calistoga. (707) 942-0859. www.frankfamilyvineyards.com

Louis M. Martini Winery

At the historic Louis M. Martini winery, the picnic grounds are in a pleasant enclosed, shaded area behind the winery.

The wines include some only found at the winery including rosé and Moscato Amabile. 254 St. Helena Hwy., St. Helena. (707) 963-2736. www.louismartini.com

Nichelini Winery

Nichelini Winery is high in the hills off highway 128 east of Rutherford almost in Chiles Valley. It's still owned by the same family who founded it in the last 19th century.

Aside from the delightful old winery and picnic grounds, it features an unusual white Sauvignon Vert as well at classic reds. Parking is just part (east) of the winery along the mountain road. 2950 Sage Canyon Rd., St. Helena. (707) 963-0717. www.nicheliniwinery.com

Rustridge Ranch

Rustridge Ranch and Winery in high Chiles Valley east of Napa is everyone's image of the wine country life. In addition to growing grapes and making fine wines, it raises thoroughbred horses, and even has a small B&B if you can't tear yourself away from the site after lunch.

If you don't want to pack a lunch, Cucina Italiana at Lake Berryessa not far away makes box lunches that you can order in advance at lest on weekends and enjoy at the ranch. 2910 Lower Chiles Valley Rd., St. Helena. (707) 965-9353. www.rustridge.com

Rutherford Grove Winery & Vineyards

Rutherford Grove features a classic picnic ground, with a square of towering trees framing the picnic tables. 1673 St. Helena Hwy., St. Helena. (707) 963-0544. www.rutherfordgrove.com

Rutherford Hill Winery

Rutherford Hill Winery has perhaps the top picnic destination in Napa Valley, and yes, that "top" is a double meaning.

The picnic tables lie high above the valley floor, above even tony Auberge du Soleil so with arguably better views. The picnic area is very popular, so be sure to call ahead. 200 Rutherford Hill Rd., Rutherford. (707) 963-1871. www.rutherfordhill.com.

V. Sattui Winery

V. Sattui Winery in St. Helena is in a class by itself. It now has the only deli at a winery in Napa Valley, and in fact, you have to buy your food and wine there if you want to enjoy the pleasant picnic grounds. 1111 White Ln., St .Helena. (707) 963-7774. www.vsattui.com

Top Breakfasts in Napa Valley

Though most inns and hotels offer breakfasts to their visitors, Napa Valley has many other great places to grab an early morning bite.

The choices include bakeries and coffee companies where you can get pastries, notably the Model Bakeries in Napa and especially St. Helena and Francophile favorite Bouchon Bakery in Yountville.

Most Mexican restaurants serve breakfast, as do the ubiquitous taco trucks, and, of course, so do chains like Denny's (still a great value) and Black Bear Diner in Napa.

Most hotels welcome those who aren't guests for breakfast, too, and the Andaz/Avia/Hyatt downtown is even positioning itself as the site for power breakfasts.

In addition, some regular restaurants offer brunches on weekends, some quite upscale. This chapter, however, focuses on the locals' favorite breakfast spots, all serving lunch, too. A few offer dinner.

American Canyon

Canyon Café

Canyon Café is one of two traditional breakfast places in American Canyon.. It serves large portions at reasonable prices, just what you expect from such eateries. 3845 Broadway St. or Highway 29. (707) 644-5011.

Highway 29 Café

The definitely funky Highway 29 Café does the same and perfectly fits the affectionate classic description of a greasy spoon. Just off Highway 29 at South Kelly Rd. (707) 224-6303 www.highway29cafe.com.

Carneros

Boon Fly Café

The Boon Fly Café at the Carneros Inn just outside Napa on the way to Sonoma is named for a local character from the past. It's an attractive upscale spot for breakfasts as well as lunch and dinner. It serves classics and imaginative breakfasts, but don't think of skipping the miniature homemade donuts, even if you're on a diet. 4048 Sonoma Hwy., Napa. (707) 299-4900. www.thecarnerosinn.com

Moore's Landing

Out on the Napa River in Carneros at the end of Cuttings Wharf Road, Moore's Landing serves breakfast Wednesday through

Sunday – but only until 11. Period. The choices are both Mexican and American favorites. 6 Cuttings Wharf Rd., Napa. (707) 253-7038. www.mooreslandingnapa.com

Napa

Alexis Bakery Co.

A local favorite is Alexis Bakery Co. on the edge of downtown. While its baked goods such as cinnamon bread have many fans, it also serves a wide variety of creative breakfasts. Order, pay and sit down – if you can find a seat. One is sure to open soon, and outside seating is an alternative in the usual good weather. 1517 Third St., Napa. (707) 258-1827.www.alexisbakingcompany.com

Black Bear Diner

The Black Bear Diner is part of a small local chain, and is famous for enormous servings (and patrons...). The slab of ham served with breakfast, for example, is more than most people would eat for dinner, not a thin slice. The best-selling breakfast is chicken-fried steak with gravy and eggs plus potatoes and toast! 303 Soscol Ave., Napa. (707) 255-2345. www.blackbeardiner.com

Buttercream Bakery and Cafe

With a name like Buttercream Bakery and Cafe, you know you're not in a health-food restaurant, but locals flock to the venerable restaurant for its delectable eats starting at 5:30 a.m. Its menu is straight diner, but it does feature a few lighter items as well as many rich bakery specialties. 2297 Jefferson Ave., Napa. (707) 255-6700. www.buttercreambakery.com

Emmylou's Diner

Emmylou's Diner is a classic American shopping center diner. You won't run into tourists, just locals chomping down on traditional diner favorites plus a few California classics like huevos rancheros and salsa. 1429 W. Imola Ave., Napa. (707) 224-6339. www.emmylousdiner.com

Gillwood's

Gillwood's, the Napa branch of the popular St. Helena eatery, is smack downtown, if hidden a bit in the Shops at Town Center. A step above a greasy spoon or diner, it offers outside seating for good weather plus some tasty choices beyond the expected, like the delicious salmon scramble of eggs with smoked salmon, cream cheese and capers, or a breakfast casserole of Italian sausage sautéed with potato, onion and tomato and topped with melted cheddar and jack cheeses and poached eggs. 1320 Napa Town Center, Napa. (707) 253-0409. www.gillwoodscafe.com

La Crepe

Almost all the vendors that sell food to eat at the Oxbow Public Market serve breakfast, from C Casa tacos and eggs and chorizo to Pica Pica arepas filled with eggs to Ca' Momi's pizza with bacon and eggs.

But La Crepe is a tempting destination for breakfast with a varieties of sweet and savory crepes, though I doubt many Frenchman eat crepes filled with sausage, scrambled egg and cheddar doused with maple syrup for breakfast. They're more likely to have a croissant and save the crepes for lunch or dessert. 610 First St., Napa. (707) 925-5410. www.lacrepenapa.com

Napa Valley Coffee Roasting Company

Napa Valley Coffee Roasting Company is a compact long-time coffee house that sells a few pastries. It's at 948 Main St., Napa. (707) 224-2233. www.napavalleycoffee.com

Ritual Roasters

To be comprehensive, we include this coffee booth in the Oxbow Public Market. You can buy food from at least eight vendors in the Market to complement the coffee drinks here. 610 First St., Ste. 12, Napa. (707) 253-1190. www.ritualroasters.com

Soscol Café

The Soscol Café is another classic greasy spoon serving huge portions at reasonable prices. Expect a wait outside to grab a seat at the bar in this tiny place, which is always packed with friendly locals, some attracted because they can get a beer for breakfast, after they get off the late shift at work, of course. 632 Soscol Ave., Napa. (707) 252-0651.

Yountville

Coffee Caboose

Coffee Caboose is a coffee shop in one of the cars in the Railroad Inn. In addition to coffee and pastries, it now makes crepes. 6523 Washington St., Yountville. (707) 738-1153. www.yountvillecoffeecaboose.com

Pacific Blues Café

Pacific Blues Café serves breakfast, but that's fine except for the crowds. A favorite of visitors as well as locals, the newly expanded and remodeled café sits in front of the popular V Marketplace.

In nice weather, sit outside on the patio. Omelettes are a specialty, but a local favorite is the massive breakfast burrito; it's very tasty, but you don't want to know all that's in it! 6525 Washington St., Yountville. (707) 944-4455. www.pacificbluescafe.com

French Blue

New French Blue is an unusual new restaurant in St. Helena: It serves breakfast, lunch and dinner, emphasizing local ingredients including from owner Leslie Rudd's gardens and pastures. Seating is on the patio and inside. It's already a local favorite, and you can see famous winemakers there almost any time. 738 Main St., St. Helena. (707) 963-9181. www.frenchbluenapa.com

Gillwood's

Gillwood's will satisfy almost any breakfast craving. Like the Napa site, it goes beyond the usual suspects, but it's a little tight – though there are some little-known tables in back. There's usually a short line, but you can shorten it by eating at the communal table, where you'll likely meet some interesting folks – perhaps a famous winemaker. 1313 Main St., St. Helena. (707) 963-1788. www.gillwoodscafe.com

Model Bakery

The Model Bakery has long been a favorite for European-style breakfasts of breads or pastries and coffee, but it does serve quiches and a few other breakfast items. 1357 Main St., St. Helena. (707) 963-8192. www.themodelbakery.com

Napa Valley Coffee Roasting Company

St. Helena's long-time Napa Valley Coffee Roasting Company is definitely a local hangout. It's off Main Street and fills with residents of St. Helena, seemingly not always welcoming of others. 1400 Oak Ave., St. Helena. (707) 963-4491. www.napavalleycoffee.com

Calistoga

Calistoga is full of coffee purveyors, most offering light breakfasts. Here are the places that serve more conventional American breakfasts.

Café Sarafornia

Café Sarafornia gets its name from the utterance of slightly inebriated town founder and Mormon Sam Brannan, who famously referred to his new town as the "Calistoga of Sarafonia" when he meant to say the "Saratoga of California."

A diner without a dining car, it's great for classic dishes as well as California favorites – plus Budapest coffee cake, cheese blintzes, apple crepes and lox and bagels with cream cheese for homesick visitors from the East Coast.1413 Lincoln Ave., Calistoga. (707) 942-0555. www.cafesarafornia.com

Calistoga Kitchen

Calistoga Kitchen serves an ingredient-driven menu with healthy choices from local farms, gardens and vineyards for breakfast, lunch and brunch on weekends.

Enjoy your meal on the patio, in the dining room or call it in to go.

The lunch menu has a house-made veggie burger with cashews, quinoa and mushrooms; avocado salad with toasted nori, togarashi, sesame, and butter lettuce; and a B.L.T. on local bakery bread with avocado.

Calistoga Kitchen. 1107 Cedar St., Calistoga,on the corner of Cedar Street and Lincoln Avenue.

It is open Thursday, Friday, Saturday and Monday from 8 a.m. to 3 p.m., and for Sunday brunch from 9:30 a.m. to 3 p.m. (707) 942-6500. www.calistogakitchen.com.

Cheeseburgers in Our Paradise

Since most people believe we live in paradise, we might note that Jimmy Buffett likes his Cheeseburger in Paradise:

> "Medium rare with mustard 'be nice; Heaven on earth with an onion slice; I like mine with lettuce and tomato; Heinz 57 and French-fried potatoes and big kosher pickle and a cold draft beer."

Cheeseburger in Paradise, © Jimmy Buffett.

But what burgers do we in Napa Valley like best? We took a survey of locals to find out what they think. We asked about both independent restaurants and chains; there was a little overlap: Is Squeeze Inn a chain? We called it one. Is Gott's? We said it wasn't. Probably inconsistent.

Even if there are a few locations, they are a long way from either to McDonald's!

Among the independent restaurants on the list:

- Andie's Café at Napa Premium Outlets. 1042 Freeway Dr., Napa. (707) 259-1107. www.andiescafe.com

- Angèle Restaurant. 540 Main St., Napa. (707) 252-8115. www.angelerestaurant.com

- Bank Café at the Westin Verasa. 1314 McKinstry St., Napa. (707) 257-1800. www.westinnapa.com

- Boon Fly Café. 4048 Sonoma Hwy., Napa. (707) 299-4900. www.thecarnerosinn.com

- Farmstead Restaurant. 738 Main St., St. Helena. (707) 963-9181. www.farmstead napa.com

- Gott's Roadside in St. Helena and Napa. 933 Main St., St. Helena. (707) 963-3486. and 644 First St., Napa. (707) 224-6900. www.gotts.com

- Norman Rose Tavern. 1401 First St., Napa. (707) 258-1516. www.normanrosenapa.com

- Silverado Grill. 1600 Atlas Peak Rd., Napa. (707) 257-5400. www.silveradoresort.com

- Red Rock Back Door BBQ & Burger Joint. 1010 Lincoln Ave., Napa. (707) 252-9250. And Red Rock North at 4084 Byway East, Napa. (707) 253-2859.

Among the chains, In-N-Out blew the competition away:

- In-N-Out Burger. 820 West Imola Ave., Napa. (800) 786-1000. www.in-n-out.com

- Squeeze Inn Hamburger. 3383 Solano Ave., Napa. (707) 257-6880. www.squeezeinnhamburgers.com

No other chain got more than two or three votes for anything except Wendy's got four third places. It's my favorite after In-N-Out, but there's really no contest.

We also asked people what *kinds* of burgers they liked best. The duck burger at Bank was a surprise favorite of many, but many respondents naturally mentioned cheese burgers with various cheeses: cheddar, blue, pepper jack and white cheddar.

Unfortunately, a few rare problems have scared most chains and many other to cook burgers well done, which is a travesty unless they meat is very juicy (i.e., fatty). Certainly the freshly ground beef at many places is not a health worry.

And finally, we got a few votes for veggie and turkey burgers, but I'd say, "Why bother?" Nothing beats a great juicy burger. You can have a salad for lunch tomorrow or enjoy a falafel sandwich instead.

Favorite Mexican Restaurants

It's really asking for trouble to try to list the ten best Mexican restaurants in Napa Valley, so we'll wimp out and call it my ten favorite Mexican – and Mexican-American -- restaurants.

As anyone who moves here from elsewhere soon learns, the Mexican food here is often distinctive, and quite unlike that you find in Texas, Arizona or Southern California, where I once lived.

That partly reflects the origins of the Mexican immigrants to the Valley, many of whom come from central western Mexico, namely Michoacán, Jalisco, Guanajuato and Zacatecas, as well as Oaxaca further south. By contrast, much of the Mexican food Americans know best comes from Northern Mexico.

Yet Mexico has a tremendously rich culinary heritage, and the various regions are as distinctive as the notoriously diverse regions of Italy or China. Fortunately, it's all tasty, just different.

Some of Napa's most popular Mexican-influenced restaurants are unabashedly Gringo, but that's not necessarily bad. The food at these restaurants, like that of most immigrants from poor areas, tends to be richer and more elaborate than "authentic" food, but we obviously love it deep fried and slathered in guacamole and sour cream.

Here's an example from Armadillo's: "Grande, a giant tortilla filled with rice, beans, lettuce, sour cream and guacamole choice of chicken, carnitas or chili verde." Maybe not a diet special and nothing you'd be likely to find in a small village in Mexico, but tasty.

Other restaurants are more authentic, serving food the people back home are more likely to eat. They're often less expensive. Some of the best places to pick up real food to take out are Mexican markets, including La Luna in Rutherford.

And how can be forget the ubiquitous taco trucks, which have great food at very reasonable prices.

At least two taco trucks, Tacos La Playita (1851 Old Sonoma Road) and Tacos Michoacán (Soscol and Lincoln), have opened small cafés, which are also favorites. That's where you can get your lengua, buches, cabeza, menudo and tripa.

I believe all of the restaurants listed serve beer (and a few token wines) and most offer "Margaritas" made from 20 percent agave wine.

A few have full bars. Many also have authentic Mexican beverages such as horchata.

First, four popular places that serve tasty Gringo-style food:

Armadillo's

Bright, cheerful place. Comfortable for anyone who's not ready for challenging selections. 1304 Main St., St. Helena. (707) 963-8082.

Compadres Rio Grill

Compadres Rio Grill offers authentic food of southern Mexico, but most people go for the Mexican-American favorites. It has a full bar and deck overlooking the river with music on Sundays during the summer. Year round, it offers $1 tacos on Taco Tuesday along with specials on beer and Margaritas, and attracts a big crowd. 505 Lincoln Ave., Napa. (707) 253-1111. www.compadresriogrill.com

Pacifico Restaurante Mexicano

Popular restaurant and bar with. Décor suggests a vacation in Mexico. A favorite for hanging around and enjoying the full bar. 1237 Lincoln Ave., Calistoga. (707) 942-4400. www.pacificorestaurantemexicano.com

Red Hen Cantina

With its large outdoor patio, the Red Hen remains popular even after moving from its former location north of Napa. Don't look for down-home traditional food, but American Mexican favorites and a happy bar scene. 4175 Solano Ave., Napa. (707) 255-8125. www.redhencantina.com

And six more authentic but also very popular places:

Puerto Vallarta

Nice hole in the wall with minimal atmosphere but tasty and authentic food. 1473 Lincoln Ave., Calistoga. (707) 942-6563.

Don Perico

My grandkids' favorite is this downtown Mexican eatery. It's a friendly, family-style place with large servings of food; enchiladas are the specialty. It has a fair number of seafood and shrimp specialties. 1025 First St., Napa. (707) 252-4(707) www.donpericomex.com

Villa Corona

Regarded by many Napans as their favorite Mexican restaurant, Villa Corona serves large portions of tasty food. It's always packed, so take out is popular, but it's not a place for lingering. 3614 Bel Aire Plaza, Napa (707) 257-8685 and 1138 Main St., St. Helena. (707) 963-7812. www.villacoronamex.com

Taqueria Rosita

Taqueria Rosita recently expanded, a result of its continuing popularity. Reasonable prices; you can get a small burrito for $3. 1214 Main St., Napa. (707) 253-9208.

Frida's Mexican Grill

Frida's gets raves from many people for its family-friendly attitude and fine food including seafood. 1533 Trancas St., Napa. (707) 252-3575. www.fridasnapavalley.com

La Taquiza Fish Tacos

La Taquiza makes fried Baja-style fish tacos (and with healthier variations and other fillings) as well as other Mexican food popular in Southern California. 2007 Redwood Rd., Napa. (707) 224-2320. www.lataquizanapa.com

Mexican markets like La Luna in Rutherford, Azteca Taqueria in St. Helena, and Market and Taqueria, and Mi Familia, La Morentina, Taco Loc, La Chiquita Mexican Market, La Mariposa Market, Latino Market, Mi Favorita Market, Pueblo Market and Quezada Market in Napa also prepare tacos and similar items to go.,

The Food Truck Phenomenon

Like other hip parts of America, Napa is being invaded by food trucks (and trailers).

The communities are still not sure how to treat them. Some see them as competition to local restaurants that avoid taxes and restrictions, while others see a manifestation of the independent American spirit offering affordable prices.

Napa has long hosted many "taco trucks" featuring Mexican food like tacos and burritos at very reasonable prices. The city mostly ignored rather than dealt with them, but an explosion of gourmet trucks and especially gatherings of the trucks forced the city to create regulations. They're still in flux, but for now, you can generally find about a dozen trucks around the city.

They serve good food at good prices (especially the taco trucks) but aren't the genre-bending efforts of Portland, Austin or Los Angeles.

They include:

- Crossroad Chicken
- Dim Sum Charlie
- La Esperanza Taco Truck
- Marks the Spot
- Pastronomy
- Phat Salads and Wraps
- Santa Maria BBQ Truck
- Tacos Michoacan
- Tacos Chavez
- Taqueria Michoacan Taco Truck

Check online at their Facebook or web pages for their locations and hours; they're as capricious as gypsies.

Restaurants by city

This listing of almost every restaurant in Napa Valley does not include chains, whether casual dining places like Applebee's, Sizzler or Chipotle, or fast food like KFC or Wendy's, though some, like In'n'Out Burger, serve superior products at amazing prices.

I've taken the liberty to mark the places you're most likely to find me with an asterisk*. That's mostly a factor of geography (I now live in Napa) and type of food rather than a reflection on the quality of the offerings.

Napa Restaurants

A note about all the restaurants making their own beer: California has some surprisingly weird liquor laws. One allows any restaurant with a brewpub license to sell spirits with the $12,000 license. Otherwise, they have to buy a liquor license on the open market for perhaps $200,000.

In the past, it took quite a bit of expensive equipment and skill to make beer, but now restaurants can buy simple and small automated equipment and buy easy-to-use materials. So many do, including Morimoto, Fish Story, Silo's and more. Since they have to make a certain amount of beer, they may sell it inexpensively since the real purpose is to allow them to sell cocktails. Some of the beer is just fine.

Alexis Baking Company (ABC)

ABC is a local favorite for breakfast and lunch as well as baked goods with a focus on pastries. It can be crowded but most people don't linger and the tables outside are pleasant in the usual good weather. 1515 Third St. (707) 258-1827. www.alexisbakingcompany.com

Allegria Ristorante

Allegria serves Italian favorites and is very popular with locals including for its happy hour specials. Housed in an impressive former bank, it has a private dining space in the old vault and a well-screened outside dining area. 1026 First St. (707) 254-8006. www.ristoranteallegria.com

Angèle*

Angèle is Napa's top French restaurant. It's also the only one, but that shouldn't detract from its reputation. It serves excellent, mostly traditional French food. It also has a great outdoor seating area on Napa River for good weather (with heaters when it's marginal). Inside, it's cozy, with a popular bar. It's a favorite of locals. 540 Main St. (707) 252-8115. www.anglerestaurant.com

Asia Café

Asia Café with its prominent "Chop Suey" sign lies on Main Street across from Veteran's Memorial Park between ZuZu and Fagiani's in one of the most visible spots in town. The scruffy place looks leftover from another era, and the only patron I've talked to said the food was cheap but mediocre. 825 Main St. (707) 224-0840.

Andaz

The Andaz hotel offers a great breakfast, no lunch, but does serve dinner. The bar in the lobby and the patio upstairs, however, are

great places to hang out. 1450 First St. (707) 224-3900.
napa.hyatt.com

A Taste of Himalaya

Vaguely connected via family relationships to restaurants in
Sonoma, St. Helena and elsewhere, A Taste of Himalaya serves
Nepalese food, which is very similar to northern Indian food – tasty
but mild. The tandoori, curries and other foods won't disappoint,
and neither will the prices. 376 Soscol Ave. (707) 251-3840.
www.himalayaca.com

Azzurro Pizzeria e Enoteca*

Azzurro serves the best thin-crust American pizzas in Napa Valley.
It also offers some pastas, appetizers and side dishes as in a
pizzeria in Italy. Interestingly, most of the menu is vegetarian and
the verde pizza with spinach, ricotta, garlic and peppers is
addictive. Azzurro is full of locals, many from the wine business,
most enjoying the intriguing wines as well as the pies. 1260 Main
St. (707) 255-5552. www.azzurropizzaria.com

Bank at the Westin Verasa

Bank Café and Bar is the "other" restaurant at the Westin Verasa
hotel. The food comes from famed La Toque, but is cheaper, more
casual and simpler. It offers burgers and other fare, but the big deal
is the nightly French regional dinners. Each week, a different part
of France is highlighted with a three-course menu for $34. 1314
McKinstry St. (707) 257-1800. www.westinnapa.com

BarBersQ

Though co-founder and chef Steve Barber is gone, BarBersQ
continues to serve excellent BBQ and other comfort food in Bel Aire
Plaza. They've created a sheltered enclave outside surrounded by
greenery; it's noisy inside. The food is uniformly good, though I'm
partial to the friend chicken and collards offered only on certain
days. The roots restaurant offers many specials and winemaker
dinners. 3900 Bel Aire Plaza. (707) 224-6600. www.barbersq.com

Bistro Don Giovanni*

Donna and Giovanni Scala's bustling Bistro Don Giovanni lies on
Highway 29 at the north edge of Napa, but even people upvalley
have always claimed it as one of their own.

If I had to pick my favorite restaurant in the whole valley, it would
likely tie with Bottega.

Crowds fight for its excellent Italian and country French specialties
prepared on the wood-burning oven and mesquite grill, as well as
other treats from Donna and chef Scott Warner.

The porch is ideal for dining and is protected during inclement
weather. It has an excellent wine list and full bar offering trendy

favorites that attracts a hip crowd. It serves lunch and dinner daily. 4110 Howard Ln. (707) 224-3300. www.bistrodongiovanni.com

Bistro Sabor

The Ceja family isn't satisfied with a winery and upcoming brewery, or a downtown tasting room and art gallery. Scion Ariel has opened Bistro Sabor serving great regional Mexican and other Latin food.

It features Salsa dancing on weekends but note that it starts late, so be patient. 1126 First St. (707) 252-0555. www.bistrosabor.com

Boon Fly Café at Carneros Inn

Great breakfast places are rare in Napa Valley since most inns and hotels offer free eats. Boon Fly Café at the Carneros Inn is one of the standouts, though it's a bit out of Napa on Carneros Highway (Highway 12/112). It also serves excellent lunches and even casual dinners. 4048 Sonoma Hwy. (707) 299-4900. www.thecarnerosinn.com

Bounty Hunter Rare Wine & Provisions

The Bounty Hunter began as a wine store and tasting bar, but it's now definitely a casual restaurant and bar with exceptional barbecue and great wine and even spirits. The wine store has shrunk into the walls. 975 First St. (707) 226-3976. www.bountyhunterwine.com

Buckhorn Grill

Buckhorn Grill is a modest steak and sandwich house, part of a small chain. Its specialty is tri-tip sandwiches. They're salty but reasonable in price. 1201 Napa Town Center. (707) 265-9508. www.buckhorngrill.com

Bui Vietnamese Bistro

Napa is weak on ethnic restaurants, not including French, Italian and Mexican, which are indigenous. Bui offers fine Vietnamese food in a casual setting. 976 Pearl St. (707) 255-5417. www.buibistro.com

Ca' Momi*

Ca' Momi in the Oxbow Public Market is a restaurant serving authentic Neapolitan pizzas and other pizzas as well as a limited selection of other Italian foods. They also serve their own wines at low prices and serve killer desserts.

Try one of Napa's bargains for value and food. Just don't ask them to change anything. They only do it their way, which includes no hot peppers or Parmesan to sprinkle on pizzas even though my experience in Italy is that the accommodating people will do anything you ask. 610 First St. (707) 257-4992. www.camomienoteca.com

Carpe Diem*

One of the new gems of downtown Napa, Carpe Diem ("seize the day") is a wine bar with small bites that has turned into a real restaurant. It's run by a young couple, Stephanie and Scott Kendall, and wine director Steve Distler.

Stephanie is the welcoming host, Scott mans the stoves, producing innovative dishes that work, and Steve finds interesting wines, some small local brands, some rare imports. Their happy hour specials can't be beat. The only downside: It's always crowded with locals. 610 First St. (707) 257-4992. www.carpediemwinebar.com

C Casa

C Casa is an innovative Taqueria offering both traditional Mexican food and innovative lighter fare. It's a long way from fried burritos and greasy chiles rellenos. They have a nice outdoor deck and music on Sundays during the summer. 610 First St. (707) 226-7700. www.myccasa.com

Celadon

You have to know where Celadon is to find it, but you'll be rewarded. Hiding in the middle of the Historic Napa Mill behind the lobby of the Napa River Inn, Greg Cole's comfort global fusion restaurant was a pioneer of great food in downtown Napa.

It has a large protected patio with heaters for cool evenings and off season as well as seating inside. The food marries the best of Asia and California and overdelivers for the price. Greg has also mastered combining innovation with producing tasty food, not a feat easily learned. 610 First St. (707) 226-7700. www.celadonnapa.com

China Light Restaurant

China Light is one of the three downtown Chinese-American restaurants. Predictable old-timey American favorites but reasonable. Fine for the family or when you hanker for sweet and sour pork or chop suey and fortune cookies. 1012 First St. (707) 226-2809.

Cielito Lindo

Cielito Lindo is a new addition to Napa's downtown restaurant scene. It features the food of Gulf and Pacific Mexico as well as familiar items. It's run by a family from Puerto Vallarta that has lived here and worked in local restaurants with a chef from Vera Cruz. 610 Main St. (707) 226-7700. www.cielitolindonapa.com

Cole's Chop House

Napa's simmering lust for giant steaks and other classic American meals is satisfied by Greg Cole, Cole's Chop House on Main Street at Napa Creek in downtown Napa.

Located in a hundred-year-old stone building, the classic steak house restaurant features a great bar where patrons sip classic martinis and Cosmopolitans, the main floor with high ceilings and a comfortable mezzanine and a patio.

The food is straight out of a traditional Chicago steak house, and that's where the meat originates. The salads include the classic Caesar — complete with whole anchovies fillets.

The specialties are steaks, naturally, but chops, fish, chicken and even a short stack of portobellos also tempt diners. A ribeye provided me two take-home lunches, and I think even a high-school football player would be filled by the huge porterhouse. It's basically the same as the famous Florentine steak served in Italy.

The portions are mostly all immense, and in fact, the classic side dishes are served for two family style.. The sides include creamed spinach, fried onion rings, and seasonable specialties such as asparagus.

The calorific desserts make no attempt at political correctness, but will tempt anyone who has appetite left.

The wine list includes many big Napa Valley Cabernets, including some difficult to find. Prices for the wine and food are fair, but not cheap, as appropriate for the quality and quantity provided. The restaurant is packed at key times, but does accept reservations. Dinner only. 1122 Main St. (707) 224-6328. www.coleschophouse.com

Compadres Rio Grille

Compadres Rio Grille is a bit of a hybrid. It's an immensely popular destination for Mexican-American classics like tacos Americans with ground beef, chips and salsa and fajitas but its Mexican chefs also make many traditional dishes as well.

It features many specials including a taco party with $1 tacos and cheap beer and Margaritas on Tuesday, happy hours, and bands on its deck along the river on Sundays.

Prices are reasonable. 505 Lincoln Ave. (707) 253-1111. www.compadresriogrille.com

Cuvée

Cuvée is the restaurant for the River Terrace Inn. It offers good food, including on the courtyard and in the lounge. It features many specials. 1650 Soscol Ave. (707) 224-2330. cuveenapa.com

Don Perico Restaurant

My grandkid's favorite Mexican restaurant is Don Perico. It offers tasty Mexican-American favorites at good prices. It also has outdoor seating. 1025 First St. (707) 252-4(707) www.donpericomex.com

Downtown Joe's Restaurant

A popular local hangout on the river featuring a microbrewery and restaurant serving pub grub. It jumps on Friday and Saturday night with live bands and young crowds. It has seating next to Veterans Park and the Napa River. 902 Main St. (707) 258-2337. www.downtownjoes.com

Eiko's

Eiko's is a Japanese restaurant combined with a hip lounge. It serves traditional and innovative food based on Japanese cuisine including excellent sushi and sashimi, and the lounge features nouveau cocktails made with liquid nitrogen and other treats beloved of millennials. 1385 Napa Town Center. (707) 501-4444. www.eikos.com

Grille 29 at Embassy Suites

No one probably chooses to eat dinner at an Embassy Suites unless they're tired and unwilling to venture out, but Grille 29 at the Embassy Suites will feed you dinner if you need it.

On the other hand, the breakfasts for guests are great, and you can eat there if you talk to the front desk. 1075 California Blvd. (707) 226-1990. www.embassysuites3.hilton.com

Emmy Lou ('Pasta Prego' at night)

Emmy Lou's Dinner is the classic breakfast and lunch café, but at night, it morphs into a white-tablecloth Italian restaurant.

The food is standard Italian-American, good and ample, but probably a bit overpriced for the location and ambience On the other hand, it's a great place to dine before productions at nearby Napa Valley Players, one of the valley's top non-professional but excellent theatres. 1429 West Imola Ave. (707) 224-6339. www.emmylousdiner.com

Farm at Carneros Inn

Farm is the "fancy" restaurant at the Carneros Inn. It offers excellent farm-to-table food from its own gardens and also has an inviting bar with extensive outdoor covered seating. The resort also has Boon Fly for casual food and a private restaurant at the top of the hill for guests. 4048 Sonoma Hwy. (707) 299-4880. www.thecarnerosinn.com

Fillipi's Restaurant

Fillipi's Restaurant is the epitome of the neighborhood Italian-American restaurant (Napa being the size of a neighborhood in San Diego, where the restaurant originated). The food is ample, cheap and filling if not gourmet. 645 First St. (707) 255-4455. www.realcheesepizza.com

Firewood Café

Firewood Café is a sleeper. It serves very reasonable and tasty wood-fired-oven thin-crust pizzas at ridiculously low prices. It also has some sides and pastas. The wine is overpriced (if not by Napa standards, but for a $9 pizza), but they charge no corkage and a Trader Joe's and Cost Plus World Market with cheap wines are only a few hundred feet away. 3824 Bel Aire Plaza. (707) 224-9660. www.firewoodcafe.com

Fish Story

Fish Story is an attractive restaurant on the Napa River in the Riverfront development. It's part of the Lark Creek Group that owns such restaurants as One Market and Yankee Pier.

Fish Story naturally highlights seafood, including some San Francisco and another traditional favorites, but also offers plenty for the meat eater. It offers nightly specials like Cioppino on Tuesday. 790 Main St. (707) 251-5600. www.fishstorynapa.com

Frati Gelato

In addition to exquisite gelati and sorbetti, Frat Gelato serves panini, coffee, pastries and even wine. It's in the Riverfront complex on the Napa River.

Gillwoods

The Gillwoods in Napa (There's one in St. Helena, too.) hides in the former Shops at Town Center downtown, which is being upgraded. It serves typical American breakfasts and light lunches and offers outdoor seating, too. 1320 First St. (707) 253-0409. www.gillwoodscafe.com

Gott's Roadside

Gott's Roadside Gourmet is the Napa branch of the exceptionally popular drive-in in St. Helena once called Taylor's Refresher. It's famous for its eclectic and upscale menu as well as serving wines you wouldn't expect in a drive in. You can eat inside or on the patio under shade. 644 First St. (707) 224-6900. www.gotts.com

Grace's Table

Grace's Table is popular with locals for its eclectic food, much with Latin inspiration. It's a block off First Street in the booming West End District and a block from the Uptown Theatre with its popular shows. Its brunches are popular on weekends. 1400 Second St. (707) 226-6200. www.gracestable.net

El Guadalajara Restaurant

Neighborhood Mexican restaurant in east Napa. 1520 Silverado Trail. (707) 253-1840. elguadalajaranapa.com

Hog Island Oyster Co.*

Hog Island Oyster Co. in the Oxbow Public Markets serves impeccably fresh shellfish, much from its own oyster and mussel beds in Tomales Bay. Along with bivalves on the half shell, you can get them grilled, fried and in soups and stews. They also serve some fish and a surprisingly popular grilled cheese sandwich. Great fried oyster sandwich – they call it a loaf, but it's on a bun. 610 First St. (707) 251-8113. www.hogislandoysters.com

Il Posto

Il Posto is a new neighborhood Italian-American restaurant in north Napa. Most of the offerings are familiar and well prepared. It's always full of locals. 4211 Solano Ave. (707) 251-8600. www.ilpostonapa.com

Joy Luck House

Joy Luck House is yet another Chinese-American restaurant, but hard to find behind Walmart. 1144 Jordan Ln. (707) 224-8788. www.joyluckhousenapa.com

Kitchen Door

The Kitchen Door is chef Todd Humphries' casual but excellent restaurant in the Oxbow Public market. Humphries has simplified his gourmet food to make it more accessible and it's tasty but not pretentious. You can eat at the bar and watch the cooks or enjoy the deck in good weather. 610 First St. (707) 226-1560. www.kitchendoornapa.com

La Strada

La Strada is an old-time Italian-American restaurant on Highway 29 south of Napa in American Canyon. It's probably most popular with those living in or staying in American Canyon. 6240 California 29 American Canyon. (707) 226-3027. www.lastradanapa.com

La Taquiza Taqueria

La Taquiza Taqueria specializes in Baja-style fish tacos, which are traditionally friend and served with chopped cabbage and mayonnaise-based sauce or crema on a corn tortilla. La Taquiza offers many other tacos, however. 2007 Redwood Rd. (707) 224-2320. www.lataquizanapa.com

La Toque

La Toque is one of the top destination restaurants in Napa Valley. Chef Ken Frank uses the freshest local ingredients, many from a garden he tends with other chefs, to produce innovative but tasty meals. The optimum experience is a multi-course tasting meal with paired wines, as he and his staff have an exceptional sense of wine and food pairing. The bad news is that the meals are expensive, but the food and experience justifies it.

La Toque is at the Westin Verasa hotel and you can enjoy food from La Toque's kitchen at the informal Bank Café and Bar in the lobby and on the pool (and river) side patio. Frank offers a truffle feast during the fungi's season at during the Napa Valley Truffle Festival. 1314 McKinstry St. (707) 257-5157. www.latoque.com

Le Crepe

La Crepe, which is owned by a Frenchman, serves authentic sweet and savory crepes made in front of your eyes in a wide variety of fillings and combinations. It also serves fresh fruit juices. It's in the Oxbow Public Market. 610 First St. (707) 925-5410. www.lacrepenapa.com

Mandarin Chinese Restaurant

Mandarin Chinese Restaurant is one of the many Chinese-American restaurants in Napa, and perhaps one of the better ones. 1675 Trancas St. (707) 224-8507. www.mandarinpalacenapa.com

VINeleven (Marriott Hotel)

Though it has little atmosphere – it 's open to the lobby of the hotel – VINeleven serves better than expected food. Prices are a pleasant surprise, too, enough that even locals eat at the hotel. Barbecue is a specialty of the chef. You can also eat outside by the pool. 3425 Solano Ave. (707) 253-7433. www.napavalleymarriott.com

Mini Garden Chinese Restaurant

Mini Garden Chinese Restaurant is another adequate Chinese-American restaurants. 3381 Old California Way at Trancas St. (707) 255-8888.

Mini Mango Thai Bistro

Mini Mango Thai Bistro is a small restaurant that's a bit hard to find (it's behind the Avia hotel) but serves excellent Thai food, both traditional and innovative. The patio is the place to be if the weather is the usual, and it's heated during the winter. 1408 West Clay St. (707) 226-8884. www.minimangonapa.com

Molinari Caffe

Molinari Caffe is a deli that sells basic sandwiches – none of the Italian favorites – and pastries as well as excellent coffee drinks. It has no relation to famed Molinari Deli in San Francisco and doesn't sell ingredients for meals but only food to eat there or take out. 815 Main St. (707) 927-3623. www.molinaricaffe.com

Monticello Deli

Monticello Deli on Monticello Road serves breakfast and a wide range of sandwiches for lunch including traditional Italian-American favorites like muffulettas and meatball subs. The prices can't be beat. 1810 Monticello Rd. (707) 255-3953.

Morimoto*

Morimoto Napa is an arm of famed Iron Chef Masuhara Morimoto's growing empire. It's a dramatic space and serves exceptional food, both traditional Japanese food like sushi, and Morimoto's inspired creations.

You can enjoy the lounge in the front, the bar in the dining room, a quieter side room or the patio on the Napa River.

Though it's a prime destination for tourists, it's also very popular with locals, including during happy hours during the week when lounge specials are discounted 30 percent. 610 Main St. (707) 252-1600. www.morimotonapa.com

Napa General Store

Napa General Store is a popular gift shop combined with a café-deli and wine bar with seating on its patio on the Napa River. It serves breakfast and lunch. 540 Main St. #100. (707) 259-0762. www.napageneralstore.com

Napa Valley Wine Train

Surprisingly, the Napa Valley Wine Train is partly a superb restaurant with the most interesting views in the Valley. The food is mostly new American cuisine, but heavy on meats to satisfy the range of customers. It pours great Napa Valley wines, mostly at reasonable prices and has a tasting bar. It's expensive but a special treat. 1275 McKinstry St. (707) 253-2111. www.winetrain.com

Nation's Giant Hamburgers

Nation's Giant Hamburgers claims to have great hamburgers and pies. 1441 Third St. (707) 252-8500. www.nationsrestaurants.com

Norman Rose Tavern*

Norman Rose Tavern is one of the standard hangouts for Napa locals, including many who work in the wine business. It offers solid and perfectly prepared comfort food, beer and cocktails with a few innovative menu items. 1401 First St. (707) 258-1516. www.normanrosenapa.com

Oenotri*

Oenotri is relatively new, but already well established as one of Napa's treasures – and the competition is tough.

Specializing in food inspired by that of southern Italy, Oenotri makes authentic pizzas, and its own pasta and salume. They even teach classes in making pizza and pasta. The menu changes constantly, but everything is good. It has interesting wine choices from both Napa and Italy. It's a bit lively inside and always crowded, so eat in the courtyard if you can. 1425 First St. (707) 252-1022. www.oenotri.com

Olive Tree Inn

Not to be confused with the Olive Garden chain, Olive Tree Inn is a local place that's been there for years serving standard American plus Italian-American favorites. Good prices. 221 Silverado Trail. (707) 252-7660. www.olivetreenapa.com

Oventi

Oventi Restaurant and Bakery is next to Napa Winery Inn at Highway 29 and Trower Ave. It serves American, Italian, Spanish, Greek and Basque at reasonable prices. 1990 Trower Ave. (707) 637-4464. www.oventirestaurant.com

Panda Garden

Another Chinese-American restaurant serving the expected food. 2940 Jefferson St.(707) 226-8881.

The Pear A Southern Bistro

Southern cooking along the Napa River in the Riverfront.

Pearl

Pearl is on Pearl Street downtown a block from First. It's bright, with innovative well prepared food and moderate prices. Very friendly atmosphere; they act like they're happy you came in to eat. Highly recommended. Owners Nicki and Pete Zeller were downtown pioneers a little too early with their previous Brown Street Restaurant, but now locals hope the intimate Pearl avoids discovery. 1339 Pearl St. #104. (707) 224-9161. www.therestaurantpearl.com

Peking Palace

Perhaps the best Chine-American restaurant of those in downtown Napa, the Peking Palace has a great location at Main and Second. Friendly staff and decent food. 1001 Second St. (707) 257-7197. www.pekingnapa.com

Red Hen Cantina

The popular Red Hen Cantina offers Gringo-style Mexican-American food. Its deck is a favorite for sucking down beers or margaritas with chips and meals. 4175 Solano Ave. (707) 255-8125. www.redhencantina.com

Red Rock Cafe

Red Rock Café is a hole-in-the-wall burger and BBQ joint. Nothing fancy, but completely satisfying. 1010 Lincoln Ave. (707) 252-9250. www.backdoorbbq.com

Rocabella

Rocabella serves a pan-Mediterranean menu with an emphasis on Greek food from a chef who used to work on Santorini. It has an extensive and eclectic wine list, indoor bar and tented, candlelit outdoor lounge on Dwight Murray Plaza in downtown Napa, Napa's feeble answer to Sonoma's or Heldssburg's squares.. 1106 First St. (707) 224-0695

Siena at Meritage Resort

Siena is the main restaurant at Meritage Resort. It offers Italian-inspired and standard American food, much with a California touch. 875 Bordeaux Way. (707) 251-1900. themeritageresort.com

Silo's Jazz Club

Silo's isn't really a restaurant, but you can get snacks, pizza and desserts to enjoy with concerts and drinks. 530 Main St. (707) 251-5833. www.silosnapa.com

Silverado Resort Royal Oak Restaurant

The Royal Oak is the fine dining restaurant at Silverado Resort. It serves the expected steaks, chops and fish. It's comfortable and old-fashioned, and open only Thursday through Saturday, traditionally only during the tourist season (not the winter). 1600 Atlas Peak Rd. (707) 257-0200. www.silveradoresort.com

Silverado Grill

Silverado Grill is the informal restaurant at Silverado Resort. It offers burgers, fried chicken and steaks as well as a few other comfortable choices. It serves breakfast through dinner. 1600 Atlas Peak Rd. (707) 257-0200. www.silveradoresort.com

Silverado Mansion Lounge

Though primarily a bar, the Mansion Lounge at Silverado Resort serves light meals as well as snacks overlooking the golf course in the main building. 1600 Atlas Peak Rd. (707) 257-0200. www.silveradoresort.com

Small World Restaurant

Small World's name is a Middle-Eastern café with excellent falafel, souvlaki, gyros and similar fare. There's zilch atmosphere – place your order at the counter and grab a drink from the cooler, but they trust you to pay when you're done. The prices are right, too. You can also sit outside. 928 Coombs St. (707) 224-7743. www.worldcafenapa.com

Soda Canyon Store

Soda Canyon Store is a deli on the Silverado Trail north of Napa at – Soda Canyon Road. The food includes fine sandwiches, Mexican specialties and some hot dishes. It has tables for picnics, and also sells wine and beer.

It's also the only store or restaurant in the 27 miles from Napa to Calistoga on the popular Silverado Trail. 4006 Silverado Trail. (707) 252-0285. www.sodacanyonstore.com

Sushi Haku

Sushi Haku is a relatively new shopping-center sushi bar with good food and prices. It's run by a Korean family – like many sushi places in Japan – but offers only one Korean dish – kalbi. 3206 Jefferson St. (707) 226-2996.

Sushi Mambo*

Sushi Mambo serves excellent moderately prices sushi in a very friendly atmosphere. The fish is always impeccably fresh, and they offer a wide range of traditional sushi but most patrons seem to go for the Baroque rolls containing half the sea and slathered with anything from Thousand Island Dressing to Sriracha.

The sushi chefs are from Mexico but trained in Japan and both gaijin owners speak Japanese. They always seem to offer a little extra or two for good customers. Downtown, but easy parking in structures a block away. 202 First St. (707) 257-6604. www.sushimambonapa.com

Sweetie Pies

Sweetie Pies is a bakery offering delectable cakes, cookies and other sweet items, but also serves breakfast and lunch. It's in the Napa Mill complex. 520 Main St. (707) 257-7280. www.sweetiepies.com

Taqueria Rosita

Taqueria Rosita is one of the most popular Mexican restaurants in downtown Napa and is always filled. It also offers take out. 1214 Main St. (707) 253-9208.

Tarla Mediterranean Grill*

Tarla serves a variety of food including steaks, but its specialty is Turkish and Greek cooking, which it does superbly. This includes beef donner kebab (gyros), lamb kebabs, imam bayildi, and many tasty mezes. Try the Turkish wine, perfect with the food. Some outside seating. It's under the Andaz hotel at First and School Streets in downtown Napa. 1480 First St. (707) 255-5599. www.tarlagrill.com

Thai Kitchen Restaurant

One of the three Thai restaurants in Napa. 1222 Trancas St. (707) 254-9271.

The Thomas Restaurant and Fagiani's Bar

The Thomas Restaurant occupies the top two floors of a venerable building in Napa, and is named after the original boarding house and restaurant. The first floor is a bar named after a long-time bar. It serves innovative food with local ingredients. The top floor has a unique patio for great views of the Napa River and eastern hills. 813 Main St. (707) 226-7821.

Tuscany

Tuscany occupies perhaps the most visible site in Napa at First and Main. It has a large dining room with a food bar where you can watch the open kitchen, and a bar. Huge windows open to the outside. The food isn't particularly Tuscan, but consists mostly of rich American-Italian concoctions. Dinner except Monday. 1005 First St.(at Main) (707) 258-1000. www.tuscanynapa.com

Crush Ultra Lounge

Crush Ultra Lounge at the Meritage resort is one of the most unique places to eat and drink in Napa Valley: Enjoy cocktails, sports entertainment, food and bowling all in one place. It's open until 2 a.m. on Friday and Saturday. 875 Bordeaux Way. (707) 251-3067. www.themeritageresort.com

Uva Trattoria

Uva Trattoria Italiana is one of Napa's most popular restaurants. A little out of the way, especially after a bridge was removed over Napa Creek, it serves reliable Italian-American favorites at good prices. Even better, it offers half portions of many items like pastas for those with smaller appetites or a desire to eat a number of courses. The bar hops with locals enjoying the live music Wednesday through Sunday. 1040 Clinton St. 707) 255-6646. www.uvatrattoria.com

Villa Corona

Almost a cult favorite, Villa Corona serves excellent and authentic Mexican food in a space in the southern back of Bel Aire Plaza. Huge portions. 3614 Bel Aire Plaza,. (707) 257-8685. www.villacoronamex.com

Villa Romano

Villa Romano is another old Italian-American restaurant left over from another era. It's where Highway 29 interests Soscol Road, admittedly in a poor location today. You can sneak under the bridge to the Meritage, however. 1011 Soscol Ferry Rd. (707) 252-4533. www.villaromano.com

Wah Sing Chinese Restaurant

Wah Sing is another ok Chinese Restaurant serving America's favorites. River Park Shopping Center, 1445 West Imola Ave.. (707) 252-0511.

ZuZu Tapas & Paella.

ZuZu Tapas & Paella is one of the gems of Napa. It serves Spanish (and some Latin American) tapas along with paella, and has an interesting choice of local and imported wines. 829 Main St. (707) 224-8555. www.zuzunapa.com

Yountville Restaurants

Yountville claims to be the gourmet capital of the United States – at least on a per-capita basis. Its 3,000 residents can choose from a wealth of restaurants, starting with the French Laundry, which has been constantly selected as one of the premier places to dine in the country, and the prices and wait for reservations reflect its status.

Fortunately, there are many other choices.

Ad Hoc

Thomas Keller's casual restaurant serving one prix fixe meal each night. Behind it is Addendum, which serves fried chicken and barbecue picnic boxes to go (or eat on picnic tables) Thursday through Saturday until they run out. 6746 Washington St. (707) 944-2487. www.adhocrestaurant.com

Bistro Jeanty

Bistro Jeanty is a homey authentic French bistro in Yountville. Its proprietor and chef is Philippe Jeanty, the highly regarded former chef from Domaine Chandon nearby. Jeanty always seems to be in the kitchen or talking with patrons.

The decor is straight out of a restaurant in a small town in France. You'll think you're there except that no one will be blowing Gaulois smoke in your face and there won't be an elegant older lady sharing her meal with a poodle at the table next to you.

Bistro Jeanty features traditional bistro fare and it's exquisitely prepared: mussels, steak frites, cassoulet, roast chicken and some French favorites that may challenge Americans like lamb's tongue, pig's feet, kidneys and sweetbreads.

Signature dishes from Jeanty's days at fancy Chandon include smoked trout and tomato soup en croute. Prices for each item are reasonable, but if you have a number of courses – starter, main course and dessert – plus wine, it adds up.

The wine list isn't lengthy, but the French and California selections are perfect with the food. By the way, if you bring wine, you'll pay corkage, no matter who you are.

Bistro Jeanty is crowded at peak times, but it's open all day so if you pretend you're French, you can eat lunch at 3 p.m. with no problem.

The bistro does have a communal table. If you're willing to share the table with others, you may be able to drop in even at busy times. It's a great way to meet people; most diners at the table are locals, some winemakers. The bar is perfect for single diners, but it's small and often full. It's also a great place to meet people.

There's a quieter room in back with a fireplace burning during cooler weather. Depending on the season, there may be al fresco seating. 6510 Washington St. (707) 944-0103. www.bistrojeanty.com

Bottega*

Michael Chiarello's Bottega restaurant in Yountville became an instant favorite the day it opened. The celebrity chef, who made Tra Vigne the top destination in Napa Valley when he was there, went on to star in cooking series on TTV, write books and start the NapaStyle lifestyle stores before returning to the kitchen.

Chiarello has crafted a menu of dishes inspired by or from southern Italy (His family is from Calabria) with a strong touch of fresh California ingredients and ideas.

The food is wonderful, and so is the ambience, warm, friendly and welcoming. The small bar is always full, and the patio is if the weather is good, as it usually is, and the main dining areas are divided up so it seems intimate.

If he's there, Chiarello visits tables, making everyone even more comfortable. Sometimes you have to eat at odd times to get in, but it's worth the wait or bother. 6525 Washington St. (707) 945-1050. www.bottneganapavalley.com

Bouchon

Bouchon is one of the most appealing restaurants in Napa Valley. It's a traditional French bistro, (Bouchon is the local term for bistro in Lyon, the gastronomic capital of France. It also means cork stopper for wine.) owned by Thomas Keller, noted chef and owner of the French Laundry.

The building seems transported from a sharp Parisian neighborhood with decor as authentic as the superb food.

The relatively small menu is what you expect, simple but excellently prepared and very French dishes. Bouchon doesn't serve weird trendy food, just classics like steak frites, mussels marinières and leg of lamb with flageolet beans.

Appetizers include seafood from an extensive raw bar, onion soup, quiche, and watercress and endive salad with blue cheese.

Desserts include a superb crème caramel, a tarte tâtin for one and great cheeses.

The wine selection is good. Many locals order carafes: The restaurant is so French it even has good local house wine. It charges everyone corkage, even winemakers used to having it waived.

Service is generally excellent, though the restaurant can get busy. The place is crowded and fairly loud, but that's part of the authenticity — at least there's no smoke or dog. The few tables outside aren't ideal for alfresco dining because they're on the street.

It's difficult to book reservations, but it only reserves half the tables. You can usually get in with ease after local typically early dining hours.

Bouchon jumps at night with staff from other restaurants — it's open until 2 a.m. on weekends.

The bar is an especially good bet if you're alone, and you're almost sure to meet someone interesting if you sit there a while. 6534 Washington St. (707) 944-8037. www.bouchonbistro.com

Brix

Brix is an attractive restaurant that's developed an excellent reputation for its food and presentation. It serves real California food, much from the extensive gardens on the property. It boasts a large wine list and wine retail shop, and large and friendly bar for eating and drinking. The patio in back is the ideal place to eat and watch the vineyard scene. 7377 St. Helena Highway. (707) 944-2749. www.brix.com

Ciccio

Ciccio serves breakfast, pizzas and Italian dinners using produce from owner Frank Altamura's garden in Wooden Valley. No lunch. 6770 Washington St. (707) 944-8246. www.ciccionapavalley.com

Coffee Caboose

Coffee Caboose serves coffee drinks from the caboose of the Railway Inn, a B&B built from old railway cars. It also offers sweet and savory crepes for breakfast and lunch. It's next to Pacific Blues Café. 6523 Washington St. (707) 738-1153. www.yountvillecoffeecaboose.com

étoile at Domaine Chandon

The Restaurant at Domaine Chandon, now called Étoile, was Napa Valley's first world-class restaurant. It offers exquisite preparations that pair perfectly with the winery's sparkling and still wines.

Much of the food is traditional French, but often reflects the California experience including local ingredients. Portions are small, so you'll definitely want to eat the French way with a number of courses.

It seems to sparkle more at lunch than dinner, but perhaps that's just because of the view and the delicious decadence of eating such superb food and drinking sparkling wines in the middle of the day.

They do serve wines other than sparkling wine, including still wines made at the winery but little available elsewhere. One California Drive. (707) 944-2892. www.chandon.com

The French Laundry

One of America's great restaurants, the French Laundry is owned and run by Thomas Keller, voted America's best chef on a number of occasions.

It features impeccable ambience, service, presentation and food. The food is French-inspired in elegance and preparation, but adapted to California ingredients and tastes. You can have the five-course meal or the nine-course tasting menu, but they throw in f little extras as you go.

Some of the food is very innovative, but unlike the inventions at many restaurants, these selections are also tasty. The servings are small, even tiny, but there are so many that you'll probably wish you could take a 24-hour break halfway through the meal. Very expensive, of course, but worth it for a memorable experience.

It's famously difficult to get a reservation. You have to call exactly two months ahead at 10 a.m. Your hotel concierge may be able to get you in – and the restaurant keeps a waiting list to call if anyone cancels. 6640 Washington St. (707) 944-2380. www.frenchlaundry.com

Hurley's Restaurant and Grill

Hurley's offers casual Italian- and French-inspired comfort food from one of Napa Valley's favorite chefs. It serves lunch and dinner daily. The patio is the place to be if the weather is good, as it usually is. 6518 Washington St. (707) 944-1500. www.hurleysrestaurant.com

Lakeside Grill

Lakeside Grill is the coffee shop at the Yountville golf course. It's little known, hence a good place for breakfast or a burger. 7901 Solano Ave. (707) 944-2426. www.vintnersgolfclub.com

Lucy at Bardessono

Lucy is the restaurant at Bardessono resort. It features food from its own and local gardens – and local farms and the ocean – prepared in elegant fashion and surroundings in the eco-friendly hotel. It also serves light food in the bar and offers alfresco dining on the patio. The extensive wine list highlights renowned small producers from around the world and many organic, sustainable and biodynamic vintners. 6526 Yount St. (707) 204-6030. www.bardessono.com

Mustards Grill

Mustards Grill is the home of "Napa Valley cuisine," Cindy Pawlcyn's popular blend of Mediterranean and American cooking. It's always packed. It's a classic American roadhouse featuring big portions of hearty comfort food made with ingredients from their garden. Don't expect gourmet food, but good food and a pleasant experience. 7399 St. Helena Hwy. (707) 944-2424. www.mustardsgrill.com

NapaStyle

NapaStyle is primarily a lifestyle store with home furnishings, kitchenware and gourmet food, but has a wine bar and counter where they make hot and cold panini and offer other treats and side dishes. Enjoy the food on the adjoining patio with wine or beer. V Marketplace, 6525 Washington St. (707) 945-1229. www.napastyle.com

Pacific Blues Café

It's a breakfast and lunch spot not a destination restaurant, but Pacific Blues Café has a pleasant setting next to V Marketplace with a deck for enjoying the good weather. It serves the expected hearty comfort food. It's also open for dinners. 6525 Washington St. (707) 944-4455. www.pacificbluescafe.com

Redd

Redd is one of Napa Valley's finest restaurants. Chef-owner Richard Reddington, formerly of Auberge du Soleil, creates innovative food in upscale surroundings. It's very popular with the local wine community and locals out for a special meal. 6480 Washington St. (707) 944-2070. www.reddnapavalley.com

Yountville Deli at Ranch Market Too

The local Ranch Market Too supermarket (There's also one in Napa) hosts the excellent Yountville Deli for sandwiches and other food to go. Great place to stock a picnic. 6498 Washington St. (707) 944-2662. www.yountvilledeli.com

Redd Wood

Chef-owner Richard Reddington of Redd took over the former pizzeria at what's now the North Branch Hotel, spent plenty redecorating it, and now it's a – pizzeria. Plus. The pizzas are excellent, as are the other food, mostly Italian in inspiration. 6755 Washington St. (707) 299-5030. www.redd-wood.com

Rutherford and Oakville Restaurants

The tiny hamlets of Rutherford and Oakville boast some of America's most celebrated wineries, and a few interesting restaurants.

Auberge du Soleil

Auberge du Soleil has both marvelous food and the best view of any restaurant in the Valley, particularly at sunset. The Auberge restaurant, being attached to a very upscale hotel, had an elegant, expensive restaurant ideal for special occasions.

The bar bistro is a great alternative, usually not too busy, and offers lighter and somewhat less expensive entrées and appetizers inside around a cheery fire or outside on a deck overlooking the Valley. Even if they don't eat here, all cosmopolitan visitors to the area should at least stop by in the evening for a drink. It's not ridiculously fancy, but don't show up in your shorts or running clothes.

The main restaurant is definitely a special occasion place, suitable for anniversaries, romantic trysts or even popping the question. The setting and service are superb, and chef Robert Curry has elevated the food to match. At dinner, the only options are prix fixe meals. It's elegantly casual and expensive. 180 Rutherford Hill Rd. off Silverado Trail, Rutherford. (707) 967-3111. www.aubergeresorts.com

Alex

Alex is a relatively new Italian restaurant in the Rancho Caymus Inn in Rutherford. The owners are Alessandro and Alessia Sbrendola from Liguria and Romagna, and the food reflects that heritage with a good dose of California ingredients and preferences. 1140 Rutherford Crossroad, Rutherford. (707) 967-5500. www.alexitalianrestaurant.com

Rutherford Grill

Rutherford Grill is a cozy and attractive roadhouse featuring popular American comfort food, big portions of rotisserie chicken, steaks, burgers, lots of delicious artery-clogging food. The restaurant is popular with locals, including a lively crowd at the bar. The outside patio and bar is popular in good weather, and in fact, fills with people waiting to eat on weekends. They never charge corkage, so it's perfect for a steak with that special bottle of Cabernet you picked up during your day. Rutherford Grill is a fine location to end up a day of winetasting. 1180 Rutherford Rd. (and Highway 29), Rutherford. (707) 963-1792. www.rutherfordgrill.com

La Luna

Modest La Luna Mexican market in Rutherford whips up some of the best and most authentic tacos and burritos in Napa Valley, just like the taco trucks. Sadly, no wineries nearby can or do allow picnics. 1153 Rutherford Rd., Rutherford. (707) 963-3211. www.lalunamarket.com

Oakville Grocery

Though it's not a restaurant either, Oakville Grocery has tables where you can enjoy the sandwiches, salads and other treats you buy inside. The farmstead in the back not only sells vegetables and fruit, but beer and other beverages at times. 7856 Saint Helena Hwy., Oakville. (707) 944-8802. www.oakvillegrocery.com

St. Helena Restaurants

St. Helena is the reserved, upscale heart of the California premium wine business. It's a quiet community that wants to stay that way. Residents fight every change, whether chain restaurants or new tourist-oriented businesses, and they have succeeded in maintaining the town's charm.

Most of the restaurants are on the same street, variously called Main St., St. Helena Highway or Route 29.

St. Helena's Umbrella Row

Though St. Helena isn't known for bargains, a delightful row of four small casual and affordable restaurants has sprung up on Main St. You can recognize them by their clustered umbrellas, and it reminds me of similar scenes all over Italy (and Belden Place in San Francisco).

All have outside seating with umbrellas for shade, hence the name. And though it's two blocks away, Tra Vigne Pizzeria is a psychic sister.

Himalayan Sherpa Kitchen

Himalayan Sherpa Kitchen seems a cousin of Tibetan-Nepalese-Indian restaurants in Napa, Sonoma and elsewhere. The food is similar to that of northern Indian, i.e., not very spicy but very tasty. It's also very reasonable. 1148 Main St. (707) 963-4439. www.himalayansherpakitchen.com

Sogni di Dolce

Sogni di Dolci (Dreams of sweets) is an Italian-inspired espresso bar, café and gelateria. It serves panini, and its coffee is roasted and imported from Italy. Like its three neighboring eateries, it features outdoor seating with umbrellas. 1142 Main St. (707) 968-5257.

Vercelli

Vercelli might be called "son of Green Valley." When very popular Green Valley Trattoria with its Ligurian food closed, the chef opened Vercelli serving many of the same classics. He certainly knew how to prepare them! The food is classic North Beach food, the pasta is freshly made there, the prices are reasonable for St. Helena and there's no corkage fee. It's also friendly and they have alfresco seating. 1146 Main St. (707) 963-3371. www.vercelliristorante

Villa Corona

Villa Corona is the St. Helena branch of one of Napa's favorite Mexican restaurants, also called Villa Corona. It features good, ample food at attractive prices. You can get anything from a taco (rolled, not fried) to combination plates and specials.

The outside seating with shade is a nice bonus. 1138 Main St. (707) 963-7812. www.villacoronash.com

Alphabetical listing

Ana's Cantina

Ana's Cantina offers a wide selection of authentic Spanish tapas, many vegetarian and seafood, and mostly familiar Mexi-Californian favorites. The atmosphere is a bit of a dive. 1205 Main St. (707) 963-4921.

Armadillo's

Armadillo's is an attractive and colorful California-Mexican-American restaurant, and if the food isn't outstanding or authentic, the tourists love it. It's a good place for families or someone who wants a comfortable if heavy meal, though service is a bit slow. Prices are a little high for the offerings, but the beer is cold. 1304 Main St. (707) 963-8082.

Cindy Pawlcyn's Wood Grill and Wine Bar

Cindy Pawlcyn's Wood Grill and Wine Bar replaces her Brassica Mediterranean Restaurant and Go Fish. This time, she's got it right: The comfortable wine country cuisine she almost invented: Farm to table from her gardens, local ingredients, food that goes well with Napa Valley wines from Mustards Grill, Buckeye Roadhouse and Fog City Diner.

Artisan pizzas, fresh-from-the-garden vegetarian dishes, desserts such as backyard blackberry-apple crumble with crème fraîche ice cream, "adult" milkshakes and a full kids' menu round out the selections.

"CP's" has a lovely shaded patio with a bar and features music on Thursdays during the summer.

It has an ambitious wine program, with many offerings including flights, Vintners pouring samples on Saturday nights, tastings, glasses to drink, bottles to drink and retail sales of a dozen hard-to-find local wines. It even serves pitchers of cocktails. 641 Main St. (707) 963-0700.

Cindy's Backstreet Kitchen

Cindy Pawlcyn's Cindy's Backstreet Kitchen lies off the Main street in St. Helena, and it's typically filled with locals, not tourists. The food is rather eclectic, with Latin American and Mediterranean influences and a good dose of American comfort food like meatloaf. She offers a special themed menu during Cindy's Supper Club on

Wednesday and Thursday. 1327 Railroad Ave. (707) 963-1200.
www.cindysbackstreetkitchen.com

Cook

Small Cook restaurant succeeded the immensely beloved Green Valley Trattoria, but the chef wisely kept many of the Ligurian favorites brought to San Francisco's North Beach by immigrants from around Genoa. This includes perfect fried calamari and gnocchi among the Italian specialties, though the main courses and desserts are more "American."

It's always tightly packed with locals including winemakers and vintners. The prices are average for St. Helena.

The former chef at Green Valley opened Vercelli down the street, and its menu is almost totally from the closed restaurant. 1310 Main St. (707) 963-7088. www.cooksthelena.com

Culinary Institute of America

The Greystone Wine Spectator Restaurant is one of the most attractive and interesting restaurants in all the Napa Valley.

Situated in the imposing Greystone Cellars that once housed Christian Brothers Winery, the restaurant is stunning yet cozy. With a number of open food preparation areas for patrons to view, it's a suitable showcase for the Culinary Institute of America, which operates a professional cooking school on the premises. Its open fires are especially welcome in winter, but even in summer, the massive stone structure insulates the dining room from the heat outside.

The food is prepared by professionals and advanced students under their direction. It includes ingredients from the student-run gardens on site.

Not surprisingly, the wine choices are excellent, and include "flights" of wines to compare and contrast. These tastes might be three small portions of the same Rhône variety, perhaps from California, or rare and dear treasures you'd have a difficult time finding in bottle elsewhere, much less to taste. 2555 Main St. (707) 967-2303. www.ciachef.edu

Dean & Deluca

Dean & Deluca is a branch of the famous New York deli, and its chefs turn out sandwiches, appetizers, main courses, sides dishes and dessert the equal of most fine restaurants in the Valley. Many locals stop on the way home from work to pick up gourmet dinners, and you can do the same for a memorable picnic lunch or dinner.

It also features an impressive cheese and charcuterie selection as well as rare gourmet food items and cookware.

In good weather, you might get some food at D&D, buy a bottle of wine at the Flora Springs tasting room next door, and picnic at its tables.

The wine selection is immense, and includes most available wines from Napa Valley. 607 South St. Helena Hwy. (707) 967-9980. www.deanandeluca.com

Farmhouse at Long Meadow Ranch

Farmhouse is an ambitious restaurant owned by Long Meadow Ranch specializing in comfort food, with many ingredients from beef and eggs to produce and olive oil coming from the Ranch.

It's part of a complex that includes a wine-tasting salon, indoor and outdoor bars and seating for meals, and gardens. It even features music on weekends during the summer.

French Blue

French Blue is a new restaurant from famed architect Howard Backen and restaurateur/vintner/distiller Leslie Rudd. The name comes from the color, not French food. The attractive eatery serves comfort food from Rudd's gardens for breakfast, lunch and dinner, and is popular with locals.

You can enjoy the heated patio almost year round. French Blue also sells many gourmet items to buy and take home. 1429 Main St. (707) 968-9200. www.frenchbluenapa.com

Gillwoods

Gillwoods serves classic breakfasts with many interesting omelets, scrambles and baked goods. Don't miss the special breakfast potatoes but be sure to ask for the onions. The café is popular with locals and tourists alike at breakfast and lunch. One feature is a communal table for singles or others; the host won't always suggest it, particularly if you look too conventional or too weird, but it's a great place to meet anyone from a local wine maker to a student from Iceland.

Unfortunately, Gillwoods' popularity creates long lines on weekends, though there's a back room so it holds more people than you'd think.

Gillwoods also serves the usual and well prepared diner favorites, from meat loaf and chicken-friend steak to chili and club sandwiches for lunch.

There's also a Gillwoods in downtown Napa. 1313 Main St. (707) 963-1788. gillwoodscafe.com

Giugni

Guigni is a Long-established Italian-inspired deli and market. It's perfect for large, inexpensive sandwiches, with so many choices some people can't deal with them and order a standard. There's a claustrophobic back room with seating as well as the few tables up front. 1227 Main St. (707) 963-4321.

Golden Harvest Chinese Restaurant

Golden Harvest offers Chinese and Chinese-American food. 61 Main St. (707) 967-9888. www.goldenharvestsh.com

La Prima Pizza

Excellent all-American pizza, the type every pizza parlor should make, with chewy crust, tasty sauce and plenty of toppings. No chèvre, arugala or porcini pizzas, just good ol' pepperoni, sausage and button mushrooms. The best American pizza in town. It also serves sandwiches and basic pastas. It serves beer by the pitcher but has no atmosphere. Reasonable. 1010 Adams St. (707) 963-7909. www.laprimapizza.com

Market

Local hangout offering classic California comfort food in a friendly setting. It serves more seafood that you'd expect. It's reasonable and popular with locals. It doesn't charge corkage either. 1347 Main St. (707) 963-3799. marketsthelena.com

Goose and Gander

Goose and Gander is a relatively new restaurant in the old residence that used to be Martini House. Its cellar bar is particularly popular, and it has garden seating in good weather. 1245 Spring St. (707) 967-8779. goosegander.com

Gott's Roadside Gourmet (Taylor's)

Gott's Roadside Gourmet started out as Taylor's, the popular local drive-in hamburger stand, but being St. Helena, it's quite upscale and even serves wine and beer. It has nice picnic tables in the trees behind the stand for patrons. Crowded but efficient at lunch. 933 Main St. (707) 963-3486. www.gotts.com

Meadowood Grill

The Grill at Meadowood is a nice casual hotel restaurant and bar overlooking the croquet course. It's really for guests who aren't up to the fancy restaurant at the resort, but offers good uncomplicated meals like steaks and simple fish. Martinis are big. A perfect answer when you want to have a nice meal on weekends in Napa Valley and forgot to call two weeks ago. 900 Meadowood Ln. (707) 963-3646. www.meadowood.com

The Restaurant at Meadowood

The Restaurant at Meadowood was extensively upgraded in décor and quality a few years ago, and is now the only restaurant in Napa Valley with three Michelin stars other than The French Laundry.

Chef Christopher Kostow knows how to produce exquisite innovation.

The restaurant serves a nine or ten course tasting menu optionally paired with wines. The current price is $225 for each. You can also enjoy the Chef's Counter tasting experience in the kitchen or dining room for $500 plus wine.

It's casually elegant and jackets are not required. 900 Meadowood Ln. (707) 963-3646. www.meadowood.com

Model Bakery

Model Bakery bakes great bread in both Napa and St. Helena, but in St. Helena, they use an ancient oven heated by a gas fire insterted into its chamber to heat up the surrounding bricks.

It also bakes pastries perfect for Continental-type breakfasts, coffee and mid-afternoon snacks. They serve sandwiches and pizza slices at lunch, too. 1357 Main St. (707) 963-8192. www.themodelbakery.com

Press

Press is Lesley Rudd's temple to beef – and Napa Valley Cabernet. Though the restaurant serves other meats and the appropriate appetizers, side dishes and deserts, it's almost a shame to eat anything but a big hunk of beef here. It's of the highest quality and perfectly cooked. It's also huge, as are the other dishes. Most are suitable to share.

If Press adores beef, however, it worships Napa Valley wines. It has an enormous collection of local wines, some well-aged treasures acquired fin estate sales and perfectly stored. Though Press offers other varieties beside Cabernet, of course, it's almost all from Napa Valley.

Only a few Champagnes and Chateau d'Yquem sneak past the county line. As Lesley says, "Why would you visit Napa Valley and not drink its wines?"

Press is a special-occasion destination, but like Cole's Chop House in Napa, meets the highest standards for its specialty imaginable. 587 St. Helena Hwy. (707) 967-0550. www.presssthelena.com

Terra and Bar Terra

One of the most-renowned restaurants in the Valley, Terra is owned by chef Hiro Sone and pastry chef Lissa Doumani. It prepares some of the most innovative food around combining Asian and European influences with California ingredients. And unlike some chefs who try to hard, Sone has a perfect touch.

The adjoining Bar Terra is ideal for drinks and smaller but impressive snacks and even meals. 1345 Railroad Ave. (707) 963-8931. www.terrarestaurant.com

Tra Vigne

Tra Vigne restaurant has deep roots in Tuscany, Napa Valley's psychic sister in Italy, and its food is an inspired marriage of Tuscan techniques and recipes with fresh local ingredients.

The restaurant — the name "means among the vines" — features one large spacious room in an old brick winery with a elegant old bar along one side. Most meals start at the bar; the restaurant is very popular and even if you have a reservation, you may spend some time there. That's not bad; in fact eating at the bar is more fun for singles or pairs who aren't couples, for you're sure to meet others at the bar. They could be other visitors, local winemakers or even Joe Montana (It's happened to me, and not being a football fan, I talked to him for half an hour about winemaking and schools before someone told me.)

There's slight encouragement to order appetizers or a meal if you sit at the bar during prime time, but it's not oppressive.

The menu changes often. Keep the wood-burning over in mind, for many of the best dishes come from it, including flatbread. The whole roasted fish is one of my favorites.

It's most fun to eat Italian style, with an appetizer, then pasta, risotto or soup, then a main course and perhaps a salad or vegetable. Most of the portions aren't huge, but they're usually happy to split salads and even pastas, or even serve half portions of some dishes if you're nice, though that option isn't listed on the menu.

If the weather is good, as it usually is in Napa Valley, the patio at lunch is a great place to eat the ultimate Napa Valley lunch. They have heaters in case the weather is marginal. 1050 Charter Oak Ave. (707) 963-4444. www.travignerestaurant.com

Tra Vigne Pizzeria

Pizzas at Tra Vigne Pizzeria have thin crusts, imaginative toppings, and of course, organic tomato sauce. They also put salads on pizza crust, an interesting idea they call piadine, sort of an Italian tostada, and serve basic pasta dishes.

It's very reasonable and doesn't charge corkage. It has outside seating as well as that inside. It's a casual, unpretentious place for dinner when you don't want to try too hard. It's good for families. It has the same owners as Tra Vigne. 1020 Main St. (707) 967-9999. www.travignerestaurant.com.

Calistoga Restaurants

Calistoga has a Wild-West look, with roofs overhanging much of the sidewalk, but it's best known for its many modest and fancy spas and mud baths. It's less fancy and formal than St. Helena, and friendlier, the part of the Valley that most appeals to visitors who want a lot to do. There are even some activities in the evening. It has an impressive collection of fine and innovative restaurants as well as some more modest but comfortable places.

Brannan's, Solbar and All Seasons are the most interesting, while Hydro is a local favorites and Bosko's and Checkers are inexpensive delights. Virtually all are on Lincoln, the short main street, so you easily check them all out, including those you'll need to call ahead on your next visit.

All Seasons Cafe

Interesting, eclectic and innovative menu with superb list of wines you won't see at many places. The featured wines, which are also offered by the glass, are good buys as well. There's even a wine store on premises where you can buy the wines you like.

The food is well-prepared American comfort food with a few Mediterranean touches thrown in. 1400 Lincoln Ave. (707) 942-9111. www.allseasonsnapavelley.net

Barolo

Barolo is an informal restaurant and wine bar that serves Italian small portions and main courses as well, it's become a favorite hangout in Calistoga. 1457 Lincoln Ave. (707) 942-9900. www.bar-vino.com

Bosko's Ristorante

Bosko's is a rustic, brick-lined Italian restaurant that sends mixed messages. You order at the register and the floor is littered with sawdust, suggesting a family-style pizza parlor, and the prices are moderate. But the food is excellent, often close to what you might find in Naples or Sicily.

Besides thin-crust pizzas, Bosko's features pasta cooked to order, soup and sandwiches. The excellent wines are moderately priced.

Bosko's is a gem easy to overlook in a small town with lots of food choices. It's perfect when you've been overwhelmed by too many fancy, expensive, pretentious meals, or when you have the bambini along. 1364 Lincoln Ave. (707) 942-9088. www.boskos.com

Brannan's

Brannan's is a big, active and attractive roadhouse, seemingly transplanted from San Francisco. Though quite large, it's broken up by partial partitions and different levels so it doesn't seem cavernous. Its bar has already become a real hangout for locals (and visitors), and it's often a challenge to find a place to belly up. You can order appetizers or full meals there. 1374 Lincoln Ave. (707) 942-2235. www.brannansgrill.com

Buster's BBQ

Buster's BBQ is a classic barbecue joint serving great food. It's very informal. 1207 Foothill Blvd. (707) 942-5605. www.busterssouthernbbq.com

Café Sarafornia

Café Sarafornia is an informal family restaurant and deli, almost a coffee shop, but with better-than average breakfasts.

The name is the reverse of Calistoga, which supposedly was invented when the Mormon founder of the town, Sam Brannan, had a few too many nips before the ceremony dedicating the town and mixed up his description of the "Saratoga of California." 1413 Lincoln Ave. (707) 942-0555. www.cafesarafornia.com

Calistoga Inn & Napa Valley Brewing Co.

The Calistoga Inn is one of the most pleasant places in Calistoga. It combines a micro-brewery, a funky bar full of locals, a nice restaurant inside, and casual seating outside next to the Napa River in season.

And don't forget the hotel. It has a number of inexpensive rooms upstairs - none of them are fancy – but the Calistoga Inn often has rooms when no one else in the Valley does. And at its low prices, you might be willing to don a bathrobe for the walk to the bathrooms down the hall.

Let's start with the micro-brewery and bar. Like most micro-breweries, the Napa Valley Brewing Co. makes a variety of beers. They vary at different times of the year. Some are quite dark and flavorful, and even the lightest is a long way from Coors. They don't serve any other beers. Why should they? Their products are excellent. You can get the beer in the restaurant or in the bar.

The bar is a narrow room with the actual seating bar along the side of the room. It's not very big, and is typically full of locals. They tolerate the tourists, but not with much enthusiasm (although unattached women seem welcome!)

The Calistoga Inn often has music on weekends, including folk music on Friday nights but check to make sure. For those who don't want beer the Calistoga Inn also has a variety of wines including interesting local wines by the glass, some difficult to find elsewhere. A few times, the bartender has warned me about wines offered that are atypical of their type, and he's always been right.

The partly covered outside seating area lies next to the Napa River, though in nice weather (Napa Valley has just two seasons, wet and tourist!), the river doesn't have much water in it. The food at the Calistoga Inn is the American comfort cuisine served in so many places in the Valley. It's heavy on steaks, barbecue, grilled chicken, mashed potatoes and other standards that go well with Napa Valley Cabernets. The portions are huge. 1250 Lincoln Ave. (707) 942-4101. www.calistogainn.com

Calistoga Roastery

The local coffee hangout, with patio seating in nice weather. It's been featured in the *New York Times*! Definitely the place for a light breakfast or even lunch as well as coffee. 1613 Lincoln Ave. (707) 942-5747. www.calistogaroastery.com

Checkers

Checkers is a moderately priced Italian restaurant featuring pizza, pastas and salads in a friendly atmosphere. Nothing too challenging here, just good casual food and service. 1414 Lincoln Ave. (707) 942-9300. www.checkers.com

Mary's Home Plate Café

Mary's Home Plate Café serves breakfast, lunch, especially burgers and sandwiches and dinner until 8. It's just north of downtown Calistoga on the way to Santa Rosa or Alexander Valley. 2448 Foothill Blvd. (707) 942-5646. www.maryshomeplate.com

Hydro Bar & Grill

The Hydro Bar is a warm restaurant and full bar featuring moderately priced American comfort food, sometimes with interesting twists. If you're interested in ribs, chicken, burgers and steaks, you're in the right place.

The desserts are scrumptious, and like the other courses, large. It has the best fried calamari anywhere. There's so much I try to get a half portion -- which they don't serve – but I end up eating it all in spite of myself.

The biggest attraction at the Hydro, however, is the friendly bar and music. The U-shaped bar dominates the room, and is always filled with locals enjoying 20 draft beers - mostly from microbreweries including the excellent Mt. St. Helena Palisades Pale Ale from Middletown over the mountain in Lake County. Some lucky tourists even happen in as well.

The bar is a good place for single diners to eat and meet people. You're likely to meet a wine maker at the bar - but he won't necessarily be drinking his own wine. There's a lot of tasting around and trading glasses among the regulars at the tables and bar.

The wines, as should be expected in Napa Valley, include some interesting choices, not the same old suspects. Sometimes the help has to run across the street for special wines from All Seasons, which has the same owners.

There's sometimes music on weekends. 1403 Lincoln Ave. (707) 942-9777.

JoLe

JoLe is one of Calistoga's upscale restaurants. It's in the Mount View Hotel, and seeks to create innovative food and serve it in an elegant setting. 1457 Lincoln St. (707) 942-5938. www.jolerestaurant.com

Kitani Sushi

Kitani is Calistoga's only Japanese restaurant and sushi bar. 1631 Lincoln Ave. (707) 942-6857. www.kitanisushi.com

Kopio Express

Kopio Express promises authentic Southeastern Asian food and coffee. 1350 Lincoln Ave www.kopioexpress.com

Pacifico Restaurante Mexicano

Pacifico's menu is tasty, with many authentic-sounding Mexican choices, and a chef from Jalisco, but service can be uneven and the food often seems like that served in other Gringo "Mexican" restaurants from Maine to San Diego. If you like Chevy's or Carlos O'Briens, you'll love Pacifico. The food prices are on the high side for the food, however, much less the overall experience.

The bar is big, and a good place for Margaritas and beer.. And Mexicans in Mexico eat limes only with Tecate, not every beer. 1237 Lincoln Ave. (707) 942-4400. www.pacificorestaurantemexicano.com

Palisades Deli Café

Palisades Deli Café in the historic Calistoga train depot serves breakfast as well as deli lunches, sandwiches, burritos, salads and more. Definitely California eclectic. 1458 Lincoln Ave. (707) 942-0145. www.palisadescafe.com

Puerto Vallarta Restaurante

Modest and unpretentious authentic Mexican cantina with some outside seating and reasonable prices. 1473 Lincoln Ave. (707) 942-6563.

Solbar at Solage

Solbar restaurant at the Solage Resort is unquestionably one of Napa Valley's better restaurants, little surprise since it's part of the Auberge du Soleil family. It features everything from light small plates to steaks in a casual setting including outside seating near the pool.

During the summer, winemakers, growers and other locals grab burgers and other simple fare and play bocce. 755 Silverado Trail. (866) 942-7442. www.solagecalistoga.com

San Marco Coffee

San Marco Coffee also serves ice cream and other sweets. 1408 Lincoln St. (707) 942-0714.

Scoops and Swirls

Scoops and Swirls serves ice cream and other sweet treats. 1473 Lincoln St. (707) 341-3132.

Soo Yuan Restaurant

Locals swear by Soo Yuan Chinese restaurant, and it's been there forever. It has a good portion of hot dishes with all the old favorites. So it's not San Francisco; it's the only Chinese food in town! 1354 Lincoln St. (707) 942-9404.

Susie's Bar

Though hardly a restaurant, Susie's Bar is a classic dive, dark and seemly still smelling of the cigarettes – and bikers – of yesterday. 1365 Lincoln St. (707) 942-6710.

Yo el Rey Roasting

Just in case you haven't consumed enough coffee in this caffeine-drenched town, Yo el Rey offers organic brews. It's just off the main drag on the way to the Sharpsteen Museum. 1437 Lincoln St. (707) 942-4358.

Village Bakery

Village Bakery has both bread and pastries to go or eat there. 1453 Lincoln St. (707) 942-1443.

The Best Places to Eat Alfresco

With our mild climate, we in Napa Valley enjoy eating outside much of the year, though heaters are necessary on many nights even in the summer.

Many eating places, including informal restaurants and even fast-food shops, offer outside seating, but a few restaurants make dining alfresco a special treat. Eating under the trees – or the stars – recalls many wonderful meals I've enjoyed in Greece, Italy, southern France and Spain. It's not surprising that many of these alfresco destinations serve Mediterranean food.

These restaurants offer the most appealing settings for alfresco dining in Napa Valley with ample shade from our searing sun. They are mostly shielded from traffic, too, and serve exceptional food at dinner (most also serve lunch).

Napa

Angéle

Angéle offers excellent French bistro food in its covered patio on the Napa River. With the opening of the river walk around the historic Napa Mill, diners can now watch the passing parade of strollers as well as the boats – and occasional sea lions – on the river. The river itself provides a constantly changing panorama from productive mud flats most people would call ugly to a shimmering expanse.

Oenotri

Southern Italian Oenotri has tables in a pleasant courtyard, though it can get hot. Check it before committing to eat there. It's great during the early evening in the summer.

Bistro Don Giovanni

Though Bistro Don Giovanni has some tables for drinks on the lawn, the tables for dining are on the attractive patio. There you get to enjoy some of the consistently best Italian food in Napa Valley yet are protected from the sun. The whole roasted fish and the pizzas from the wood-burning oven are some of my favorites, but the pastas are universally praised.

Yountville

Bottega

Bottega is one of the best restaurants in Napa Valley. It has a large covered patio that wraps around the restaurant. The part near the door is lounges for drinks, the rest tables for food. It can be enclosed and heated if needed.

Brix

Brix has a lovely patio in the back overlooking the restaurant's own extensive gardens as well as vineyards and the nearby Mayacamas Mountains. It is also being reborn with an emphasis on its own produce and the culinary traditions of the winegrowing regions of Provence and Northern Italy. It features its own wine along with others from its rare restaurant wine shop, and features a fresh look.

Rutherford

Auberge du Soleil

The restaurant at Auberge du Soleil is a special occasion for most of us, but the deck shared with the bar is simply the best view from a restaurant in Napa Valley. The prices are creeping up, but the bar offers reasonable choices to enjoy with a glass of wine – especially considering the ambience and vistas. A pizza or hamburger is about $18, for example.

St. Helena

Tra Vigne

When you eat in the patio at Tra Vigne, you could well be dining as a guest of a Marchese at his family's castle in Tuscany. The shading trees and surrounding walls provide an ambience unique to Napa Valley. The Italian food is authentic and excellent, too. Many of the best bets come from the brick oven, but pastas are home-made and the wines are always interesting.

Cindy Pawlcyn's Wood Grill and Wine Bar

Cindy Pawlcyn's Backstreet Kitchen has a cozy patio, but her Wood Grill and Wine Bar has one of the best outdoor eating sites in Napa Valley. Mulberry trees and awnings filter the sunlight and a fireplace provide a warm glow at night. The food is even inspired by Mediterranean cuisines, though it's definitely Californian.

They have music on Thursdays during the summer.

Calistoga

Calistoga Inn

The Napa River is little more than a creek except during the winter, but the extensive patio at the Calistoga Inn exploits its presence to provide privacy and ambience. You can enjoy the Inn's own microbrews or a fine Napa wine with your meal. The inn features music inside and at its bar many evenings and weekend afternoons.

Solbar at Solage

Solage is the Valley's newest resort and its Solbar is its restaurant. Solage is the "family" resort from romantic Auberge du Soleil, so encourages informality and active sports. Solbar offers terrace dining in a true California setting designed by famed local architect Howard Bakken where you can enjoy classic ingredient-driven fresh California cuisine while taking in the dramatic mountain views. A fire place helps cheer cooler nights.

Other choices

Some other restaurants have pleasant outside dining, including Meadowood, Rutherford Grill, Étoile at Domain Chandon, Bouchon, Bistro Jeanty, Redd, Downtown Joe's and Ristorante Allegría.

For informal lunches, you can't beat enjoying food from Oxbow Public Market vendors or the Kitchen Door on the river deck with a glass of wine from Oxbow Wine Merchants, or at Napa General Store as well as the Gott's Refreshers in Napa and St. Helena.

Where to stay in Napa Valley

One thing a Napa Valley insider doesn't know about is lodging. I've stayed in few local hotels and inns, and none in years. After all, I have a perfectly good house and a needy cat. So these descriptions are necessarily sketchy. Remember that the Internet is the best place for data and details, while this book is about opinions.

The valley contains big hotels, boutique luxury hotels, business-type chains and motels and intimate inns including traditional bed and breakfasts, though that name isn't very descriptive.

Some of these inns are converted houses or mansions, some restored old hotels, some newly built small places. You might share a bath with the family or have a secluded cottage of your own. In general, inns have 20 rooms or less.

The county also contains a number of motels and lower-end hotels in the cities. Most are modest but relatively expensive compared to those found elsewhere.

About vacation rentals

Finally, a world should be said about short-term vacation rentals in Napa County's rural areas. They are illegal. Period. It's against the law to rent a home in the unincorporated area (called "county" locally) for less than 30 days.

Napa County is not issuing any more hotel, inn, vacation rental or B&B permits in the unincorporated area, either, except for small hotels (under 50 units) in the few commercial areas like the airport area, one has appeared.

Napa and St. Helena have legalized some of these rentals, but many people advertise illegal rentals online.

There are a number of reasons these illegal rentals are forbidden:

- They don't necessarily meet health and safety codes.
- They don't pay the transient occupancy taxes licensed places do.
- Many are in places unsuited for visitors, particularly large groups that party hard.

So far, the county (and cities) have gone after landlords, not guests, but they have closed down some places leaving people who've reserved the homes without accommodations – and perhaps without their deposits.

Some places advertised as being in "Napa" are in nearby Solano or Sonoma where they may be allowed. That may not be a problem. Both have areas as attractive as Napa County, but they may be a long or challenging drive away from the attractions of Napa Valley – though Sonoma certainly has its own.

Napa County has two time-share developments. Vino Bello Resort next to the Meritage Hotel south of Napa is a modern development whose guest can use the amenities of the Meritage including its bowling alleys, spa and chapel. (707) 251-1900, 865 Bordeaux Lane, Napa

RiverPointe Napa Valley Resort is a bunch of trailer cottages near the Napa River in Napa that have to be moved in case of potential flooding. It's basically an upscale RV park where you rent the trailers, though they don't really look like trailers. The only attraction nearby is Compadres Rio Grille, a popular Mexican restaurant and bar. RiverPointe is not the vacation most people envision in Napa Valley. (888) 430-9988 500 Lincoln Ave., Napa

Stay at a Winery?

While Napa County ordinances prohibit inns and hotels at wineries, a few wineries have lodging that was grandfathered in or avoids the county regulations by being in one of the cities. So you may be able to spend the night at a winery, but that doesn't mean your accommodation will be luxurious.

The county isn't being unreasonable, however. There are more than 400 bonded wineries in Napa Valley, and it would simply be untenable for very many to open inns or restaurants. It would be nice if a dozen could, but who's to select which ones qualify?

Here are the places you can stay at wineries:

Sunny Acres B&B

Sunny Acres B&B is on the grounds of 20-acre Salvestrin Vineyard & Wine Company almost in downtown St. Helena. The restored building was originally constructed in 1879. In the middle of a vineyard. All rooms have private baths.

Milat Vineyards

Small Milat Vineyards and Winery south of St. Helena has two suites available for rent in the middle of its vineyards. They're nothing fancy, but almost unique in Napa Valley. 866.270.5669 1091 St. Helena Hwy. South St. Helena

Prager Port Works

Prager Port Works close to downtown St. Helena rents two modest suites to visitors. The Prager family makes wines including "port" on site, and visitors always get to meet members of the family and their pets.

RustRidge Ranch & Winery

RustRidge Winery in very rural Chiles Valley is truly unique: The only lodgings in a remote winery in Napa County. The three-room getaway has a full professional kitchen in case guests don't want to drive the windy road to St. Helena or Rutherford, too.

The winery owners also raise thoroughbred race horses, though the county won't allow them to offer trail rides.

(707) 965.9353 2910 Lower Chiles Valley Rd, Chiles Valley

Guest houses

If you work in the industry, note that many wineries have guest houses available to the trade. Some are quite elaborate like the Beaulieu House, virtually a small luxury hotel. I've never heard of wineries renting these spaces in those not in the trade., both because of the consequences if they're caught but also because they're generally filled with legitimate guests.

Christian Brothers Retreat

The Christian Brothers Retreat & Conference Center is not your usual hotel, but could be a very nice getaway among the vines.

When the conference center isn't fully occupied, you can rent a quiet room and even enjoy meals with the brothers. They used to run Christian Brothers Winery, now the Culinary Institute of America's Greystone Cellars campus in St. Helena. They're definitely not teetotalers and wine is served with dinner.

The retreat is next to the Hess Collection up in the Mayacamas Mountains west of Napa. (707) 252.3703 4401 Redwood Road Napa

Hotels in Napa

Napa Valley has a huge range of accommodations, from modest motels – though not as inexpensive as they would be elsewhere – through mid-market business-type hotels, luxury resorts, big hotels and a wide range of intimate inns and bed and breakfasts.

Information on small inns and B&Bs and modest chain-type lodging follows in the next sections.

Downtown Napa hotels

Andaz hotel

The upscale Andaz hotel was the Avia until it was bought by Hyatt. It has brought luxurious accommodation to downtown Napa, joining the elegant Napa River Inn in the restored Historic Napa Mill.

It has an elegant bubble bar featuring sparkling wine in the lobby and a restaurant that's busy mostly at breakfast.

Napa River Inn

The Napa River Inn was cleverly and lovingly built into the restored Historic Napa Mill. Once grinding wheat and making pet food, the buildings were long abandoned, but now contain meeting rooms, suites and lobby for the Napa River Inn, while new buildings designed to compliment the ambience contain most of the rooms, all along the river.

The Napa Mill complex also contains two fine restaurants, Celadon and Angèle, informal Napa General Store, which is also a café, Sweetie Pies, Napa Sweet Shop, a gift shop and Silo's Jazz Club, which acts as the hotel's bar as well as a performance venue. T

The Napa Mill, also called the Hatt Building by locals, is next to the large Riverfront development with the visitor's center, Fish Story and hot Morimoto restaurants and a number of stores and a new gelato and coffee shop.

If I were staying in Napa, the Napa River Inn would be my first choice, both because it's very nice and because it's so convenient to so many things from great food to entertainment. (707) 251.8500 500 Main St. Napa

River Terrace Inn

The River Terrace Inn, also recently bought and moved upscale, has a Yosemite lodge feel. It is only a few blocks from downtown on the Napa River and easy walking distance to the Oxbow Public Market and its Cuvée Restaurant as well as the elegant La Toque next door. It's a nice place. (707) 320-9000 1600 Soscol Ave. Napa

Westin Verasa

The larger Westin Verasa is next to the River Terrace on the Napa River. It's even closer to the Oxbow Market, downtown and across the street from the Napa Valley Wine Train Station.

It houses Ken Frank's famed La Toque restaurant, which is in the top tier of Napa Valley restaurants if not as famous as the French Laundry or Meadowood. The kitchen staff there also prepares meals for the informal Bank Café and Bar in the lobby, which serves a three-course dinner from a region of France each night at a very reasonable prices.

The Westin generally has a car to deliver guests to nearby restaurants and other attractions just for the donation of a tip to the driver, though it's only about six blocks to First and Main, the center of downtown. Westin Verasa Napa (707) 257-1800 1141 First St. Napa

Medium-size boutique hotels

Napa Winery Inn

The Napa Winery Inn is new. It was formerly the moderately priced John Muir Inn, but hotelier Rick Swing, who also owns the elegant Harvest Inn in St. Helena, has bought and upgraded it. It's more affordable that most hotel upvalley yet still very nice. (707) 257.7220 1998 Trower Ave. Napa

Rural luxury

Carneros Inn

Carneros Inn is a luxury resort in the rural Carneros area surrounded by vineyards. Its lodging is in private cottages, all beautifully appointed, and its boasts a spa, private dining area and pool on the hill above plus elegant Farm Restaurant, informal Boon Fly Cafe and even a small store that sells picnic foods and local items. It's managed by the PlumpJack Group. (707) 299.4900 4048 Sonoma Highway Napa

Big hotels

Few vacationers would probably choose to stay at large chain hotels, but all are nice and well run.

Marriott Napa Valley

The Marriott Napa Valley is very convenient in North Napa, and has recently been heavily upgraded to move it upscale. It naturally attracts many conferences and business travelers, but has a private lounge for guests. The restaurant open to the lobby has little charm, but the food is cuts above that found in most hotel restaurants. The hotel has an extensive spa. (707) 253.8600 3425 Solano Ave. Napa

Embassy Suites

The Embassy Suites is at First Street and Highway 29 near downtown Napa but not really walking distance for everyone. It's a big hotel that serves breakfast and happy hour to guests, and has a typical hotel restaurant called Highway Grill 29 that's okay for basic food. The hotel is now being upgraded and expanded. (707) 253.9540 1075 California Blvd. Napa

The Meritage Resort and Spa

The Meritage Resort and Spa is big and recently doubled in size. Though in a corporate park south of Napa, it does have vines around.

It now has about 340 guest rooms, each with patio or balcony, an extra 12,500 square feet of conference space, a sports lounge with bowling lanes, a café and an outdoor wedding area over looking hillside vineyards in addition to the current Siena restaurant, and a spa and tasting room for the owners' Trinitas wines in the estate wine cave. It even contains a chapel.

Most of what a visitor wants is available onsite, but the hotel has a shuttle that makes runs to downtown Napa regularly.

(707) 251-1900 875 Bordeaux Way Napa

Silverado Resort and Spa

Silverado Resort and Spa is a large resort with two 18-hole golf courses, tennis courts and pros, two restaurants and a first-class spa. Accommodations are in suites that are now being upgraded under new management.

The resort also is a country club, and locals usually call the whole resort Silverado Country Club. The headquarters is in a 19th century mansion that has a friendly bar overlooking the fairway. It has a formal and an informal restaurant and a lobby bar that serves burgers and snacks. (707) 257.0200 1600 Atlas Peak Rd. Napa

Hotels in Yountville, Oakville and Rutherford

Napa Valley Lodge

Napa Valley Lodge looks like a motel, but its 55 rooms are nice after renovation into a luxury inn. 2230 Madison St , Yountville, (707) 944.2468, ww.napavalleylodge.com.

Villagio

Villagio is a luxury inn that suggests an Italian village with its 112 rooms in separate buildings arranged among plantings and waterways. It has a popular spa and a rare (for Napa Valley) lobby bar. 6481 Washington St., Yountville, (707) 944.8877. www.villagio.com.

Vintage Inn

Vintage Inn is the French-inspired counterpart and sister property to Villagio with 80 rooms., 6541 Washington St., Yountville, (707) 944.1112, www.vintageinn.com

Hotel Yountville

Hotel Yountville is another pleasant hotel in "downtown" Yountville. It was recently expanded and upgraded from an inn into a hotel. 6462 Washington St., Yountville, (707) 944.5600, www.yountvilleinn.com.

Bardessono

Bardessono is an environmentally sensitive luxury hotel. Every step has been taken to use sustainable materials and design, but it's not brown rice and tofu. It's attractive and the rooms spare no luxuries, even hiding a massage table for in-room massages.

It also includes an unusual roof-top pool, spa, on-premise gardens for its Lucy Restaurant and comfortable courtyard.

North Branch Hotel

North Branch Hotel, formerly Hotel Luca, seems a street in a Tuscan town. It's definitely luxurious, and even has upscale furnishing from Restoration Hardware. On site is Redd Wood Pizzeria plus.

Auberge du Soleil

Auberge du Soleil is one of Napa Valley's top properties. Splayed across the hills of a small valley east of Rutherford, it seems transplanted from the Mediterranean. Rooms are mostly cottages, and service is unmatched. One attraction is an amazing sculpture garden-gallery of works you'd expect to find in top museums. The restaurant is also one of the valley's standouts, and the restaurant and bar deck offers the best views from any restaurant in Napa Valley.

Rancho Caymus Inn

Rancho Caymus Inn is in Rutherford's tiny downtown behind Rutherford Grill and next to Beaulieu Vineyards. It specializes in quiet luxury. Alex Italian Restaurant is a bonus, though La Luna market across the street makes some of the best tacos and burritos you could find.

Hotels in St. Helena

El Bonita

El Bonita started as a modest motel that was once the only place to stay in the area. It still looks that way, but the interiors have been upgraded over time. It's in a convenient location not far south of St. Helena's downtown. And, yes, it should be La Bonita; a man called El once owned it and liked that name better. (707) 963.3216. 195 Main St. St. Helena

Harvest Inn

Harvest Inn is an elegant mock-Tudor complex almost in downtown St. Helena but its 54 luxury cottages are well screened from outside intrusion. It has a wine bar, too, and hosts special events and music at times. One Main St., St. Helena, (707) 963-9463, www.harvestinn.com

Hotel St. Helena

Some would call this small hotel a B&B, but is was built to be a hotel, and its location can't be beat: In the middle of St. Helena's charming downtown Main Street within walking distance of a dozen restaurants. It has its own wine bar, too. (707) 963.4388 1309 Main St. St. Helena

Hotel Wydown

Hotel Wydown is a relatively new 12-room hotel that once was apartments in downtown St. Helena. It's very convenient and the rooms are luxurious. (707) 963.5100. 1424 Main St. St. Helena.

The Inn at Southbridge

The Inn at Southbridge offers luxury one block from downtown and adjacent to popular Tra Vigne Restaurant. It includes a complete health club. 21 suites. 1020 Main St., St Helena, (707) 967-9400, www.innatsouthbridge.com.

Meadowood Napa Valley

Meadowood Napa Valley Resort is just minutes from downtown in its own private valley accessible only from a gap in the surrounding hills; you can drive by on the famed Silverado Trail only a short distance way and have no idea the 250-acre resort is hiding nearby.

The 85-unit resort and private club is one of the most sought-after lodgings in Napa Valley, not only because of the privacy, but for its exquisite food, spa, pools, nine-hole golf course, tennis courts and rare formal croquet court as well as hiking on trails in the surrounding hills.

Each June, Meadowood Napa Valley hosts the world-renowned Auction Napa Valley organized by the Napa Valley Vintners.

A big draw for many is the other clientele, including most top vintners in Napa Valley, who belong to the club and use its facilities.

Not surprisingly, Meadowood offers guests the finest wines as well as wine courses and tours. Each afternoon resort guests are invited to enjoy a tasting of outstanding Napa Valley wines.

Meadowood guests can also enjoy a taste of the good life in accommodations ranging from cozy cottages to elegant suites and spacious lodges, all sited in a private forested setting. Fireplaces add a romantic glow to most guest rooms and terraces offer ideal settings for quiet contemplation or intimate dining.

Meadowood offers many dining options. The Restaurant at Meadowood offers a casually elegant dining experience featuring a modern approach to Napa Valley cuisine by Chef Christopher Kostow. The Restaurant is one of Northern California's two three-star Michelin restaurants. The other is the famed French Laundry.

Kostow also supervises the cuisine at the informal Grill, which serves breakfast, lunch and dinner; The Restaurant Bar & Terrace; in-room dining; poolside; and special occasions and events. The resort will even furnish picnic lunches to be enjoyed at wineries in Napa Valley.

Meadowood Lane, St. Helena (707) 963-3646. www.meadowood.com.

Hotels in Calistoga

Calistoga Ranch

While other elegant resorts in Napa Valley attract their share of celebrities, Calistoga Ranch stands alone for its exclusivity – and privacy.

Its location ensures that privacy. Because it's at the end of an obscure road in a narrow canyon in the eastern hills of Napa Valley, all guests and visitors must leave their cars with the valet when they arrive, and after that, all transportation is by staff-driven electric carts – or on foot.

That's only part of the reason the resort owned by the Auberge du Soleil group has become a haven for celebrities, high-powered executives and members of royal families, some of whom own homes there. While all enjoy the low-keyed luxury and privacy, they also appreciate the level of service and luxury.

Lady Gaga can – and has – walked around without notice, and the queen of Jordan receives no attention other than the attentive service given all guests.

The resort starts in the canyon near a small vineyard, restaurant garden, pool, exercise facilities and poolside bar and lunch area. It winds up the canyon on both sides of an attractive creek, and at the top of the canyon is gourmet Lakeside Restaurant and Bar, as well as a wine cave and the luxurious spa overlooking Lake Lommel.

At a casual look, Calistoga Ranch seems like a pleasant summer camp of rustic cottages set in a lush western valley. Look closer, however, and you'll notice the tailored landscaping and meticulous maintenance. Enter a suite and you'll immediately be struck by the elegant design, quality of construction and attention to detail.

The unusual resort contains consists of 48 guest cottage suites and 27 shared-ownership homes. Most of the suites consist of two modules, a living room with fireplace and a bedroom joined by an inviting outdoor covered living room that's even comfortable in inclement weather due to fireplaces and heaters.

Three suites mimic the homes and add a second "guest" bedroom and fully equipped Viking gourmet kitchens and dining areas for those rare times when the outdoor space isn't inviting. A Viking grill is on the patio for outdoor cooking.

Not surprisingly, most guests don't cook with the resort's gourmet Lakeside Restaurant nearby and lunch served around the pool during season, while Napa Valley's famed gourmet delights are on a short ride away. However many guests use private chefs or the hotel chefs to prepare private meals. Renowned San Francisco restaurateur Gary Danko owns a home here, and can help with meals and events.

All of the master bedrooms boast private outdoor showers as well as whirlpool tubs, and of course large screen televisions and upscale audio systems. Their outdoor spa pools are always warm and inviting, and the pools are emptied and sanitized after each guest, with the drained water irrigating the vineyard.

In spite of the lure outside the gates, many guests don't leave the grounds. The resort boats private hiking trails, yoga in the morning, and the spa, exercise equipment and pool are open around the clock. If guests want to see Napa Valley, new Mercedes are available for their complimentary use.

One attraction of the resort is its many vintner members, who often host events including in the wine cave. Famed wine expert Andrea Robinson is a member and often leads tastings and classes. The resort also has classes in winemaking and blending, and even in processing olives in season.

Like the rest of the facilities, the restaurant is exclusively for guests, though those staying at nearby Solage and Auberge du Soleil can eat there, too. It has a deck overlooking the lake, but also contains private rooms for those who prefer seclusion.

The spa was rated #1 in California by Conde Nash, and includes outdoor treatment areas as well as Watsu water massages, too.

(707) 254.2800 580 Lommel Rd. Calistoga.

Calistoga Inn, Restaurant & Brewery

Calistoga Inn is an old hotel with rooms upstairs and baths down the hall. It's also very reasonable and the location is perfect on Calistoga's main street, Lincoln Avenue. The inn has a hopping bar with music on weekends, a microbrewery (Don't ask for Coors Light!), a good restaurant and a nice patio by the Napa River (here a creek) for the usual nice weather. (707) 942.4101 1250 Lincoln Ave. Calistoga

Mount View Hotel & Spa

Mount View Hotel & Spa is a nice small hotel and spa right in the middle of downtown Calistoga. Two restaurants share the building, JoLe and Barolo. (707) 942-6877 1457 Lincoln Ave. Calistoga

Solage

Solage is Auberge du Soleil's "more affordable" brand, but it's no Motel 6. A luxurious resort by any standards, it consists of detached cottages spread over a walkable area with a first–class restaurant (Solbar), luxurious spa and pool and bocce court. It's an easy bicycle into town, and the resort has bicycles to borrow. You can also walk. (707) 226.0800 755 Silverado Trail Calistoga.

Boutique inns & B&Bs

Napa

- 1801 First (707) 224.3739 1801 First St. Napa
- Arbor Guest House (707) 252.8144 1436 G St. Napa
- The Beazley House (707) 257.1649 1910 1st. St. Napa
- Bel Abri Napa Valley Inn (707) 253.2100 837 California Blvd. Napa
- Blackbird Inn - A Four Sisters Inn (707) 226.2450 1755 First St. Napa
- Brookside Vineyard B&B (707) 252.6690 3194 Redwood Road Napa
- Candlelight Inn (707) 257.3717 1045 Easum Dr. Napa
- Cedar Gables Inn (707) 224.7969 486 Coombs St. Napa
- Churchill Manor (707) 253.7733 485 Brown St. Napa
- The Cottages of Napa Valley (707) 252.7810 1012 Darms Lane Napa
- De Mar House (707) 299.0009 Napa
- Hennessey House Napa B&B (707) 226.3774 1727 Main St. Napa
- Hillview Country Inn (707) 224.5004 1205 Hillview Lane Napa
- The Inn on First (707) 253.1331 1938 First St. Napa
- Inn on Randolph (707) 257.2886 411 Randolph St. Napa
- La Belle Epoque (707) 257.2161 1386 Calistoga Ave. Napa
- La Casita (707) 738.0682 Napa
- La Residence Country Inn (707) 253.0337 4066 Howard Lane Napa
- McClelland-Priest B&B Inn (707) 224.6875 569 Randolph St. Napa
- Milliken Creek Inn 888.593.6175 1815 Silverado Trail Napa
- The Napa Inn Bed & Breakfast (707) 257.1444 1137 Warren St. Napa
- Oak Knoll Inn (707) 255.2200 2200 E. Oak Knoll Ave. Napa
- Old World Inn (707) 257.0112 1301 Jefferson St. Napa
- Stahlecker House B&B (707) 257.1588 1042 Easum Dr. Napa
- White House Inn & Spa (707) 254.9301 443 Brown St. Napa

Yountville

- Bordeaux House (707) 944.2855 6600 Washington St. Yountville
- Lavender, a Four Sisters Inn (707) 944.1388 800.522.4140 2020 Webber Avenue Yountville
- Maison Fleurie, a Four Sisters Inn (707) 944.2056 6529 Yount St. Yountville
- Napa Valley Railway Inn (707) 944.2000 6523 Washington St. Yountville
- Oleander House (707) 944.8315 7433 St. Helena Highway Yountville
- Petit Logis Inn (707) 944.2332 6527 Yount St. Yountville
- Poetry Inn (707) 944-0646 6380 Silverado Trail Yountville,

St. Helena

- Adagio Inn (707) 963.2238 1417 Kearney St. St. Helena
- Ambrose Bierce House B&B (707) 963.3003 1515 Main St. St. Helena,
- Black Rock Inn (707) 968.7893 3100 North Silverado Trail St. Helena
- Ink House B&B (707) 963.3890 1575 St. Helena Highway St. Helena
- The Red Door Inn (707) 963.5400 1523 Main St. St. Helena
- Shady Oaks Country Inn (707) 963.1190 399 Zinfandel Ln. St. Helena
- Spanish Villa Inn (707) 963.7483 474 Glass Mountain Road St. Helena
- Wine Country Inn is on a knoll north of St. Helena. Built to be an elegant B&B, it has 24 guest rooms and five private cottages. 1152 Lodi Lane, St. Helena, (707) 963-7077, www.winecountryinn.com
- Zinfandel Inn (707) 963.3512 800 Zinfandel Lane St. Helena

Calistoga

- Aurora Park Cottages (707) 942.6733 1807 Foothill Blvd. Calistoga
- Bear Flag Inn (707) 942.5534 2653 Foothill Blvd (Hwy 128) Calistoga
- Brannan Cottage Inn (707) 942.4200 109 Wapoo [sic] Ave. Calistoga

- Calistoga Spa Hot Springs (707) 942.6269 1006 Washington St. Calistoga
- Calistoga Wayside Inn (707) 942.0645 1523 Foothill Blvd. Calistoga
- Calistoga Wine Way Inn (707) 942.0680 1019 Foothill Blvd. Calistoga
- Carlin Country Cottages (707) 942.9102 1623 Lake St. Calistoga
- CasaLana B&B (707) 942.0615 1316 South Oak St. Calistoga
- Chanric Inn (707) 942.4535 1805 Foothill Blvd. Calistoga
- Chateau de Vie B&B (707) 942.6446 3250 Highway 128 Calistoga
- Chelsea Garden Inn (707) 942.0948 800.942.1515 1443 Second St. Calistoga
- Christopher's Inn (707) 942.5755 1010 Foothill Blvd Calistoga
- Cottage Grove Inn (707) 942.8400 1711 Lincoln Ave. Calistoga
- The Craftsman Inn (707) 341.3035 1213 Foothill Blvd. Calistoga
- Dr. Wilkinson's Hot Springs (707) 942.4102 1507 Lincoln Ave. Calistoga
- Euro Spa & Inn (707) 942.6829 1202 Pine St. Calistoga
- Fanny's Napa Valley (707) 942.9491 1206 Spring St. Calistoga
- Golden Haven Hot Springs (707) 942-8000 1713 Lake St. Calistoga
- Hideaway Cottages (707) 942.4108 1412 Fairway Dr. Calistoga
- Hillcrest B&B (707) 942.6334 3225 Lake County Hwy. Calistoga
- Hotel d'Amici (707) 942-1007 1436 Lincoln Ave. Calistoga
- Indian Springs Spa & Resort (707) 942.4913 1712 Lincoln Ave. Calistoga
- Larkmead Country Inn (707) 942.5360 1103 Larkmead Lane Calistoga
- Luxe Calistoga (707) 942-9797 1139 Lincoln Ave. Calistoga
- Mayacamas Ranch (707) 942-5127 3975 Mountain Home Ranch Road Calistoga
- Meadowlark Country House (707) 942.5651 601 Petrified Forest Road Calistoga
- Oakwood B&B (707) 942.5381 1503 Lake St. Calistoga

- The Pink Mansion (707) 942.0558 1415 Foothill Boulevard Calistoga
- Roman Spa Hot Springs (707) 942.4441 1300 Washington St. Calistoga
- Trailside Inn (707) 942.4106 4201 Silverado Trail Calistoga
- Villa Palma (415) 420-2263 north of Calistoga
- Zinfandel House (707) 942-0733 1253 Summit Dr. Calistoga

Chain, business and other lodgings

American Canyon

- DoubleTree Hotel & Spa Napa Valley (707) 674-2100 3600 Broadway St. American Canyon
- Fairfield Inn & Suites (707) 643.3800 3800 Broadway St. American Canyon
- Holiday Inn Express and Suites (707) 552-8100 5001 Main St. American Canyon

Napa

- Best Western PLUS Inn at the Vines (707) 257.1930 100 Soscol Ave. Napa
- Best Western Premier Ivy Hotel Napa Valley (707) 253.9300 4195 Solano Ave. Napa
- Chablis Inn (707) 257.1944 3360 Solano Ave. Napa
- Chardonnay Lodge (707) 224.0789 2640 Jefferson St. Napa
- Discovery Inn (707) 253.0892 500 Silverado Trail Napa
- Hawthorn Suites by Wyndham (707) 226.1878 314 Soscol Ave. Napa
- Hilton Garden Inn (707) 252.0444 3585 Solano Ave. Napa
- Napa Valley Hotel & Suites (707) 226.1871 853 Coombs St. Napa
- Napa Valley Redwood Inn (707) 257.6111 3380 Solano Ave. Napa
- SpringHill Suites Napa Valley (707) 253.1900 101 Gateway Road East Napa
- Wine Valley Lodge (707) 224.7911 200 South Coombs St. Napa

Calistoga

- Best Western PLUS Stevenson Manor (707) 942.1112 1830 Lincoln Ave. Calistoga
- Comfort Inn Calistoga (707) 942.9400 1865 Lincoln Ave. Calistoga

Camping and RV spaces

Though many might not be tempted to camp in Napa Valley, plenty of people do. The following are campgrounds or TV parks.

- Bothe-Napa Valley Park had recently been taken over by Napa County and volunteers. It has camping sites and hopes to restore some cabins for overnight stays. (707) 942.4575 3801 St. Helena, Hwy. North St. Helena

- Napa County Fairgrounds (707) 942.5111 1435 Oak St. Calistoga

- Napa Valley Exposition (707) 253.4900 575 Third St. Napa

- Safari West is a wild animal retreat. It rents permanent tents to guests and serves barbecue. It's actually in Sonoma County. (707) (579) 2551 3115 Porter Creek Rd. Calistoga

- Skyline Wilderness Park (707) 252.0481 2201 Imola Ave. Napa

At Lake Berryessa

- Lake Berryessa is about a half hour drive from Napa Valley. Check about facilities as the area is in a state of flux.

- Chaparral Cove Resort (Putah Creek): Tent and RV camping. (707) 966-9088, www.lakeberryessashores.com reservations@lakeberryessashores.com

- Foothill Pines Resort (Spanish Flat): Tent and RV camping. 707-966-9088, www.lakeberryessashores.com reservations@lakeberryessashores.com

- Lupine Shores Resort (former Steele Park): Tent and RV camping, 707-966-9088, www.lakeberryessashores.com reservations@lakeberryessashores.com

- Pleasure Cove Marina: Two dozen RV sites with full or partial hookups and over 100 tent campsites with water only. Cabin rentals. (707) 966-9600, www.goberryessa.com

What to Do Beside Eat and Drink

Top Views in Napa Valley

Few places on earth have more dramatic views than Napa Valley. With its ever-changing vistas from season to season, and even as the sun scoots across the sky, almost anywhere you go can make you want to pull out your camera.

From the bright yellow of the mustard season to the green of spring and dramatic color of vines with viruses in the fall, every season has its treasures.

Even the cities have picturesque aspects – certainly St. Helena's downtown and Calistoga's wild west look are intriguing, but there's little question that the best views of all occur among the vineyards, at the wineries and in the hills.

With that in mind, we tried to identify what we thought were the best vistas in the valley.

They all are accessible to the public, though some require taking a tour or other expenditure.

Artesa Winery

It's in Carneros Valley rather than Napa Valley, but the Artesa Winery also features views from its deck as interesting as those of the attractive winery itself. After climbing the front stair, you're treated to views of the bucolic valley – and maybe the sheep grazing among the vines – while from the deck by the tasting room, the di Rosa Preserve, Carneros and San Francisco Bay opens. On clear days, you can see Mount Diablo, Mount Tamalpais and even the skyscrapers of San Francisco.

Auberge du Soleil

Oddly enough, Napa Valley has few elevated restaurants where you can enjoy the views as you dine. This isn't likely to change because of today's zoning restrictions, but the deck at the Auberge du Soleil east of Rutherford remains one of the nicest places to enjoy a repast.

The bar isn't the bargain it once was, but it's still a nice place for a cocktail at sunset, and is not outrageous for a light lunch at noon. The restaurant, however, is one of the valley's best, with charges to match.

Deck at Bistro Don Giovanni

Surprisingly few restaurants in Napa Valley are nestled among the vines, but you can enjoy those views – as well as interesting sculpture – from the deck at Bistro Don Giovanni in Napa.

You can also grab a glass of wine and wander out to the tables on the lawn to wait to be called for dinner, but the bar is more fun.

Castello di Amorosa

In addition to being a view in itself, Castello di Amorosa offers impressive views from its towers and parapets. It's also a view east, so is ideal in the late afternoon as shadows play tricks on the hills. It provides a great view of Sterling Vineyards, so you can imagine yourself on a Greek island.

Wine Spectator Restaurant at Greystone Cellars

The only elevated other restaurant deck in the valley besides Auberge is at the Wine Spectator Restaurant at Greystone Cellars, the home of the Culinary Institute of America. The restaurant has expanded its seating there, and you *know* the food is good, making it one of the top destinations for an alfresco meal as well as one with a view.

Ghost Cairn Vineyard

Though most of our choices of views are from above, we can't forget the Ghost Cairn Vineyard nestled in the western Yountville hills just across from Brix. It's no wonder that tourists line the road with their cameras on weekends to capture the organic old vineyards rising into the hills long sacred to the Wappo people.

Rutherford Hill Winery

Just above Auberge, the vistas from Rutherford Hill Winery top even its views. You can even picnic there. You're supposed to call for reservations and expected to buy some of their wine to complement you meal, but that's hardly a hardship as the wine is excellent. They're best known for their Merlot, but the rosé is the ideal accompaniment for a picnic.

Silverado Vineyards

One of the few places to enjoy a view in southern Napa County – except in some vineyards and other places not accessible to the public – is the tasting room deck at Silverado Vineyards in the Stags Leap District.

Silverado Vineyards looks like a Tuscany walled city from the valley floor before, but once you ascend the knoll, you find a hidden treasure. The wines are among the best in the valley, if not promoted heavily, and if you search, you can find a single reminder that the winery is owned by members of the Disney family.

Sterling Vineyards

The deck at monastery-like Sterling Vineyards south of Calistoga offers some of the most dramatic views of Napa Valley imaginable. You have to take the gondola to the winery, but that's a treat in itself and you can often get a $5 discount from the $25 cost on Sterling's website. Under 21 are $10. They're generous in the wine-tasting salon, too, even offering treats to kids. You get a nice view of Castello di Amorosa, transporting you to a hilltop in Italy.

You can also catch fleeting views from roads into the mountains all over the valley, including Atlas Peak, Soda Canyon, and of course, Deep Park Road and Highway 29 heading over Mount St. Helena.

The Sign

We can't forget the famous signs that state, "The Wine is Bottled Poetry," quoting Robert Louis Stevenson. There's one in Oakville and one south of Calistoga on Highway 29. If you want to take a picture, be careful, particularly if you have to cross the highway – or the train tracks, though the train moves so slowly that more cars have run into it than it's run into cars.

The Statue

On the hill just before the high crossing of the Napa River south of town sits a famed statue of a man pressing grapes, though it's universally called "The Crusher." Reach it from the road that runs under the bridge, off Soscol Ferry Road.

Farmers Markets in Napa Valley

Napa Valley cities have Farmers' Market weekly during the summer, from May until October typically. Note that state law prohibits animals in any place where food is sold.

Napa Farmers Market

The Napa Farmers Market is held on Tuesday and Saturday from 7:30 a.m. until noon in the Oxbow Parking lot next to the Oxbow Public Market. It's very popular; parking can be challenging.

It features produce vendors, as well as suppliers of meat, eggs, prepared food and crafts. Charitable organizations and businesses as well as government agencies sometimes exhibit, too.

A number of the vendors sell food ready to eat, but that's not an emphasis as it might conflict with the restaurants and food vendors in the Oxbow Market. In fact, La Crêpe started as a booth in the Farmers Market before graduating to a space inside the Market.

The Chefs' Market in Napa on Thursday evening during the summer also has a small farmers market.

St. Helena Farmers' Market

The St. Helena Farmers' Market Friday morning is the best one in the valley. Held in out-of-the-way Crane Park, it attracts the best vendors, products not seen in the other Napa Valley markets, and, it seems, most of St. Helena's residents.

Locals socialize as they walk and shop, enjoy pastries and coffee under towering redwood trees as the kids play and even play bocce.

Calistoga Farmers' Market

Calistoga Farmers' Market is held Saturday morning between the city hall and Sharpsteen Museum just north of downtown.

Yountville occasionally has a market, but the town is too small and close to Napa to make it very successful.

During the summer, local farm stands also sell produce. They include those at Highway 12/112 and Stanly Lane, on Big Ranch Road, at Oakville Grocery, at Farmstead restaurant in St. Helena and at Deer Park Road and Silverado Trail.

Oxbow Produce Market is a virtual year-round farmers market.

And a number of farms in the valley offer Community Supported Agriculture boxes full of ripe produce weekly for customers. They include Boca Farm, Hudson Ranch and Clif Family Farm.

Napa Chef's Market and Cheers!

One of the best attractions in Napa Valley is a transitory one. Every Thursday evening during the summer, downtown Napa holds its own version of a Caribbean Jump-Up, a street fair and party rocking with music, food, people – and wine.

The highlights of Chef's Market are naturally demonstrations by local chefs, who make a dish, then offer small tastes with a complementary wine; the classes and tastes are free.

A number of different organizations sell wine at the Market, but I'd be sure to frequent those run by Napa Valley wineries or organizations offering Napa Valley wines, not places selling cheap wine from elsewhere at the same price. The wine is served in a small Go Vino "glass," and if you remember to bring it back, you're supposed to get a $1 discount.

There's always a selection of music for different tastes, from rock for the young to mellower sounds for the older folks.

Vendors offer a wide selection of food. Much comes from local restaurants, caterers and organizations, some of gourmet quality, but a few outsiders slip in with favorite items like giant smoked turkey legs and barbecued oysters.

Chefs' Market also has activities for kids, a small farmers market, crafts for sale and political, civic and commercial organizations hawking their wares and views

Local restaurants and wine bars are open during the Market, and if you can get into one, most offer wines by the glass, bottle and taste. My favorite restaurants for light meals are ZuZu, with its tapas, Carpe Diem and Bistro Sabor.

Azzurro Pizzeria bakes and sells pizzas from its portable oven, but I'd rather walk a few blocks to the restaurant, sit down and eat comfortably.

It's mostly a local crowd, and not surprisingly, the highlight for many people is seeing their friends. It's always great fun.

Cheers! St. Helena

St. Helena has a monthly street party called Cheers! on the first Friday of each month during the summer, and it's even better than Napa's.

It's all local wines and food, and its seems that the whole town turns out. The shops are interesting, even if you don't (or can't afford) to buy their merchandise. You can even take a special train to Cheers! from Napa or Yountville, which multiplies the fun.

Auction Napa Valley

The big social and charity event in Napa Valley every year is Auction Napa Valley held in early June each year at Meadowood Resort and locations around Napa Valley.

Auction Napa Valley is the most successful charity wine auction in the world and has raised and donated more than $100 million to local medical, youth, and other nonprofit programs in Napa Valley.

It was inspired by Robert and Margrit Mondavi to raise money for good causes and also promote the quality of Napa Valley wines and the Napa Valley lifestyle. From humble beginnings, it has grown be a four-day celebration of wine, food and the good life, all for a good cause.

The annual fundraiser is hosted by the Napa Valley Vintners, which represents most wineries in the Valley. Hundreds of them combine with community volunteers to put on the impressive show.

The auction starts Wednesday with an elegant dinner for past big bidders.

For most attendees, who pay up to $2,500 each to attend, the festivities start Thursday night with small, generally creative dinners at vintners' homes, wineries or vineyards featuring meals prepared by top chefs from Napa Valley restaurants and wineries, restaurants around the country or even the owners themselves.

Friday brings the famed Barrel Auction and Marketplace, with its extensive Taste of Napa Valley featuring local chefs and wineries, then more intimate vintner dinners. People from around the world can participate in the global E-Auction.

Saturday, attendees head to Meadowood Napa Valley to inspect the impressive lots, many combining rare wine with unique experiences in a glen where they can interact with donors, then enjoy lunch.

The heart of the Auction, of course, is the auction itself. The fun and tension is incomparable as bidders from across the country and around the world compete for the lots from large format bottles to vertical wine collections, vintner-hosted travel and luxury goods.

As the auction wraps up, attendees enjoy a memorable al fresco dinner followed by dancing under the stars.

The Auction ends with a sparkling wine brunch on Sunday at Meadowood as guests prepare to head home, hopefully with a little bit of Napa with them.

Not everyone can attend the Auction as a guest, but hundreds of local volunteers make it happen. If you'd like to participate next year, be sure to check the details at www.napavintners.com, where you can also get more information about the event. Locals get first consideration, however.

Everyone has fun, and successful bidders enjoy unique treasures and everyone in Napa Valley benefits from the funds the generous donors spend at Auction Napa Valley.

Music Festival for Mental Health

Though it doesn't include a wine auction and raises all its donations from tickets, the one-day Music Festival for Mental Health held annually at Staglin Family Vineyards in Rutherford by the International Mental Health Research Organization is one of the most important mental health fund-raising events in the world. It has raised more than $140 million through direct and leveraged funds in its 18 years.

It is held in mid September.

The Music Festival includes a free scientific symposium featuring a leading mental health researcher, then an impressive wine tasting in the Staglin cave and a concert performance by a leading performer and an exclusive VIP dinner featuring top chefs preparing a feast paired with Staglin Family wines.

All expenses are underwritten by its sponsors, and all proceeds go directly to scientific research and treatment programs, including those at UCSF, John Hopkins University, UCLA, Mt. Sinai School of Medicine, University of Texas Southwestern Medical Center, the Roskamp Institute studying Alzheimer's, plus Aldea of Napa and Sonoma.

Of late, tickets for the lecture, reception and concert have been $1,000. Tickets for the lecture, reception, concert and exclusive dinner are $5,000. Admission to the scientific seminar is free with prior registration.

For more information call (707) 963-4038 or visit www.music-festival.org.

School and Charity Auctions

Little known to most visitors to Napa Valley, many of the best events in the valley are fundraising benefits for local schools and other nonprofit organizations. Their auctions often include wine and experience treasures at bargain prices.

In Napa Valley, almost every school, cultural event and charity involves winemakers and vintners, and they donate great wines to the causes they support.

In addition, most chefs have ties to many of these groups, so they volunteer to prepare killer food.

Almost every weekend, two or three of these events happen. Most are reasonable to attend – at least compared to the $2,500 to attend Auction Napa Valley – and it's generally easy to out-bid the local attendees.

For someone who doesn't live in the valley, the easiest way to keep track of events is to check the exhaustive calendar compiled by the Arts Council of Napa Valley, which goes far beyond the "arts." You can find it at www.nvarts.org, and search ot in many ways, including for benefits.

The *Napa Valley Register* and winecountry.com also maintain calendars of events. If you visit often, you might consider a subscription to *NapaLife*, the insider's guide to Napa Valley published weekly (www.napalife.com). You can request a sample from paul@napalife.com.

If you do attend a school auction, you may run into friendly people curious about why you're there, but they'll be appreciative if you help support their favorite causes – even if you outbid them,

The Napa Valley Wine Library tasting

One of Napa Valley's little-known but most interesting events is the annual wine tasting of the Napa Valley Wine Library Association.

Each year, it picks a theme, such as a specific varietal or type of wine, for winery members to pour for two hours under giant oaks at Silverado Resort and Country Club. It naturally benefits the Wine Library, an impressive collection housed at the St. Helena Library.

Local wineries that participate donate wines, and typically more than 100 participate. Only members are admitted to the tasting, but you can joint at the door for a reasonable amount.

The focus changes each year. It might be the obvious, Napa Valley Cabernet, but rotates among Chardonnay, blends, other whites and reds and even obscure varieties.

The day before the big tasting, the Napa Valley Wine Library sponsors an in-depth seminar on the wine focus for the weekend. In the seminar, grape growers, winemakers and winery principals (vintners, in local parlance) present their philosophies, techniques and views about the subject and wines.

The seminar naturally includes wine tasting as well as a question and answer period with the presenters. You have to be a member to attend, but you can pay your membership and seminar fees together.

For further information and reservations about either Wine Library event, visit www.napawinelibrary.org call Napa Valley Wine Library at (707) 963-5145 or e-mail info@napawinelibrary.org.

The V Foundation Wine Celebration

The V Foundation for Cancer Research's annual fundraiser, The V Wine Celebration, has raised more than $120 million for cancer research since 1993, typically about $4 million in a recent year.

It's held in early August in Napa Valley.

The V Foundation's signature fundraising event attracts attendees from all over the U.S. to the Napa Valley for a gala weekend of events and activities with a serious underlying purpose — to support significant cancer research at major institutions and research centers nationwide.

The V Foundation for Cancer Research was founded in 1993 by ESPN and the late Jim Valvano, legendary North Carolina State basketball coach and ESPN commentator.

The annual V Wine Celebration kicks off Friday evening with a party at Vintage Estates in Yountville with food prepared by some of Napa Valley's renowned chefs accompanied by an array of wines from equally famed Napa Valley wineries.

Guests bid on silentand barrel auction lots of unique wine, sports, art and travel packages, and then they dance.

Saturday morning the foundation presents a public Cancer Research Symposium, where prominent physicians and research scientists from around the nation gathered to present the most current advances and discoveries in clinical applications, new diagnostics and alternative treatments for cancer. The crowd can pose questions to these leading researchers during a Q&A session.

The weekend's activities culminate with a gala dinner and live auction at Nickel & Nickel Winery.

The Foundation awards 100 percent of all direct cash donations and net proceeds of events directly to cancer research and related programs. The V Foundation awards grants through a competitive awards process strictly supervised by a scientific advisory board. For more information, visit www.jimmyv.org or www.winecelebration.org.

Flavor Napa Valley

Though new, Flavor Napa Valley is already becoming a major festival for Napa Valley, amazingly the first to focus solely on Napa Valley's world-class food and wine.

It features an impressive array of Napa Valley-based celebrity chefs and graduates of the Culinary Institute of America, restaurants, vintners, sommeliers and artisan food producers.

It is held in mid November and lasts six days.

It features intimate and grand tastings of food and wine, dinners and lunches, classes, seminars and workshops led by top chefs and vintners as well as wine experts at wineries, restaurants, Silverado Resort and Spa and the Culinary Institute of America campus in St. Helena.

The festival's net proceeds support student programs and scholarships at the CIA at Greystone Campus in St. Helena.

For more information including a complete lineup of festival events and activities, visit www.flavornapavalley.com.

The Arts in Napa Valley

As we know, wine reigns supreme in Napa Valley, but food is close behind, and the arts are moving up fast.

That's not surprising. Civilizations that celebrate food and wine also appreciate the arts, from Athens to Florence. The same phenomenon has occurred in Napa Valley. Supported by wealthy patrons of the arts, most involved in the wine business, the visual and performing arts are becoming increasingly important in the valley.

This includes both ongoing activities but also an increasing number of festivals focusing on specific arts. Napa Valley has had two chamber music festivals for years, one called Music in the Vineyards, the other Chamber Music in Napa Valley.

Calistoga has supported a jazz festival. Recently, the valley has added the Napa Valley Film Festival and Festival del Sole with more festivals like one for Mozart's music and time in the works.

There are also festivals for visual arts, too, including Arts in April, Open Studios in the fall and numerous weekend events.

Festivals attract fans from elsewhere, but visitors might well notice the ongoing performances and exhibitions that take place regularly. Check the schedule at nvarts.org and you're likely to find something you'd like to attend any week during the year.

Visual Art

Napa Valley has always hosted exceptional art at some of its wineries and other institutions and mansions,, but the level and quality of art has risen dramatically in the last decade.

One of the most exciting trends is the public art than now adorns downtown Napa and Yountville. Both have impressive art walks with significant pieces of sculpture situated around town. They tend to rotate, so are worth checking regularly.

In addition, Napa places art in vacant store fronts downtown; we hope they won't stay vacant too, but enjoy the Art on F1rst.

Auberge du Soleil sculpture garden

Auberge du Soleil has an amazing and little-viewed sculpture garden-gallery. You're supposed to have a representative from the gallery office there show you around. 180 Rutherford Hill Road, Rutherford, 963-1211, www.aubergedusoleil.com

Ca' Toga

Ca' Toga is a bizarre but interesting home and gallery in Calistoga.

di Rosa Preserve

di Rosa Preserve hosts an incredible collection of contemporary Northern California art. You couldn't appreciate it all in a week of visits, but it's worth starting. 5200 Carneros Highway, Napa, 226-5991, www.dirosapreserve.org

Napa Valley Museum

The Napa Valley Museum in Yountville includes art among its exhibits. 55 Presidents Circle, 944-0500 www.napavalleymuseum.org

Robert Louis Stevenson Museum

Robert Louis Stevenson Museum at the St. Helena Library has many interesting exhibits. The Napa Valley Wine Library is also based there. 1492 Library Lane, St. Helena, 963-5145. www.napawinelibrary.org.

Sharpsteen Museum

Sharpsteen Museum focuses more on local Calistoga history. 1311 Washington St., Calistoga, 942 5911, www.sharpsteen-museum.org.

Gordon Huether's Studio and Huether Gallery

Gordon Huether's Studio and Huether Gallery are in Napa. The working studio where internationally know artist Gordon Huether creates his masterpieces is on Monticello Road. He welcomes visitors and the site also have a gallery that exhibits his and other artists' work.

Huether also has a gallery in downtown Napa with his works on display.

Art at wineries

Beyond that, many wineries have impressive art collections.

Art has always accompanied wine and food in the good life, and many wineries in Napa Valley join in offering exceptional art displays. Some have established galleries, while others integrate it into their grounds and public spaces.

Best of all, you can view the art at these wineries for free, though most people would want to taste wine while they do so.

Cliff Lede Vineyards

The Gallery at Cliff Lede Vineyards features four exhibits per year. It's a serious gallery with the feel of a top space in New York and the works are for sale. 1473 Yountville Cross Road, Yountville. cliffledevineyards.com.

Clos Pegase

While Clos Pegase Winery is exceptional architecture in itself, the walls, spaces and grounds of the winery showcase part of Jan Shrem's collection of paintings and sculpture.

Most photographed is a frivolous giant thumb in the garden, but the modern sculptures and originals of the wine labels also deserve careful attention. 1060 Dunaweal Lane, Calistoga. (707) 942-4981. www.clospegase.com.

Hall Wines

Craig and Kathryn Hall are passionate art collectors, and some of their work remains on display around and in the tasting room at their winery in St. Helena as well at their jewel of a winery in the hills of Rutherford. 401 St. Helena Highway South, St. Helena. (707) 967-2620. hallwines.com.

The Hess Collection

The Hess Collection Gallery is in a class by itself. Part of Donald Hess' personal collection, the extensive gallery could easily stand alone as a major attraction in any large city without any connection to the winery. Its most famous work is Johanna, the haunting giant image of a young woman created from thousands of tiny dots. 4411 Redwood Road, Napa. (707) 255-1144 www.hesscollection.com.

Markham Vineyards

The Harley Bruce Markham Gallery features periodic art shows, presently a photographic retrospective of Rock n' Roll's biggest stars and events as captured by Baron Wolman, *Rolling Stone*'s first chief photographer. 2812 St. Helena Highway N, St. Helena. (707) 963-5292. www.markhamvineyards.com.

Michael Mondavi Family Winery

Michael Mondavi's tasting room offers a fluid collection of art for sale. 1285 Dealy Lane, Napa. (707) 256-2757. www.foliowine.com.

Robert Mondavi Winery

Robert Mondavi Winery has always been a bastion of art thanks largely to its cultural director, Margrit Biever Mondavi.

The most obvious sign is the Bufano and other sculptures dotting the grounds, a delight for children of any age, but the winery has a permanent collection and the Vineyard Gallery hosts changing shows that are open to the public. Frequent receptions introduce the artists and their works. Highway 29, Oakville. 1-888-766-6328. www.robertmondaviwinery.com..

Mumm Napa Valley

Mumm Napa Valley includes one of the world's leading galleries of photographic art. Though former owners removed part of the famed Ansel Adams collection, benefactors have replaced them, and temporary exhibits provide an excuse to visit often. 8445 Silverado Trail, Rutherford. 800-686-6272. mummnapa.com.

St. Supéry Vineyards and Winery

There's an art gallery upstairs at the St. Supéry Visitor Center featuring changing seasonal exhibits by local and internationally renowned artists. 8440 St. Helena Hwy., Rutherford. (707) 963.4507. www.stsupery.com.

Turnbull Winery

Like Mumm, Turnbull features a gallery featuring famous black and white photography. The exhibit changes every six months. It is in the reserve room of the winery, so requires appointments. 8210 Saint Helena Hwy., Oakville. (707) 963-5839. www.turnbullwines.com.

Many standalone tasting rooms also feature art. Ceja Vineyards' salon in downtown Napa and Jessup Vineyards in Yountville, for example, have extensive galleries.

St. Helena has many first-class commercial art galleries, and Yountville, Calistoga and Napa all have commercial and association galleries as well. See the listings following

Commercial Art Galleries

In this listing of art galleries, I'll make no attempt to impose my taste on you, so include all I know of, not just the ones showcasing "serious" art:

Calistoga

- Calistoga Art Center 1506 Lincoln Ave., (707) 942-2278
- Lee Youngman Galleries (707) 942-0585 1316 Lincoln Ave.,
- Santa Fe West (707) 942-2100 1421 Lincoln Ave, Calistoga
- Ca' Toga Galleria D'Arte (707) 942-3900 1206 Cedar St.
- Stix and Stones Gallery 1409 Lincoln Ave. (707) 942-6002
- Donlee Gallery of Fine Art 1316 Lincoln Ave. (707) 942-0585

Napa

- Artists of the Valley Gallery of the Napa Valley Art Association 1307 First St. www.nvart.org
- Ceja Vineyards Wine Salon Lounge and Art Gallery 1248 First St. (707) 226-6445
- di Rosa 5200 Carneros Highway (707) 226-5991 www.dirosaart.org
- Gordon Huether Gallery 1465 First St. (707) 255-2133
- Gordon Huether Studio 1821 Monticello Rd. (707) 255-5954 www.gordonhuether.com
- Grand Hand Gallery 1136 Main St. (707) 253-2551
- Jessel Gallery 1019 Atlas Peak Rd. (707) 257-2350 www.jesselgallery.com
- Quent Cordair Fine Art 1301 First St. (707) 255-2242 www.cordair.com
- Thomas Kinkade 1390 1st St. (707) 258-8200 www.thomaskinkadeofnapavalley.com
- Volakis Gallery421 Walnut St. (707) 320-8796 www.volakisgallery.com

St. Helena

- Art On Main 1359 Main St. imagesnapavalley.com (707) 963-3350
- Caldwell Snyder Gallery 1328 Main St. (707) 200-5050 www.caldwellsnyder.com

- Christopher Hill Gallery 1235 Main St. (707) 963-0272 www.chgallery.com
- Findings 1269 Main St. (707) 963-6000 findingsnapavalley.com
- Wolk Gallery 1354 Main St. (707) 963-8800 www.iwolkgallery.com
- Pavati Collections 1150 Main St. (707) 967-8797 www.pavaticollections.com

Yountville

V Marketplace 6525 Washington St. www.vmarketplace.com:

- 1870 Gallery (707) 944-9670
- Art Of Dr Seuss Yountville (707) 944-2523
- Blue Heron Gallery (707) 944-2044 www.blueheronofnapa.com
- Generations A Fine Art Gallery (707) 944-1778
- Starz Gallery Inc. (707) 944-1990

Other locations in Yountville:

- Gordon Gallery 6484 Washington St. (707) 944-0823
- Hope and Grace 6540 Washington St. (707) 944-2500 www.hopeandgracewines.com
- Jessup Cellars Tasting Room 6740 Washington St. (707) 944-8523 www.jessupcellars.com
- Ma(i)sonry 6711 Washington St. (707) 944-0889 www.maisonry.com
- North Bay Gallery 6525 Washington St. (707) 945-0145 www.northbaygallery.net
- RASgalleries www.rasgalleries.com 6540 Washington St. (707) 944-9211
- Somerston Wine 6490 Washington St. (707) 944-8200
- Visions of the Napa Valley 6540 Washington St. (707) 944-1277

The Most Interesting Winery Architectures

Ever since the Beringer Brothers built their Rhine House to remind them of their home in Germany, winery owners have created wineries that evoke exotic and artistic visions.

Though some vintners erect sturdy and practical insulated steel structures, many make stronger statements. Many are remain controversial. Some wineries disappear into the background, or are even build completely underground, while others proclaim, "Here I am!" and some critics wish they weren't.

There are three historic models for wineries in Napa Valley, all based on local materials: redwood barns, stone buildings and farm houses. To those have been added contemporary designs and exotic structures, most honestly done in pretty good taste.

With that in mind, we chose the most interesting architecture at Napa Valley wineries.

We didn't try to judge their worth as great architecture, or whether they are appropriate for their site or even Napa Valley – just which are most interesting to view and visit.

Artesa Winery

Artesa Winery was built as a natural apex for the hill it crowns. Clean and contemporary, it's unobtrusive but attractive. The interior, with its enclosed courtyard, evokes its Catalonian ownership.

Chappellet Winery

Chappellet Winery is out of the way, and hence seen by few visitors, but the modern pyramid on Pritchard Hill is worth a visit. It doesn't dominate the setting, but when you enter it, you'll appreciate the scale.

Clos Pegase

Clos Pegase was one of the most controversial buildings constructed in Napa Valley. Designed by a top architect, it suggests a Phoenician temple, though the architecture may be overshadowed by Jan Shrem's remarkable art collection scattered around the winery.

Castello di Amorosa

Dario Sattui's Castello di Amorosa is every boy's dream of his own castle. Expected to raise howls of derision, it's been well received both because it's been incredibly well implemented and because Sattui has made it ground zero for worthwhile charitable events. Even the most skeptical are won over after a tour – though they may mutter that it doesn't belong in Napa Valley.

Darioush Winery

Darioush Winery was created as an homage to owner Darioush Khaledi's Persian origins and his namesake, Darius the Great, and any visitor is immediately drawn to ancient images as he enters.

Domaine Carneros

Domaine Carneros is a faux chateaux, a copy of a palatial home of its owners, the Taittinger family of Champagne. The deck is a great place to enjoy a glass of sparkling wine as you prepare to begin – or end – a visit to Napa Valley.

Dominus

You can't visit Dominus, but you can look at it, hidden by its design west of Yountville. Built of boulders encased in a steel frame, it disappears into the landscape.

Greystone Cellars

Greystone Cellars, no longer a working winery, is the largest stone building in Napa Valley, and evokes the sense of boom times in the 1900s. It now houses the Culinary Institute of America, which has restored it sensitively.

Inglenook

Inglenook, until recently Rubicon Estates but now restored to its original name, is the largest of the many stone wineries still dotting the valley that still a winery. Many have been converted to other uses. One great example of a smaller one that has been restored to its former appearance and use by Leslie Rudd is Edge Hill Winery in St. Helena.

Long Meadow Ranch

Long Meadow Ranch, the largest rammed earth building in America. It contains both Ted and Laddie Hall's winery and their olive mill or frantoio.

Robert Mondavi Winery

Robert Mondavi Winery is the icon of Napa Valley. Constructed in pseudo-mission style – though there were no missions here – its arch and bell tower say "California wine" to most observers.

Opus One

Opus One, a distinctive circular structure, stands out like a lost Mayan pyramid, but blends surprisingly well into its vineyard setting.

Ovid Vineyards

Ovid Vineyards is an exquisite example of famed architect Howard Backen's rustic contemporary designs. Though not large, it dominates its site overlooking central Napa Valley from Pritchard Hill. Open on three sides, it lets the environment set the stage.

Quixote Winery

Quixote Winery is probably the most unique winery in a valley full of distinctive designs. The design by eccentric Austrian artist Friedensreich Hundertwasser features no parallel or perpendicular lines, lots of curves, bright colors and a gold dome.

Sterling Vineyards

Sterling Vineyards evokes a hilltop monastery on a Greek isle. Napa Valley's most dramatic winery in the most dramatic setting, it is as impressive from below as on an extended tour.

Trefethen Vineyards

Trefethen Vineyards probably wasn't built as architecture but as a working barn and winery, but the magnificent redwood building provides a link with our past with few frills or encumbrances.

Cave wineries

Honorary mentions must also go to two wineries that seem less architecture than anti-architecture.

Palmaz and Jarvis Wineries are both build entirely underground, and are almost invisible from outside. Yet each is magnificent and deserves a visit.

Jarvis is shaped like a wheel, with an underground stream and waterfall and giant caverns.

Palmaz stretches the equivalent of 14 stories underground with one huge domed room five stories high containing fermentation vats on a giant carousel.

Music, Drama and Entertainment

Performance Venues

Napa Valley Opera House

The Napa Valley Opera House in the heart of downtown Napa is the gem of Napa Valley.

It is a national historic landmark originally built in 1879 and used for vaudeville, melodramas, concerts and musical comedy – but not operas. "Opera" sounded classier than music hall in those days.

A public drive restored it in 2002 after more than 70 years of neglect. Its intimate second-floor, 500-seat Margrit Biever Mondavi Theatre was named after a major benefactor.

The theater is run by a non-profit performing arts organization.

Patrons enjoy an eclectic array of performing arts including theater, dance, comedy, jazz, blues, folk, world music, classic movies and family programming in a world-class setting. An occasional small or semi-staged opera graces its stage, too. (www.nvoh.org)

Uptown Theatre

The Uptown Theatre was built as a movie theatre in 1938, but has been restored to its Art Deco glory as Napa's leading commercial venue for today's popular, rock and country music as well as occasional comedians or other performers.

The 850-seat auditorium offers intimate views, and its bar and café nourish patrons, who are allowed to take beverages to their seats. (www.uptowntheatrenapa.com).

Lincoln Theater

Lincoln Theater, which was built for residents of the California Veterans Home in Yountville, was upgraded into a modern 1,000-seat performance venue that attracted top acts but was also the home of the Napa Valley Symphony.

Unfortunately, it is temporarily closed and the symphony disbanded. It's likely the theater will eventually reopen.

The Napa Valley Opera House has formed smaller Orchestra Napa Valley to present classical music.

Napa Valley College Performing Arts Center

A new addition to the Napa Valley cultural scene is the Performing Arts Center at Napa Valley College. Napa Valley College Performing Arts Center is dedicated to theater and music instruction and performance.

The Theater wing houses the Studio Theater, scene shop, costume studio and acting studio as well as theater support.

The Music wing features the Silvagni Recital Hall, music rehearsal space, choral rehearsal, orchestral rehearsal, practice rooms and piano classrooms.

Common areas include the Main Theater performance space, dressing rooms and green room, box office, service kitchen, Paul Ash Lobby, terrace and administrative offices.

It offers many concerts and plays during the school year. (www.napavalleytheater.org)

The White Barn

The White Barn in St. Helena is an 1872 Carriage House that was once part of U.S. Civil War General Erasmus Keyes' home and winery estate. Located at the end of Sulphur Springs Avenue in a bucolic vineyard setting,

The White Barn was transformed into an intimate 75-seat performing arts venue without loss of its historic charm.

The White Barn has nurtured local, San Francisco Bay area, West Coast and international talents for more than 22 years under the guidance of artistic director Nancy Garden, and is staffed by volunteers. It often features folk and other local performers.

All proceeds from White Barn events benefit local and international charitable organizations. Complimentary Napa Valley wines and desserts are served during performance intermissions. (www.thewhitebarn.org)

The Cameo Cinema

The Cameo Cinema is St. Helena's historic and intimate single-auditorium film theater. It's one of few still left in the United States. It shows current hits, art films, family movies and occasionally hosts live concerts. It also features special programs like film classes

Though small, it boasts first-class digital video and audio equipment. (www.cameocinema.com)

Silo's Club

Silo's Club is an intimate 100-seat nightclub that hosts eclectic music and comedy performers including jazz, rock and folk. It is in the resurrected Historic Mill in downtown Napa. It has a full bar as well. (www.silosnapa.com)

Uva Trattoria

Uva Trattoria Italiana in Napa has music from Wednesday to Sunday each week in its lounge, with an emphasis on jazz and related music.

It's also a popular Italian restaurant and bar. (www.uvatrattoria.com)

Downtown Joe's

Downtown Joe's microbrewery and pub in downtown Napa features music for a younger crowd. It has seating on a patio and along the Napa River, too. (www.downtownjoes.com)

Calistoga Inn

The Calistoga Inn features music in its brewpub and patio nightly during the high season. (www.calistogainn.com).

Wineries and restaurants throughout the valley offer music on occasion.

Music and Art Festivals

Arts in April

Arts in April is a month-long celebration of the arts, with wineries partnering with artists and art organizations for exhibits, performances and other events.

Throughout April, the annual Napa Valley Arts in April celebrates the famed wine region's other collection of priceless vintages – important 20th and 21st century artwork.

Winery art collections include work by notable contemporary painters Francis Bacon and Jean Dubuffet, as well as sculptors George Rickey and Richard Serra. Napa Valley Arts in April lets mad-about-art vintners collaborate with collection curators and favorite artists to turn the Napa Valley into a month-long art and wine crawl, made up of a variety of interactive art programs, curator-led tours, special exhibitions and inspired tastings. Visitnapavalley.com

Festival del Sole

Napa Valley's top festival of the arts and good life occurs each July, when world-class musicians perform at wineries and other venues throughout the valley. Exclusive dinners and other events complement the Festival of the Sun.

Festival del Sole operates under the auspices of Napa Valley Festival Association, a not-for-profit charitable organization established to enrich the region's cultural and economic vitality by presenting performances of the highest international quality, to nurture young talent, to build the audiences of tomorrow and to showcase the exceptional hospitality, wine and cuisine of the Napa Valley. www.festivaldelsole.org.

Napa Valley Shakespeare in the Park

Each July, Napa Valley Shakespeare presents one of Shakespeare's comedies – and sometimes more – in the amphitheater of Veterans' Memorial Park in downtown Napa.

Music in the Vineyards

Music in the Vineyards during July and August is the valley's venerable chamber music festival. Concerts are held at wineries and other local venues like the Napa Valley Opera House. www.musicinthevineyards.org.

Napa Valley Film Festival

The new Napa Valley Film Festival is quickly establishing itself as one of the industry's top venues for premieres and screening of films of all types.

The Napa Valley Film Festival is a five-day festival in early November spread over four of the valley's cities and towns, Napa, Yountville, St. Helena and Calistoga.

The Film Festival is produced by Cinema Napa Valley, a registered 501c3 non-profit organization headquartered in Napa.

The festival's co-creators – and Cinema Napa Valley co-chairs – are Brenda and Marc Lhormer, producers and distributors of the feature film *Bottle Shock* about the historic upset victory by Napa Valley wines over the French at the famous 1976 wine-tasting competition in Paris.

The husband-and-wife team also ran the successful Sonoma Valley Film Festival from 2001 through 2008.

In addition to producing the annual film festival, Cinema Napa Valley presents special film programs throughout the year and provides support to student filmmaking programs in Napa Valley schools. NapaValleyFilmFest.org

Chamber Music in Napa Valley

John and Maggy Kongsgaard organize Chamber Music in Napa Valley, which features ten concerts from November to April. It sells out quickly. chambermusicnapa.org

Special events year round in Napa Valley

There's always something happening in Napa Valley. Here's a summary of other events during the year. You can find details on most of them at visitnapavalley.com.

Napa Valley Restaurant Month

During January, restaurants throughout Napa Valley offer special deals on meals. These include special prices, discounts on wine, special prix fixe offerings and more. Many are tied to offerings at local lodgings, too.

Yountville restaurants even extend the specials through February with its Moveable Feast celebration.

Napa Valley Truffle Festival

Napa Valley is best known for its wine, but a few growers are looking at an even more lucrative gourmet crop – truffles. The Napa Valley Truffle Festival in January covers the planting and business of truffles, and also features truffle feasts and treats.

Napa Valley Marathon

The Napa Valley Marathon in March is one of the top runs in America, and certainly covers the most attractive course. It's widely seen as a warm up to the Boston Marathon, and attracts top runners.

Historic Wineries of Napa Valley Tour

A new tour of the many Historic Wineries of Napa Valley debuts in March in 2013.

Live in the Vineyards

Live in the Vineyards bring today's popular music to Napa Valley twice during the year, in April and in September. The festival, which was formerly private, now welcomes fans.

Appellation St. Helena Bash

The wineries of St. Helena join local restaurants and winery chefs for a celebration of local wine and food in April. Other appellations throughout the valley hold similar festivals.

St. Helena Sidewalk Sale

St. Helena is ground center for high-end clothing, art and lifestyle shopping in Napa Valley. Its annual sidewalk sale in May attracts those seeking great prices on unique items.

Napa County Fair

Though a relatively small county, Napa Valley has two county fairs. The official one is held in Calistoga in June, and is a classic small town celebration.

Fourth of July celebrations

Independence Day lights up the skies from American Canyon in the south to Calistoga in the north, with home-town parties in all the cities and towns. Silverado Resort even jumps the gun with a big show on July 3.

Napa Valley Writers Conference

The long-running Napa Valley Writers Conference in July collects famed fiction writers and poets with students and fans for an orgy of literature and learning.

Napa Town & County Fair

The valley's unofficial second county fair is held in Napa each August. It's larger than the official fair, and features the expected treats: 4H animals to a carnival, a destruction derby to country music concerts, and being Napa Valley, its local specialty as well – wine.

Hands Across the Valley

One of the Valley's biggest parties in August attracts celebrities to support the local food bank and other programs to fight hunger.

Harvest Stomp

The Napa Valley Grapegrowers' Harvest Stomp in August is an old-fashioned harvest festival, with picnic food, plenty of Napa Valley wine and music and dancing.

Napa Main Street Car Show

One of the most popular events in downtown Napa is the annual car show featuring classic and exotic cars in August.

Napa Valley Art Festival Yountville

The Napa Valley Art Festival held in Yountville during August supports Connolly Ranch, which provides a farm experience for children. The one-day festival showcases famed representational artists in a juried show.

American Folk Art Festival Napa

Each year, the American Folk Art Festival in September attracts fans to view and buy a wide range of naïve and folk arts and crafts.

Napa River Wine & Crafts Fair

Another big festival in downtown Napa, the Napa River Wine & Crafts Fair in September is one of the largest art and craft shows in California.

Manaleo Hawaiian Festival

Homesick Hawaiians throw an annual festival featuring Hawaiian music, arts and culture in Napa during September.

Napa River Rock & Stroll (September)

The Napa River Rock & Stroll is an easy walk and party that benefits families in need.

Dada di Rosa Benefit Art Auction

di Rosa's annual art auction in October gives collectors a change to acquire some of Northern California's top contemporary art.

Napa Valley Bike Tour

The Napa Valley is ideal for bicycling, from flat rides on shaded lanes to steep climbs. This tour in November provides them all.

Calistoga Tractor Parade

The Calistoga Tractor Parade in December is small-town fun at its best; it's accompanied by a street part.

Twelve Days of Christmas

Meadowood Resort's three-Michelin-starred restaurant invites the world's top chefs to join local cult wine producers in incomparable meals during December.

Holiday Historic Tour & Taste Napa

Both historic properties and B&Bs conduct festive tours for the holidays in downtown Napa during December.

Festival of the Lights and Winterscape

Yountville kicks off the holiday season with its Festival of the Lights the day after Thanksgiving.

It segues into its Winterscape celebration until the start of the new year.

On-going events during the summer

In addition, many festivals and other celebrations are held weekly or monthly during the summer. They include:

Napa Chefs' Market (Thursday nights)

Cheers! (St. Helena, first Friday)

Napa Farmers Markets (Tuesday and Saturday)

St. Helena Farmers Market (Friday)

Calistoga Farmers Market (Saturday)

Concerts in the Park (Friday, Napa)

Locals Night

Oxbow Public Market sponsors festive Locals Night on Tuesday nights year round.

Wellness and Sports in Napa Valley

A nice complement to all the fine wine and food in Napa Valley is some outdoor activity to burn off the calories. Though it may be cold and rainy in the winter, Napa's weather is usually perfect for sports, exercise and just plain fun outdoors.

Golf and tennis

Though golf isn't the draw in Napa Valley it is in areas with fewer other attractions, Napa Valley has its share of golf courses and tennis courts.

- Silverado Resort boasts two 18-hole golf courses, and new owners are renovating the course and other facilities in hopes of returning the facility to the glory of the days when it hosted PGA championships. (www.silverado.com 1600 Atlas Peak Rd., Napa (707) 257-5460)

- Chardonnay Golf Course (www.chardonnaygolfclub.com 2555 Jameson Canyon Rd. (707) 257-1900) and Eagle Vines Golf Course (www.eaglevinesgolfclub.com 580 S. Kelly Rd. (707) 257-4470) south of Napa are full courses, too, while the city of Napa has an 18-hole public course at John F. Kennedy Park. (www.playnapa.com 2295 Streblow Dr., Napa (707) 255-4333)

- Napa Country Club offers reciprocal privileges. (www.napavalleycc.com 3385 Hagen Rd., Napa (707) 252.1111)

- The valley has truncated 9-hole courses, too:

- Meadowood Resort www.meadowood.com, 900 Meadowood Lane, St. Helena (707) 963-3646)

- Mt. St. Helena Golf Course (www.mtsthelenagolfcourse.org (707) 942-9966 2025 Grant St., Calistoga)

- Vintner's Golf Club is on the grounds of California Veterans Home in Yountville (www.vintnersgolfclub.com 7901 Solano Ave., Yountville (707) 944-1992.

- Over the mountains in Pope Valley, a short course at Aetna Springs was reportedly the first in California. It is open weekends. (www.aetnasprings.com, 1600 Aetna Springs Rd. Pope Valley (707) 965-2115)

Silverado also has an ambitious tennis program, and Meadowood has courts, too.

Bicycling

Bicycling may be the most popular active sport for visitors. The flat floor of Napa Valley seems designed for bicyclists, while the mountains attract the more ambitious peddlers.

Many hotels and resorts offer bicycles for guests to ride, and bike companies from Napa to Calistoga both rent bicycles and lead tours.

One day, the Vine Trail will stretch from Calistoga to the ferry to San Francisco in Vallejo; for now, many pieces are in place and connections on roads join them together.

Most of Silverado Trail has bike lanes, while Highway 29 is mostly narrow and uninviting. Fortunately, quieter roads and bike paths parallel the highway from Napa to north of Yountville, in St. Helena and south of Calistoga. Traffic is generally fairly slow along Highway 29 from Yountville to St. Helena.

For minimal traffic, many head to bucolic Pope Valley or the rolling hills of Carneros. The truly dedicated can tackle rugged climbs like Oakville Grade or Sage Canyon Road, or mountain trails like Oak Hill Mine Road.

Bicycle rentals

- Calistoga Bikeshop (1318 Lincoln Ave. www.calistogabikeshop.net, Calistoga (707) 942-9687.
- Getaway Adventures (301 Post St. on the Silverado Trail, Napa (707) 753-0866. www. getawayadventures.com)
- Napa Valley Adventure Tours (www.napavalleyadventuretours.com, (707) 224-9080)
- Napa River Velo (680 Main St., Napa (707) 258.8729 www.naparivervelo.com)
- Napa Valley Bike Tours and Rentals (6795 Washington St., Yountville) www.napavalleybiketours.com. (707) 251-8687)
- St. Helena Cyclery (1156 Main St. Helena, (707) 963-7736, www.sthelenacyclery.com)
- Velo Vino (709 Main St., St. Helena (707) 968-0625 www.velovinonapavalley.com

Hiking

The mountains harbor many hiking trails, too.

Among the most popular are those in Robert Louis Stevenson State Park on Mount St, Helena, the nearby and challenging Palisades Trail and Oak Hill Mine Trail, and walks in Napa-Bother Park and Skyline Park east of Napa. Trails along the Napa River in Napa are also popular.

Many trails can be found in lands owned by the Land Trust of Napa Valley, which hosts frequent hikes. Some are easy, some difficult and steep. Some are open to the public, but joining the Land Trust is reasonable and supports a good cause, too (napalandtrust.org).

Water activities

Water sports aren't what first comes to mind for most visitors to Napa Valley, but the Napa River is one of the few navigable rivers in California, and is certainly a magnet for kayaks and canoes. These are available for rent at Napa Valley Adventure Tours (www.napavalleyadventuretours.com, (707) 224-9080) and Getaway Adventures (301 Post St. on the Silverado Trail, Napa (707) 753-0866. www. getawayadventures.com).

The county's large lakes, especially Lake Berryessa, hosts all sorts of water activities. The amenities around the lake are in transition, but basic launching sites, supplies and camping are available now, and the area should boast everything from primitive camping to luxury resorts in the future.

Lake Hennessey allows boating with sail, row and small powered boats.

And of course, most hotels and resorts, and many spas and other facilities, offer pools and opportunities for more formal exercise. Many also host yoga, pilates, classes and other training. The spas also allow you to recover in case you overindulge – in exercise as well as food and wine.

The Best Bike Rides in Napa

Many people like to ride their bikes, but their abilities and ambitious vary widely. If you're ready to tackle Oakville Grade or Howell Mountain Road, this isn't really for you, however. It's ten relatively easy rides of 10 to 20 miles over mostly level ground, most in circles so you don't have to retrace your tracks – and most with a treat waiting for you at the end of the trip — a winery, casual restaurant of at least a store where you can get a snack.

Brunch in Yountville

One of the delightful bike trips in Napa Valley just became even better with the opening of the new bike trail along the Napa Valley Wine Train. Pick it up near Soscol Ave. in downtown Napa, then follow it to Solano Avenue parallel to highway 29 to Yountville, where you can turn right, then left on Washington Street past restaurants, galleries and shops.

You can also bypass Yountville on a new bike path between highway 29 and the town, but you can't get off it until the end at Madison Street.

At the north end of town, continue east on Yountville Cross Rd. and south on Silverado Trail through the Stags Leap district and numerous wineries. Right on Oak Knoll Rd. gets you off the busy trail, back to where you started. It's 15 miles with some gentle hills on the Silverado Trail.

Touring the Napa River

Napa's river trail starts at Trancas and the river, providing a path south to Lincoln Avenue. Soon, there will be a great bike route beyond, but the riverfront from River Terrace Inn and Westin Verasa to First Street is impassable at present, though you can find your way on surface streets.

It picks up again just south of the Bounty Hunter and continues past the Napa Mill. Then you can bicycle along the river, then slip over to South Coombs, and past the old Sawyer Tanner to Imola, where it's a steep climb over the bridge, then right on the bike path through Kennedy Park. It ends at the boundary of the park, but may eventually continue to Vallejo. Head back along Soscol to downtown Napa. 15 miles round trip. No hills, one big bridge.

The eastern frontier of Napa

The eastern foothills of Napa are called Coombsville and are bucolic and uncrowded yet little known. You can head north on Main Street or Soscol from downtown to Lincoln, then up the Napa River Trail, then east on Trancas, which becomes Monticello Road, to Atlas Peak Road, where you can visit Silverado Resort. Back to

Monticello, turn right on Vichy, where you glide through the back roads, and left on Hagen, following it around Napa Valley Country Club on 3rd, and back through North Avenue and south on First to Coombsville to downtown. 17 miles, mild hills.

Gliding through West Napa

The western edge of the valley is quite interesting. Head up Foothill Blvd. at Old Sonoma Road, then follow Laurel to the left until you get to Browns Valley Road. Left on there, and you can stop for snacks at La Fôret Chocolates or Brown's Valley Market, then head west on Browns Valley, which turns right to go north. At Redwood, turn right unless you want to climb to the Hess Collection, then left on Dry Creek by Allston Park. Turn right on Orchard to return to Solano and to the start. There's a secret bike path just before First Street. 6 miles, flat.

Cooling off in Carneros

The Carneros Region is a great one to visit when it's hot upvalley, for it's almost always cooler there. A good place to start is the Carneros Inn, which has a deli as well as the Boon Fly Restaurant. You should cross Highway 12/121 at the light at Old Sonoma Road. Crossing carefully, turn left on 12/121, then right on quiet Los Carneros Road till it ends, then jog left to Cuttings Wharf Road. Right there. At the end is funky Moore's Landing burger and beer bar on the Napa River. You have to retrace to Las Amigas to get to the Napa Valley Marina on Milton Road, then along the homes behind levees along the river. The road ends at a wildlife preserve in the marsh. Then back and left at Las Amigas past Bouchaine and Acacia, and right at Duhig and enjoy a glass of bubbly at Domaine Carneros. Cross the highway and return. 16 miles; almost flat.

The heart of the valley

A trip through the heart of the valley starts at Yountville and tours Oakville and Rutherford, avoiding main roads as much as practical. Start at V Marketplace, and follow Yount St. behind Hurley's north on peaceful Yount Mill Road. Turn right at Highway 29, through Oakville, then into tiny Rutherford. Go east on Rutherford Road, then right on Conn Creek, then left where it ends at Skellenger Lane. Then it's right on the Silverado Trail to Yount Cross Road and returns. 5 miles and flat.

South from St. Helena

One of the most popular bike trips in Napa Valley starts in downtown St. Helena, traveling south along Highway 29 past numerous wineries to Rutherford, where a left turn takes you across the valley on Rutherford Road, curving north to join the Silverado Trail. From there, it's left and back to Pope Street, across its narrow bridge, and a return to the start and many places for a snack or glass of wine. 15 miles, almost flat.

You can also turn left (east) at Zinfandel Lane and visit Raymond Vineyards, a worthwhile stop.

North from St. Helena

A symmetrical tour heads north from downtown St. Helena past famed Beringer, historic Charles Krug Winery and the Culinary Institute of America and up to Larkmead. Just ahead on the left is the entrance to Napa Bothe Park; you can actually bicycle inside it from the south. Turn right on Larkmead past the new Larkmead Cellars and then the friendly Frank Family Vineyard before getting to Silverado Trail and a zip down to Pratt, when a right across the little-used road returns you to downtown St. Helena. If you're not energetic, you can take a shortcut on Bale Lane or Lodi Lane. 15 miles, almost flat.

A circle of Calistoga

The north end of the valley holds many possibilities, including a new bike path along the Napa River in Calistoga at the end of Washington Street ending at Dunaweal Lane. Catch its beginning in the center of town at Lincoln Ave., and on Dunaweal, turn left. You can take the gondola up to Sterling on the right, or visit Clos Pegase's incredible artwork on the left as you head east. At Silverado Trail, turn left to head back into Calistoga. You'll pass the Aubert Winery just before "Mount Washington," see B Cellars on the right, and can visit Solage Resort just beyond on the left. A quick jog takes you up to Lincoln Avenue and a return to the center of Calistoga and its many restaurants and stores.

Bicycling East of Eden

If you're tired of crowds, you might like to head over the mountain to East of Eden, the back country of Napa County. If you are up to bicycling up the hill you probably have long since turned the page from these easy rides, but otherwise, drive over Howell Mountain through Angwin and park near the Pope Valley store, the only place you can buy any snacks or drinks (other than wine) in the whole valley. All these trips retrace, I fear, north by Litto's Hubcap Ranch to interesting Aetna Springs, which is being restored into a private club. Or you can go south, then across Pope Canyon Road and down Hardin Road to really get away; make sure you bring some water and a lunch. Then it's back with a shortcut across Pope Valley Cross Road for a slightly different route. Flat, but different distances.

Hiking Napa Valley

Eating fine food and drinking fine wine inspires many visitors to Napa Valley to get some exercise. Hiking and biking are naturals in Napa Valley, where the options range from mild walks or bike rides along the Napa River to challenging hikes in the mountains that frame the valley.

To start with the mild, you can enjoy a hike or walk along the Napa River in south Napa at Kennedy Park, downtown along the riverfront, or on the trail through Yountville or south of Calistoga.

Most hikes, however, extend into the foothills or higher. A number of parks offer interesting trails. Skyline Park in east Napa offers a range of hiking trails, some pretty level, but others rising high into the Vaca Range. Watch out for aggressive swans by the lakes. The Native Plant Garden at the park groups plants by natural habitat and is a very worthwhile detour.

Two state parks being turned over to local operation due to the state budget crisis also offer many opportunities: Bale Mill and nearby Bothe Napa Park.

The Mill is fascinating, for it still grinds wheat and corn on weekends, and there's a fairly serious hike through the backwoods to Bothe. It passes a poignant pioneer cemetery before ending up at Bothe, which was once a resort hideaway for Hollywood Royalty. Little remains of that day except an unheated pool, but the park has interesting exhibits of natural and history including the life of the Wappo Indians who lived in this Eden, plus hikes along a creek and into the hills.

Plans are in place to restore disused cabins and add yurts to provide overnight accommodations; for now, it has camping spaces.

The other state park remains open mostly because there's nothing to shut or any practical way to close access: It's Robert Louis Stevenson State Park high up on 4,300-ft. Mount St. Helena. You can hike to the old mine where the writer got inspiration for his *Silverado Squatters* and enjoy great views of Napa Valley.

Heading the other way down the mountain from that park is the challenging Palisades Trail across the mountains to Oak Hill Mine Trail, which wanders down to Calistoga or over the mountains to the east to Aetna Springs in Pope Valley. These trails are for serious hikers, even going downhill from the mountain.

Other opportunities wait at the far end of the valley. The di Rosa museum is best known for its impressive collection of contemporary Northern California art, but it also contains a number of hiking trails, one to the height of Milliken Peak, the southernmost peak of the Mayacamas Mountains and highest spot in the Carneros region.

Beginning in April, di Rosa offers a series of spring nature hikes, when guests join experienced guides for the rare opportunity to hike to the top of Milliken Peak. In addition to sweeping views of the North Bay, hikers can view sculptures along the moderately strenuous climb. For more information, visit www.dirosaart.org.

Though seemingly a world away from Napa Valley, public lands around large Lake Berryessa in eastern Napa County offer many opportunities for hikes as well as boating and even swimming. Most are a bit primitive as the area transitions from its former life of long-term trailer parks to ambitious plans for overnight accommodations, however, and facilities are limited. You can get the latest information at www.usbr.gov/mp/ccao/Berryessa.

The Land Trust

That brings us to some of the most interesting trails in Napa County, those owned or controlled by the Land Trust of Napa County. This organization dedicated to the preservation of Napa Valley protects more than 45,000 acres from development (10 percent of the county), including 26,000 acres of pristine wilderness. These areas include fabulous vistas and wildlife corridors, and naturally have many hiking trails.

The Land Trust acquired many of these spaces intending to turn them over to the state for parks, but unfortunately, the state's finances preclude that at present and the Land Trust doesn't have the staff or resources to operate them as public parks and recreational areas.

Fortunately, throughout the year, the Land Trust offers unique and invigorating field trips, from hikes to wildlife sanctuary explorations or jeep-led tours for members and the public.

For example, the Land Trust is offering a free six-mile "Maggie's Peak Trail Run." The new hike features a trek up the mountainside to the dramatic Devil's Well waterfall and into a serene redwood grove.

During spring, the Land Trust offers its member series program focused on new ways to connect with the Napa Valley's protected lands, including a yoga/meditation session at Archer Taylor Preserve, a century-old redwood forest, and field trips involving lessons in outdoor art and photography.

The hikes range from short 1-mile trips suitable even for families with small children to vigorous climbs that would challenge even the most fit.

The program also includes boating, sessions on photography, sketching and blockprinting, yoga and meditation as well as viewing wildflowers, owls and other wildlife. Some are at night.

Most of the activities are open to the public. Some of the activities are for members only, but the worthwhile membership starts at only $30.

For a schedule of events and sign-up, visit www.napalandtrust.org.

The Top Gardens in Napa Valley

Napa Valley has many beautiful gardens, but many are hidden on estates where only the owners and their guests can enjoy them.

Fortunately, many more available are to the public, and they're very varied, from formal to rustic, from utilitarian vegetable plots to elegant formal gardens.

Here are some of our favorites:

The Martha Walker Native Habitat Garden

The Martha Walker Native Habitat Garden at Skyline Park has to be one of the top destinations. It shows you the beauty of native plants adapted to our climate, and hence requiring minimal water and care. The 2.5-acre garden was designed for school groups, garden and hiking clubs and the casual visitor. Here, the native plants are assembled within a garden plan that is both attractive and beneficial for the plants. As a bonus, the garden propagates native plants from seed and cuttings, and hosts sales where you can buy the plants. Visit www.ncfaa.com/skyline/garden.htm.

Connolly Ranch

Connolly Ranch is an educational resource for kids, but no one says that excludes big kids. It features a wide variety of plants typical of working farms with a bonus of complementary farm animals, too. Connolly Ranch is at 3141 Browns Valley Road in Napa. Call (707) 256-3828 or visit www.connollyranch.org.

Napa Country Iris Garden

Napa Country Iris Garden is one of Napa's best-kept secrets. It's a garden specializing in tall bearded irises. The spring bloom season is for April to May, but weather can affect bloom season. The garden is open during bloom season. Admission is free. You can also order bulbs from the garden website. You can get more at www.napairis.com or (707) 255-7880. The garden is at 9087 Steele Canyon Road at Lake Berryessa.

Brix

Many restaurants in Napa Valley grow some of their own food, but perhaps none is more extensive and attractive than that at Brix just north of Yountville. The garden was created to provide fresh herbs and vegetables for the restaurant's seasonal menu and consists of eleven 6-by-20 foot raised beds. About 80 percent of the fresh ingredients on the tasting menu during season are picked from the garden. Brix also own 16 acres of olive trees and vineyard land, all visible from the dining area and patio. Call (707) 944-2749 or visit www.brix.com.

Rutherford Gardens

Rutherford Gardens on Highway 29 between Rutherford and St. Helena has been producing organic fruits and vegetables in season since the 1930s. It's owned by Ted and Laddie Hall of Long Meadow Ranch, pioneers in organic agriculture as well as beef, olive oil, and wine.

The 5.8-acre garden is open on weekends during the season and offers organic produce including tomatoes, figs, corn, basil, beets, beans, chard, cucumber, melons, strawberries, and potatoes.

The gardens and roadside stand are open to the public beginning in April. You can enjoy a walk through the beautiful demonstration gardens, and also buy fresh vegetables, fruits, eggs, grass-fed beef and flowers grown on site. Its website is www.longmeadowranch.com/RutherfordGardens

Kuleto Estate Family Winery

Pat Kuleto's Kuleto Estate Family Winery high in the hills above Lake Hennessey can only be visited with an appointment, but it's well worth the planning – and the effort. It's the closest we have in Napa Valley (along with Long Meadow Ranch) to a self-sustained estate like the great tenute of Tuscany. Pat has extensive vegetable and fruit gardens, livestock, fruit and olive orchards— and of course, great wine. www.kuletoestate.com 2470 Sage Canyon Road east of Rutherford (707) 302-2209

Raymond Vineyards

By far the biggest "gardens" in Napa Valley are those that grow wine grapes, and you can see them up and down the valley in countless places.

Perhaps the best place to see a lot of varieties and how they grown, however, is Raymond Vineyards in Rutherford. It has one of the best demonstration vineyards, and it's also adjacent to other gardens, great tours and exhibits about growing grapes—and fine wine to taste as the end of your tour.

Its garden focuses on Biodynamic framing and includes animals like chickens and goats. www.raymondvineyards.com 849 Zinfandel Lane, St. Helena (707) 963-3141

Frog's Leap Winery

Another winery that's a must visit on many counts is Frog's Leap in Rutherford. Owner John Williams doesn't take himself too seriously, unlike many local vintners, but he's very serious about his farming and wine.

Frog's Leap is one of very few dry-farmed (unirrigated) vineyards still left in the valley, and his grapes and other plants are organically farmed, another term for traditional farming.

The winery also has extensive vegetable, herb and flower gardens as well as fruit orchards and lots of other delights for the eye as well as the tongue.

And the wines are like the superb Napa Valley wines of yesterday, not the over-ripe over-extracted wines that all taste alike. You need an appointment to visit. www.frogsleap.com 8815 Conn Creek Rd., Rutherford (707) 9634704.

Sutter Home Winery

It's very difficult to select the last garden from among all those at wineries in Napa Valley, but one that's both beautiful and accessible in that at Sutter Home Winery in St. Helena. It's in front of the winery's Victorian guest house, and next to the tasting room, one of the few in Napa Valley that doesn't charge for tasting, at least its basic wines. The garden is full of roses and other flowers and plants, all lovingly tended and labeled. 277 St. Helena Hwy (Hwy. 29) South St. Helena (707) 963-3104 www.sutterhome.com.

Nurseries

Napa Valley also contains a number of nurseries where you can both view and buy plants:

- Napa Valley Ornamental Nursery 453 Fulton Ln., St Helena (707) 287-2028
- Central Valley Builder's Supply 1100 Vintage Ave., St. Helena (707) 963-3622
- Cottage Gardens Nursery 1450 S. Whitehall Ln, St. Helena (707) 963-0800
- DJ's Growing Place 1289 Olive Hill Ln, Napa (707) 252-6445
- Home Depot 225 Soscol Ave., Napa (707) 251-0162
- Mid City Nursery 3635 Broadway/Hwy 29, Amercan Canyon (707) 642-4167
- Napa Valley Orchids 2536 MacGregor Court, Napa (707) 255-8266
- Napa Valley Ornamental Nursery 453 Fulton Lane, St. Helena (707) 963-9157
- Orchard Supply Hardware 3980 Bel Aire Plaza, Napa (707) 224-3410
- Russell Levy Bonsai 3348 Atlas Peak Rd, Napa (707) 226-3963
- Van Winden Garden Center 1805 Pueblo Ave., Napa (707) 255-8400

Do remember that's it's illegal to bring uninspected plants into Napa County to avoid pests. Your county may have restrictions.,

Skyline Park Native Habitat Garden

If you haven't visited the Martha Walker Native Habitat Garden in Skyline Park, you'd be amazed at its present state.

In the last three years, an enormous amount of work by volunteers has transformed the 25-year old garden. The garden had gotten a little tired, but under curator Kathleen Chasey, a landscape designer who volunteers extensive time, it's like a new garden – except that it's taken advantage of many plantings long ago.

Among the changes are reorganizing the garden to reflect the habitats found here in Napa County. One area shows the plants that grow in meadows, another in chaparral, still another in oak woodlands, one shows what plant life is among the redwoods, while still another shows a typical riparian (creek side) habitat complete with a spring-fed creek that runs year round.

The meadow, for example, replaces an area that was overgrown with tall – and aggressive – thistles.

Many of those habitats can be found elsewhere in Skyline park, though the huge oaks in meadows around the garden are its native environment.

Other areas show plants that attract birds and butterflies, show plants used by native Americans for food, health and other parts of their life like baskets, and children can plant in the kids' area.

The garden also has newly defined paths, new gates, but most of all, it's acquired informative signs that explain each area. A stroll through the park-like setting beats reading books or even sitting in the classroom to learn about our environment.

The signs were supported by fines paid for wildlife transgressions.

The garden was founded by Ralph and Evelyn Ingols. The garden was named after the late Martha Walker, a garden expert and long-time garden columnist for the *Register*.

Spring, of course, is a great time to visit, for many perennial and annual flowers are in bloom. Everyone knows the California poppy, but many of these rarer wildflowers and flowers perennials are beautiful and fascinating, too, and a few are rare and endangered.

Quail patrol the garden – foundlings are released in the garden, and tall fences prove the garden's appeal to local deer.

You can picnic at the garden, too. Just carry out your trash. The garden and nearby community hall can be rented for events, too.

There's an admission charge if you drive into Skyline Park, which has been privately owned but is being acquired by Napa County Regional Park and Open Space District.

The garden in Skyline Park is maintained by volunteer members of the Napa Valley chapter of California Native Plant Society, which also runs a nursery that grows native plants for use in the garden, elsewhere in Skyline Park, other restoration projects and for sale at semiannual sales, one just past but another coming up in the fall, the best time to plant native plants.

The chapter will also sell plants in a planting and BBQ on Earth Day in April.

It also participates in the Bay-Friendly garden tour in May. The tour features 12 gardens in and near Napa that provide inspiration for all kinds of home landscapes.

The chapter also holds weekly wildflower hikes each Tuesday.

Volunteers also work with children and school classes as well as maintaining and improving the garden and growing plants in the nursery.

For more information, visit www.napavalleycnps.org, email mail@napavalleycnps.org or call 253-2665.

You can reach Kathleen Chasey at her business, Direct to Earth Landscape Design at kathleen@dtelandscapedesign.com or 320-8895.

Why plant native plants?

Native plants have many advantages over introduced plants in our yard and landscaping: They don't require site preparation or soil amendment except removing weeds.

Native plants are adapted to our dry summers, unlike many plants, and don't generally require irrigation once established. They also often exclude weeds and don't require the use of pesticides – they have natural resistance or tolerance.

Natives usually grow to their mature size, and then stay that way. Many landscape plants continue growing and filling our landfills or compost piles.

One of the most compelling reasons to plant natives is that they support and attract native birds, butterflies, other insects and even animals, including ones endangered by loss of habitat.

Most of all, they provide our natural environment, the one that was here before we started messing with it.

Up, up and Away In a Beautiful Balloon

If you've ever stayed one night too long in Napa Valley and had to return early Monday morning, you've probably been greeted by the magical sight of colorful hot-air balloons floating above your car as you've driven through Yountville or other parts of the Valley.

It looks like fun, but you don't know the half of it. It's simply unforgettable, better than you could even imagine. Slowly floating where the wind wants to take you over vineyards, farms and towns, you get a perspective unimaginable from any other experience.

That's especially true over the narrow Napa Valley defined by steep mountains, compressing the scenery and ride to a compact area over and among some of the most beautiful views in America.

A number of companies offer balloon rides. The rides typically last about an hour, the experience three or four, including coffee and pastry before the ascent, and a post-flight brunch featuring Napa Valley sparkling wine.

The balloons get their lift from hot air generated by nozzles that burn propane. The flames can shoot 10 feet high only a few feet above your head. A warning: if you're bald, wear a hat!

The best time for ballooning is at sunrise, when the winds are typically light in Napa Valley. Obviously, the early morning time is perfect in the warm summer, but the balloons do operate year round. Fortunately, the heat from the burner keeps passengers warm even when it's cool. If it's raining or too windy (over 10 mph), the balloons don't fly.

The passengers get to watch the inflation process. The balloon is stretched out across the lot while a powerful fan partly inflates it with cold air. Then the giant blow torches start and soon the balloon is stretching skyward. At that point, everyone scrambles aboard, climbing gracelessly in most cases, into the gondola. A number of ground crew hang on as the hot air is again ignited and when the pilot says so, the crew lets go (or jumps off) and the balloon slowly rises above the parking lot, then the winery.

There's no jumpy sensation in your stomach as in an airplane because of the slow and gentle motion.

The balloons typically travel about 500 ft. up, though they can hover just above the vines or rise thousands of feet up, high enough to cross the mountains.

As you glide along, jack rabbits and deer bolt from their forbidden pleasures munching on grapes and tender grape vines, and the occasional cow looks up curiously. A red-tailed hawk eyes the balloon, trying to figure out whether it's a threat or a treat, but soon zooms away seeking better prospects for breakfast.

The winds typically take you south, but sometimes travel north.

Your pilot identifies sights as you pass their site, here Robert Mondavi's former villa on Wappo Hill, there Trefethen vineyards, famous for its Chardonnay and Cabernet. If it's in the fall, you see the patchwork of fields dotted with beautiful red and purple grape leaves that betray vines infected with viruses.

The distance you travel depends solely on the winds. You may go only a few miles, allowing you to inspect every sight, or you may travel about 15 miles over the city of Napa, looking at its huge collection of Victorian houses.

The landing is exciting but the balloon comes down with only a few gentle bumps and bounces. Then the ground crew, with a little help from passengers, furls the balloon.

There may be a better way to start a day than gliding over Napa Valley in a balloon, but if there is, I've never found it.

Balloon companies in Napa Valley

- Balloons Above the Valley (707) 253-2222 603 California Blvd Napa

- Napa Valley Aloft (707) 944-4400 6525 Washington St., Yountville

- Bonaventura Balloon Co. (707) 944-2822 1458 Lincoln Ave. Railcar #15 Calistoga

- Calistoga Balloons (707) 942-5758 1458 Lincoln Ave. Railcar #15 Calistoga

- Napa Valley Balloons (707) 944-0228 300 Post St., Napa

- Bennett Lane Winery in Calistoga also has a balloon. It hosts flights combined with winetasting and other luxury touches. 3340 Highway 128, Calistoga www.bennettlane.com (707) 942-6684

Shopping in Napa Valley

Most people don't got to Napa Valley to shop. They go for the wine, the food, the art and music and theater, maybe for healthy excursions. But there certainly are plenty of places to shop for interesting and unique treasures.

Starting with the most mundane, Napa Premium Outlets offers discounts from many of American's top retailers and brands.

Napa itself is a bit sparse for retailing downtown, but does have interesting art galleries and vintage and contemporary clothing shops.

Two stores, West End Napa and Poor House in the Oxbow Public Market complex, have very interesting upscale lifestyle furniture and accessories.

Perhaps some of the most interesting treasures are found at Oxbow Public Market, but a serious foodie can go lost in Shackford's Kitchenware.

Yountville is better, notably with it V Marketplace, a font of art, food and more.

St. Helena is ground central for interesting shopping, with numerous women's clothing and shoe stores, serious ($$$) art galleries and more.

Calistoga is the home for eclectic art.

And, of course, there's always the wine and gourmet goodies...

Harvest in Napa Valley

Harvest is a magical time in Napa Valley. All year long, the valley waits and anticipates the time when the grapes are ripe and ready to begin their transformation into Napa Valley wine.

The time to harvest grapes depends on the variety, where they're planted, how they're tended, what kind of wine they'll be used for – but especially the weather. It takes heat to ripen grapes. Ripeness is a subjective term, however.

The most common measure of maturity is the sugar content of the grapes, which is very easy to measure in the vineyard with a simple optical instrument called a refractometer. Grapes for table wines have traditionally been picked at 23 to 25 percent sugar, while those for sparkling wine are picked underripe at 19 degrees or less, and dessert wines are harvested at higher levels, even into the 30s.

The higher the sugar, the higher the alcohol, of course. If the grapes are too sweet, the yeasts used to convert sugar to alcohol die before converting all the sugar to alcohol, resulting in a sweet dessert wine.

Sugar is only one indicator of ripeness, however. Another measure is acidity: acidity drops as sugars rise, and a wine with insufficient acidity can taste sweet and cloying (and be more susceptible to unwanted bacteria and disease).

In California, it is legal to add acid to wine if necessary, but not sugar, as is done in cold regions like Germany. Low sugar is almost never a problem in California's generally warm climate, however.

The other indication of ripeness is more difficult to measure with instruments. It's the so-called physiological ripeness, the time when the natural tannins mellow and the flavors fully develop. As this occurs, the grape's seeds turn brown and the grapes soften.

Though some wineries analyze grape tannins and other properties in laboratories, most winemakers just taste the grapes. With experience, they can tell when it's time to pick.

Cool weather delays sugar production, but not necessarily flavor development. In a cool year, the grapes can 'hang' on the vine a long time before they're picked, and that can mean luscious flavors without excessive sugar or low acid, as happens in a hot year.

In Napa Valley, summers are always dry, and winemakers want to pick grapes before the rains start. Though it rains during harvest (and during the growing season) in other wine regions, moisture can also encourage fungus and mold. The growers have to treat that with chemicals.

Rain can also cause grapes to burst, inviting spoilage, and can dilute flavors and sugar levels. And if ripeness is delayed too long, a freeze is even a possibility.

In a cool year, growers and winemakers bite their nails, praying that their grapes are ripe enough to pick before the rains start.

The first grapes to come in are for sparkling wine. Wineries in Napa Valley usually start to pick grapes for sparkling wines in mid August, but in cool years, that happen until the end of August or even early September.

Grapes for white wines come in next. Reds are picked later. Some grapes may not come in until late October, possibly even November.

The harvest time does depend on the part of the Valley the vineyards are in, however. Southern Napa Valley is cooler than mid-valley, and the vineyards north of the Yountville Hills are warmer. Some of the mountain vineyards are cool, and their grapes ripen later, too.

If you want to see harvest activity, some wineries along Highway 29 are happy to have you watch the process as the grapes arrive. They include Robert Mondavi, St. Supéry and Grgich-Hills. At some wineries, safety considerations and lack of access discourage viewing the crushing.

And while large wineries will be processing different varieties of grapes from different areas for months, at some smaller wineries, the most intense activity can all be over in a day or two. Call ahead if you want to visit your favorite winery; wine club members often get special treatment.

Many wineries host harvest parties, many limited to wine club members, though sometimes others can pay to attend. A inevitable feature of many is the "Lucy" grape stomp, named after an infamous episode of "I Love Lucy," though no winery can actually use this method for commercial wines due to sanitation concerns.

All the parties feature wine, often including samples of just-pressed, fermenting or barrel samples. The parties range from simple affairs with snacks to blow-out parties with whole roasted lambs and music.

Because of the vagaries of the weather, wineries can't plan very far in advance, so the best way to observe the crush is to call or email your favorite wineries; some use Facebook or Twitter to notify fans or post schedules on their websites.

Even small or late, harvest is a great time to visit Napa Valley. It can be crowded, however, so plan as far ahead as you can, and consider visiting midweek if possible. The crowds will be smaller and you will likely receive more personal attention.

What about global warming?

Though many wine regions of the world are definitely heating up, Napa Valley has been cool the last few years, and that may continue.

The reason is its location close to the Pacific Ocean and San Francisco Bay. As the Central Valley of California heats up, the hot air there rises, sucking cool (or cold!) air in from the Pacific and Bay. The result is cool weather in California's Northern Bay Area, including Napa.

That's not necessarily bad, for it can lead to more flavorful wines – and slightly lower alcohol levels, making it easier to drink more delicious Napa wine.

Winter in Napa Valley: Cabernet Season

When the weather turns cold and rainy – yes it does happen even in Napa Valley – it's time for hearty flavors, and that includes both foods and wine.

That's why it's the perfect time to visit Napa Valley. Napa Valley is the world center for luscious Cabernet Sauvignon – even its ancestral home Bordeaux grows more Merlot than Cabernet.

In Bordeaux, historically the wines were blends of different grapes, including Cabernet Sauvignon, Merlot, Cabernet Franc, Malbec and Petite Verdot. The grapes complemented each other, for some didn't always ripen fully in that area's climate, and Merlot, for example, is softer and ripens sooner, and can partially balance under-ripe and overly tannic Cabernet Sauvignon.

In Napa Valley, however, all five varieties ripen fully most years and Cabernet on its own can mature fully, softening tannins and dissipating 'green' flavors that most people don't appreciate.

Here, the grapes get riper and more intense, and not only exhibit muted tannins, but tend to be more lush with have strong aromas and flavors of tasty black fruit.

The wines also tend to be a little higher in alcohol than European versions because the grapes ripen more fully, producing a bit more sugar that is converted to alcohol by yeast. That's not necessarily a problem, for it's only a small increase, and when the wine is drunk with food – where Cabernet excels – it's inconsequential.

Fortunately, though the legendary Napa Valley Cabernets of the past – like the famed 1941 and 1974 – required long aging to reach their peak, improved farming and winemaking create wines that can be enjoyed much younger.

Though most continue to improve for a decade at least, they can typically be enjoyed after only three to four years and many peak in five to 10 years.

Some can also last much longer, but most people who buy fine wine want to drink it, not save it for their children!

The most famed Cabernets come from central and upper Napa Valley, and particularly from the foothills (benches they're called locally), hills and mountains that ring the valley floor, but great Cabs come from all over the Valley.

In addition to wines made from single varieties ('varietal' is an adjective, by the way), many wines labeled 'Cabernet Sauvignon' have other grapes blended it for enhanced flavors; they're not required to compensate for weak years.

If labeled 'Cabernet,' they have to contain at least 75 percent Cabernet, but many producers tell you the other varieties, too.

Cabernet's cousins from Bordeaux have similar but distinct characteristics. Merlot is softer but tends to get overripe in hot climates. Many fine Merlots come from southern Napa Valley and Carneros.

Petite Verdot is intense and adds purple color and violet notes. It is generally used to spice up blends, not bottled on its own. Cabernet Franc is a bit lighter and ripens sooner, and Malbec is becoming increasingly popular.

Blends in which no variety reaches 75 percent are becoming increasingly popular. Some blends are called Meritage (rhymes with heritage) but increasingly they have proprietary names.

And though Napa Valley is famous for its big Cabs, many wineries produce lighter, more 'European' wines – in cool years, they have little choice, in fact. Anyone who thinks vintages don't change in California hasn't tasted many of its wines.

What to eat with Cabernet

Cabernet Sauvignon is a legendary partner for big red meat – beef steak and roast, as well as duck, lamb and game. The flavors are a perfect complement to each other.

Cabernet is also good with hearty stews and strong cheeses and some people even find big Cab goes well with dark chocolate since both share bitter tannic undertones.

Lighter styles of Cabernet wines, which some people consider more elegant, are also good with red meat, but they can also work with well-flavored poultry and pork. Salt and acid from lemons always improve affinity between wine and food, and garlic, pepper and other strong flavors help, too. Cabernet Franc and Merlot are a bit lighter than Cabernet Sauvignon.

Beyond wine, Cabernet Season is also the time when the yellow mustard blooms, providing welcome color amidst the drab winter landscape. The mustard grows as a cover crop in vineyards and is an important part of organic grape growing as it adds organic matter to the soli as its rots.

Visitors to Napa Valley during Cabernet season will find smaller crowds and a less frantic pace. You get more personal attention at wineries and it's easier to score reservations at popular restaurants. Many hotels and inns offer special prices and packages, too.

Napa Valley's top wineries, restaurants and hotels welcome guests to cozy up with educational tastings, hearty fare that pairs best with the Valley's legendary Cabernet Sauvignon and other great red wines, and restorative spa treatments.

And in-between sipping and nibbling, guests can enjoy the Valley's growing arts and entertainment options at the Napa Valley Opera House, Uptown Theater and more.

Cabernet Season is the perfect time to visit Napa Valley. For information on events and special offers, visit www.visitnapavalley.com.

Visiting Napa Valley Alone

Much of the world seems designed for couples, and that's especially true for romantic getaways like Napa Valley. Nevertheless, a single person can have a great time in 'Wine Valley.'

He or she might even meet someone for a future visit together, but if your goal is to meet someone, you may be disappointed. It's better to plan to have fun, and see what happens.

Getting to Napa

A great way to get to Napa is via the ferry from San Francisco. It's an hour of relaxation. You can even have a glass of wine on the way to get yourself in the proper mood.

There *is* bus service from the Vallejo Ferry to downtown Napa, thence to Calistoga on clean, modern busses run by VINE, the local transit agency. Check the schedule at www.napavalleyvine.net as it changes occasionally – and don't be discouraged if the bus is running a little late. The busses from Vallejo to Calistoga and back run about every hour.

There's also bus service from both Oakland and San Francisco Airports provided by Evans Transit. Amtrak buses connect the train station in Martinez to Napa a number of times a day.

Once you're in the Valley, city buses serve many popular destinations. Most attractions in Napa itself are within walking distance of hotels and inns.

There are shuttles in each of the Valley's towns (Yountville, St. Helena and Calistoga), though most of the attractions for visitors are close enough for walking.

The Wine Train can't offer conventional passenger service, but it's still fun to take the train and you can just take the trip and buy wine in the bar rather than buying an excellent but pricey meal. The train does offer tours of a few wineries.

Where to stay

In the past, most visitors stayed up valley north of Napa if they could find a room and afford it.

Some of the nicest inns and resorts and best restaurants are in Yountville and St. Helena in mid Valley. Unfortunately, their limited accommodations fill quickly, and few of their rooms are reasonably priced.

Calistoga at the north end of the Valley and Napa at the south have a wider variety of lodgings.

Staying in Napa or Calistoga isn't a hardship, however. Both boast many attractions, restaurants and bars, mostly within walking distance. Napa, in fact, has become a major tourist destination with many new attractions and restaurants.

The city of Napa contains some large chain hotels that often offer special prices. One of the nicest places to stay is the Napa River Inn in downtown Napa within walking distance of almost everything you'd like to see there. The Hyatt chain's Andaz is in the hot West End of downtown and the Westin Verasa and River Terra Inn are close to downtown.

In Calistoga, The Calistoga Inn, which also has a popular microbrewery and restaurant, has inexpensive rooms, though the bathrooms are down the hall.

Many modest spas in Calistoga have inexpensive rooms, too. The ambience is about like a Motel 6, but they're clean and you won't care much about surroundings after a relaxing mud bath and massage.

One place I wouldn't recommend is a B&B. Most target couples on a romantic weekend and you'll feel left out.

What to do

Visiting wineries and tasting wine is the prime attraction in Napa Valley, but it's worth planning ahead if you want to get the most out of your visit.

Robert Mondavi Winery offers the widest variety and some of the best classes, tours and events, but you need reservations. You also need reservations at most other outstanding venues, like the sit-down tastings at Joseph Phelps and Duckhorn Cellars, and visits to hot small wineries.

Frank Family Vineyards is notoriously fun, particularly when the bachelorette parties descend. Other friendly places include Peju Province, V. Sattui, Castello di Amorosa winery, and the sparkling wine producers such as Domaine Chandon, Domaine Carneros and Mumm Napa.

Many wineries host meals, parties and special events that aren't too widely publicized. Some are only for their wine club members, but many are open to the public, usually for a charge. Many singles attend these events.

In addition, many wine bars and tasting rooms have opened in downtown Napa. Their formats range from single-winery tasting rooms like Mason and Craig to operations shared by a number of wineries like Vintners Collective.

A number of wine bars. and wine-tasting salons seem to attract more singles than couples. The Bounty Hunter seems more a friendly wine bar than a retail store, as does Back Room Wines, which has special tastings each Thursday and Friday night. All attract many single tasters.

Of course, tasting wine is a friendly pastime, and particularly later in the day, it's easy to meet people at tasting rooms. Do be prudent and watch your consumption, however. The police take their responsibility seriously. That's another good reason to stay downtown and walk.

More than wineries

Napa Valley boasts many other activities to enjoy beside wine tasting. One real treat though pricey is an early-morning balloon ride, an unforgettable experience.

There are classes on wine, food and other topics galore throughout the Valley, too, and they often attract singles. The local college offers many short courses, and wineries and restaurants also provide a chance to both learn and enjoy.

The Culinary Institute of America at Greystone Cellars offers many cooking classes for enthusiasts.

Napa Valley is also a treasure-trove of art. Among the art collections you can see for free are those at Clos Pegase Winery, Mumm Napa, the Hess Collection, and the sculpture garden at the Auberge du Soleil.

You should definitely see the di Rosa Preserve at least once. It's an incredible collection of contemporary art, some bizarre but all worth viewing. The preserve is in the Carneros Region of southern Napa County, and requires reservations for tours, though you can visit its Gatehouse Gallery free.

The Valley also has a number of museums and they offer classes.

The Napa Valley Museum in Yountville is a must. The Sharpsteen Museum in Calistoga and Robert Louis Stevenson Museum at the St. Helena Library (which also hosts the Napa Valley Wine Library) are also worth visiting.

And though Napa Valley was once a desert for performing arts, it's becoming an oasis. The Napa Valley Opera House's remarkable upstairs theater may be the best intimate concert venue in America and has a variety of eclectic performances at reasonable prices. Its downstairs café hosts performances, too.

Napa Valley is becoming a center for drama, too, including Lucky Penny Productions, Napa Valley Players and Napa Valley College's Napa Valley Conservatory Theater.

The restored Uptown Theatre offers many popular acts and the Cameo Theater in St. Helena screens critically acclaimed current films as well as current popular favorites.

There is also a mundane multiplex behind the Home Depot.

Where to eat

The only thing locals and visitors in Napa Valley love as much as wine is food. The valley hosts many incredible restaurants, including famed French Laundry, which is definitely a couples place, as are Étoile at Domaine Chandon, Auberge du Soleil and La Toque, the other world-class romantic restaurants.

Other restaurants welcome singles, and most have bars intended as much for eating as drinking. The bars offer full menus, friendly bartenders and the likelihood of meeting winemakers and vintners as well as visitors including occasional celebrities.

Friendly locals at bars happily offer suggestions about places to visit and eat, assuming people are welcoming unless proven otherwise. The bars are also comfortable for women alone, and bartenders discourage anyone who goes over the line.

A few restaurants like Bistro Jeanty, Lucy and French Blue even have communal tables where you're sure to meet someone to talk to.

Some of the best bars for singles to eat are ZuZu and Carpe Diem in downtown Napa as well as Angèle and Oxbow Public Market.

Uva Trattoria has great Italian-American food at reasonable prices, live music and a friendly atmosphere and almost no tourists find it.

Bistro Don Giovanni's bar is small, but always crowded and friendly, and the restaurant is a local favorite. So is Fumé Bistro.

Favorites in Yountville include Bouchon, Redd, Hurley's and Bistro Jeanty, while Rutherford Grill is popular and doesn't charge corkage.

St. Helena has a number of fine restaurants with friendly bars for eating: Goose & Gander, Press, Cindy Pawlcyn's Wood Fire and Wine Bar, Market, Cook and Tra Vigne. Calistoga boasts the Calistoga Inn, Brannan's, Barolo and Hydro Bar.

But if you're seeking a quieter time, the same bars that serve meals attract locals and visitors alike after dinner. It's a good place to meet people – and maybe even find someone to help explore the Valley the next day or on your next visit to Napa Valley.

Things to Do on a Cold, Rainy Day

They say that Napa Valley has two seasons, tourist and rainy.

There's always plenty to do when the weather is good, but there's also lots of fun indoors on a cold, rainy day. It's the favorite time for locals to visit the local wineries and tourist haunts while the hoards are still at bay.

The most obvious thing to do in Napa Valley on a cold, wet day is taste wine at your favorite winery, but let's look beyond that. Many wineries would be fascinating places to visit even if you're a teetotaler, so we'll break those wineries out separately in this list of ten things to do on rainy days. I bet you'll try the wines, too.

Check out a local museum

While Napa Valley isn't New York or even San Francisco, it still has a number of museums worth a careful look. The most obvious is Napa Valley Museum in Yountville, which someday hopes to open a location in Napa. It hosts art, history and other exhibits and programs.

The Sharpsteen Museum in Calistoga is a wonderful look at the way Napa Valley once was, and is ideal for kids.

The Robert Louis Stevenson Museum in St. Helena chronicles Napa Valley's first publicist. While you're there, the adjoining Napa Valley Wine Library collection in the St. Helena Wine Library also has an amazing collection of books and historic documents.

Take a tour of a winery

Many local wineries give good tours, but perhaps none is more enjoyable than that at Raymond Vineyards with a hall where you can sample wine aromas, a "laboratory" where you can blend your own wine or taste in a room filled with Baccarat Crystal or even in a Belle Epoch Bordello.

At Sterling Vineyards, you have to lead your own tour after you rise in the gondola, but it's comprehensive and well annotated and the views can't be beat. Neither can the tram ride – though they use a van if it's too windy – and even kids will enjoy the tastings, too, for they get fruit juice while their parents sit and enjoy the wine.

Explore historic caves

There's something spooky about a cave, and the hand-dug tunnels at Schramsberg and Beringer are the oldest and among the most extensive in the valley. Just as caves are cool in the summer, they're warm (relatively) when it's cold outside, and the tasting at the end of the tour is even more warming.

Visit a winery in a cave

Of late, a few wineries are building their whole production facilities in caves, not just storing wine there. Some do it to minimize impact on the environment, but no one can dispute the appeal to visitors, either.

Jarvis Winery's cave includes an underground stream and a small waterfall as well as huge rooms containing giant amethysts, while Palmaz Vineyards' cave stretches the equivalent of 14 stories from top to bottom, with its fermentation cavern an enormous five-story high dome blasted out of Mount St. George. The Staglin wine cave is more utilitarian, but still worth a visit.

See fine art

Many wineries feature original art, not none can compare with the three-story art museum at the Hess Collection. From the flaming typewriter, a mystery to kids in this computer era, to the giant portrait of Johanna, you can spend hours studying the art.

Jan Shrem's collection of art at Clos Pegase is impressive and eclectic, though part is sculpture outdoors. Cliff Lede Winery features an art gallery.

Visit a photo gallery

Some art galleries specialize in photographs, including Mumm Napa's impressive gallery in Rutherford. It's best known for its collection of Ansel Adams works, but has permanent and traveling exhibits of other photographers as well. Turnbull Winery also has an impressive collection of rare photos. So does Markham, famous for its *Rolling Stone* covers.

Enjoy a food demonstration

The Culinary Institute of America in St. Helena offers demonstrations of cooking along with samples or even lunch or dinner almost daily. If you want to get yourself involved, the CIA, some wineries, individuals and the Napa Valley Cooking School at the Upvalley Campus of the Napa Valley College have tasty classes.

Shop for special treats

Obviously, there are many places to eat in Napa Valley, including the French Laundry, where you can while away a long rainy afternoon or evening as well as your children's inheritance. But you could also spend as long looking, tasting and eating at the Oxbow Public Market or even the Whole Foods Market or Trader Joe's in Napa if you don't have them back home. You can also find special treats at Dean & DeLuca, Oakville Grocery, Sunshine Market and the Napa Valley Olive Oil Company in St. Helena and Genova Deli in Napa. V Marketplace in Yountville hosts many shops inside an old winery

Visit a hilltop castle in Italy

See your ultimate fantasy at Dario Sattui's Castello di Amoroso in Calistoga. The formal tour takes an hour and a half, and while few now visit just for the wines, the tasting of the excellent wines at the end of the tour will convince you that it really is a top winery, not just a tourist attraction.

Even the most cynical anti-tourist local will be impressed with the care and details Sattui has devoted to his "castle of love," and most would happily enjoy the wine while they pretend they're in a hilltop near San Gimignano or Monteriggioni.

Sit by the fire

Few things are more pleasant on a rainy day that sitting by the fire, perhaps reading a book while you sip a glass of sherry. You can do that at many resorts and bars in Napa Valley, including the bar at Auberge du Soleil, in the lobby bar around the original mansion fireplace at Silverado Resort, in the Harvest Inn or St. Helena Hotel's lobby, in the front lobby at Villagio, which has the least-known public bar in Napa County, in the comfortable sofas in the lounge at Cuvée or in the bar at Meadowood. At Meadowood, you might even just read in the lobby as if you're waiting for someone or for dinner. Who knows if they just don't show up or you change your mind about dinner...

About Author Paul Franson

Paul Franson lives in Napa Valley, where he writes regularly about life and wine in Napa Valley and elsewhere in his *NapaLife* weekly newsletter, the insider's guide to Napa Valley both for locals and those who wished they lived there.

He also writes about life in Napa Valley for other publications including *the Napa Valley Register* and *Napa Valley Life*.

In addition, he writes about wine for *Senior Connection, Wine Business Monthly* and *Wines & Vines*, the *Napa Valley Register,* including a weekly news posting at *winesandvines.com* and a wine business column every other Friday in th*e Register.* He has written for the *Wine Enthusiast, Food & Wine, Decanter,* the *San Francisco Chronicle* and many other publications.

He has traveled extensively to wine regions of the world, from Chile to the Republic of Georgia.

He also writes about food and travel.

His writing can be found on the Internet at www.*NapaLife.com*, a web site about Napa Valley for locals and visitors, and at *www.TravelTastes.com,* a web site about wine, food and travel.

Franson formerly managed a public relations agency he founded in Silicon Valley, worked in corporate public relations, and was a business and trade magazine writer and editor. He has published three books about marketing.

He's lived in Napa Valley since 1996 following a year in San Francisco's North Beach, and two years on his sailboat in Antigua.

He's an avid home cook and vegetable gardener. He was long a home winemaker but quit after he moved to Napa Valley and found so much good wine to drink.

Cover photo by Mars Lasar

Lasar moved to Napa Valley in 2006 after spending 20 years in the music industry as a composer and producer in Hollywood. When he moved to Napa Valley, he was taken by the different kinds of light and color combinations within the valley and vineyards and set out to capture their seasonal variations. His landscapes are hanging in various venues and homes throughout the country.

The Last Word

A Request for Updates

If you find anything mentioned in the book has changed – or is simply wrong – please pass along your comments and changes so we can update it for future readers. Send comments to paul@napalife.com

Subscribe to *NapaLife*

NapaLife is a weekly update on what's happening in Napa Valley. In a sense, it's an ongoing supplement to this book. It provides news – generally scoops – on restaurants, wineries, the arts and entertainment and shopping in Napa Valley. It also lists all events each week. *NapaLife* arrives by email to print every Monday; a link points to a web version.

You can subscribe for $50 per year, which is only $1 per week, 14 cents per day. You could save that much just taking advantage of one special deal.

To subscribe, visit www.napalife.com, where you can use a credit card or Pay Pal. You can also send a check to

Paul Franson
2035 Oak St.
Napa, CA 94559

If you have any questions or want this week's issue, email paul@napalife.com.